THE GRANT WRITING GUIDE

SKILLS FOR SCHOLARS

The Grant Writing Guide: A Road Map for Scholars, Betty S. Lai

The Secret Syllabus: A Guide to the Unwritten Rules of College Success,
William Germano and Kit Nicholls

*The Economist's Craft: An Introduction to Research, Publishing, and
Professional Development*, Michael Weisbach

The Book Proposal Book: A Guide for Scholarly Authors, Laura Portwood-Stacer

The Princeton Guide to Historical Research, Zachary Schrag

You Are What You Read: A Practical Guide to Reading Well, Robert DiYanni

Super Courses: The Future of Teaching and Learning, Ken Bain

Syllabus: The Remarkable, Unremarkable Document That Changes Everything,
William Germano and Kit Nicholls

Leaving Academia: A Practical Guide, Christopher P. Caterine

A Field Guide to Grad School: Uncovering the Hidden Curriculum,
Jessica McCrory Calarco

How to Think Like Shakespeare: Lessons from a Renaissance Education,
Scott Newstok

The Craft of College Teaching: A Practical Guide, Anton Borst and
Robert DiYanni

The Grant Writing Guide

A ROAD MAP FOR SCHOLARS

BETTY S. LAI

PRINCETON UNIVERSITY PRESS
PRINCETON & OXFORD

Requests for permission to reproduce material from this work should be sent to permissions@press.princeton.edu

Published by Princeton University Press
41 William Street, Princeton, New Jersey 08540
99 Banbury Road, Oxford OX2 6JX

press.princeton.edu

ISBN 9780691231877
ISBN (pbk.) 9780691231884
ISBN (e-book) 9780691231891

Library of Congress Control Number: 2022943033

British Library Cataloging-in-Publication Data is available

Editorial: Peter J. Dougherty, Matt Rohal, and Alena Chekanov
Production Editorial: Karen Carter
Jacket/Cover Design: Matt Avery (Monograph LLC)
Production: Lauren Reese
Publicity: Alyssa Sanford and Kathryn Stevens
Copyeditor: Cindy Milstein

This book has been composed in Arno

10 9 8 7 6 5 4 3 2 1

For Tom

CONTENTS

Introduction   1

TASK A. DEVELOP AN IDEA   9

1   The Landscape: Find Available Grants   11

2   Your Values: Generate Ideas   20

3   External Values: Further Your Career Goals   31

4   The One Pager: Create Phenomenal Pitches   43

TASK B. TARGET A FUNDER   57

5   Talk to a Program Officer: Fit with a Funder   59

6   Get Samples: Signal That You Belong   69

7   A Grant's Anatomy: Outline and Timeline   79

8   Evaluation Criteria and the Mission: Make It Easy
    to Advocate for You   91

TASK C. DRAFT YOUR GRANT   101

9   The Literature Review: Clear and Simple Communication   103

10 Your Research Plan: Living up to the Hype   119

11   Structure Your Draft: Consistency Is Comforting   139

12   Go Figure: Images That Deliver Value   151

TASK D. POLISH YOUR GRANT   161

13   Style Strategies: Increase Readability   163

14   The Pick Me Factor: Sell Your Expertise and Team   170

15   Critical Critiques: Identify Weaknesses   181

Conclusion   193

List of Tips and Frequently Asked Questions   197
Submission Checklist   203
Glossary   207
Acknowledgments   211
References   215
Index   223

THE GRANT WRITING GUIDE

Introduction

THIS BOOK is about grant writing skills. It focuses on helping scholars from every discipline learn to craft compelling grants for any funder.

That's because this book is about you. It's about developing your skills so that you lead research in your field. It's about gaining independence in your career and sharing incredible ideas. And this book is about making sure the best discoveries and insights in every field are heard.[1]*

Research is shaped by men who are white and older. Look at data from the National Institutes of Health, the largest funder of biomedical research in the world.[2] Men receive $39,000 more in first-time funding from the National Institutes of Health than do women.[3] White investigators are 10 percent more likely to receive funding than African American and Black investigators, and white investigators are 4 percent more likely to receive funding than Asian investigators.[4] The age at which people receive their first major grant has also steadily risen. In 1980, researchers were 36.1 years old when they received their first major grant. By 2016, the average age was 45.2 years.[5] Biases are not unique to the National Institutes of Health; they have been documented at funders around the world.[6–8] Funding goes to select portions of our talented workforce.

It's time to invest in the voices we are missing. Funding biases matter because grants are a gateway to influence. In 2020, the United States invested over $57.8 billion in funding at three agencies alone: the National Science Foundation, the National Institutes of Health, and the Environmental Protection

---

* In 2020, I attended a training run by the OpEd Project. Its message about missing voices in op-eds was transformational. It made me realize that we are missing voices in the grant writing world for many of the same reasons that diverse voices are missing from op-eds. We need to hear from our missing voices. I drew great strength from the OpEd Project's message, and I hope this message gives you strength as well.

Agency.[9–11] Every year in the United Kingdom, UK Research and Innovation invests £6 billion in science and research.[12] That's enormous buying power swaying research, policy, media attention, and support for our next generation of scholars.

There are many systemic and structural reasons why funding biases exist. *The Grant Writing Guide* addresses the piece of the puzzle you control: submitting your ideas. Women, scholars of color, and those at early career stages submit fewer grants than older white men.[13–16] Submitting less translates directly to less funding. As former basketball player Michael Jordan said, you miss 100 percent of the shots you don't take.[17]

This book is about taking your shots.

Equity and Access: Uncovering the Hidden Curriculum

When I moved to New England, I knew I had to get ready for cold winters. I bought a jacket that looks like a sleeping bag and snow boots that repel water.

And still I froze through my first winter. I figured that's what life is like in New England. But a year into living here, I said to my partner (who's from New England), "I wish my toes would thaw." He looked at me, perplexed. He said, "Why don't you put on your wool socks?"

I didn't have wool socks. I didn't know wool socks would make a difference. I never asked anyone how to keep my toes warm because I didn't know that was possible in this environment. And no one from New England thought to tell me about wool socks. To insiders, it's obvious that sock fabric makes a difference.

Being a scholar is like moving to New England. You prepare. You know the environment will be tough. But you may be missing inside knowledge that will make a difference in your survival (e.g., whether you are able to secure funding).

This inside knowledge is so expansive it has a name: the "hidden curriculum." The hidden curriculum of grant writing includes strategies that make it easier to secure funding (e.g., how to talk to a program officer or write to evaluation criteria).

The hidden curriculum is a barrier to your success. Because strategies are "hidden," you can only learn them by training with a seasoned mentor. Yet access to seasoned mentors is inequitably distributed across groups. Thus funding flows to insiders and their trainees. Among organizations that receive National Institutes of Health funding, the top 10 percent of organizations receive 70 percent of the research funding. The bottom half of organizations receives less than 5 percent of the research funding.[18]

Luck of the draw in training and social privilege shouldn't determine who gets funded. All scholars should have access to grant writing strategies.

That's why I'm uncovering the hidden curriculum of grant writing in this book. I'm sharing everything I know as a tenured professor at a Research 1 university. I've had success in this process. I've been funded by the National Science Foundation, the National Institute of Mental Health, and the National Academies of Sciences, Engineering, and Medicine, just to name a few funders of my work. My research has been recognized with awards from the American Psychological Association and the American Psychological Foundation. And I've published over seventy peer reviewed articles. I understand parts of the hidden curriculum that may help you.

But sharing what I know isn't enough. I only know what helped me succeed. Additional strategies may help *you* succeed. To uncover these additional strategies, I interviewed a hundred experts. Experienced grantees, program officers, researchers, administrators, and writers in every phase of their careers contributed their knowledge.[†] They shared their best advice for navigating the grant writing environment.

They took the time to do this because we share the same dream. We believe in creating a world where talented researchers get the information they need to grow in their careers, advance our fields, and find solutions to our world's most challenging problems.

Confront Your Limiting Beliefs

Grant writing skills won't help you if you're holding onto limiting beliefs. Limiting beliefs are those that keep you from aiming high and putting in effort to get results you care about. Everyone has limiting beliefs. Let's challenge limiting beliefs that will get in the way of your success.

[†] Social science colleagues may be interested in my interview approach. While planning my interview strategy, it was important to me that this book represent diverse voices with a range of experiences. I reached out to colleagues and experts with these goals in mind. The interviews were approximately thirty minutes long, and took place via phone and Zoom (with one exception, where an interviewee emailed me their responses). I took notes during the interviews. When referring to interviewees in this book, I do not use people's full titles. I chose to do so because titles seemed likely to shift relative to this book's publication. I also felt titles could overshadow people's stories about choices that shaped their careers. Titles, however, are a crucial sign of respect. Thus I want to underscore that I have the utmost gratitude and respect for the people who shared their wisdom for this book. The interviewees are listed in the acknowledgments section.

1. **Grants aren't worth the effort**. I felt this way when I started. There was too much to learn. All of that work probably wouldn't pay off because grants are so hard to get. I spent my time on papers instead because I knew how to write papers and get them published. That felt like a better use of my time. But consider this. The stakes are high for learning how to write a fundable grant. A survey of forty-seven hundred researchers worldwide found that 36 percent considered grant funding to be one of the most important factors in their career.[19] Another study examined tenure and promotion criteria in biomedical sciences. Among ninety-two randomly selected institutions worldwide, 67 percent listed securing grant funding as a key criterion for promotion and tenure.[20] Grant writing can shape your career.

2. **I don't need the money**. We've all worked for relatively low pay in the process of getting into graduate school or earning our degrees. We're used to running studies on zero to slim budgets. Maybe you're in a hard money or clinical position already. A grant isn't necessary to pay your salary. We're not talking about pocket change, though. At the National Institutes of Health, the median amount given to first-time awardees is $165,721 for men and $126,615 for women.[3] Imagine the opportunities this money could create for your work and the communities you serve. And consider the doors you could open for the next generation with a grant. About 20 percent of the positions funded by grants from the National Institutes of Health are for trainees.[21]

3. **They're not going to fund me**. I don't have enough expertise. I haven't published enough yet. I don't have a new enough idea. No one likes to fund scholars from my field. What would happen if you turn these limiting beliefs around and ask why *not* you? In 2017, the National Science Foundation directly supported over 350,000 people.[22] And about one in four awards from the National Science Foundation go to first-time awardees.[23] That's just one agency. There are many, many agencies and foundations out there that want to fund promising scholars. Everyone recognizes how important it is to fund and develop talented scholars in every field. Why shouldn't it be you?

4. **Grant training doesn't help unless it covers the exact type of grant I want**. Here's the secret. Grant writing skills let you call the shots. You choose where you pitch your ideas. You aren't tied to one agency or one type of grant. That's been true for me and my colleagues. It can be true for you too if you practice strategic skills.

Grant writing is just a skill. You can learn how to write a fundable grant. Senior scholars get funded at higher rates than early career scholars.[24] That's partly because senior scholars have learned more grant writing skills than early career scholars. If you learn these same skills, you will be on a faster track to success.

How to Use This Book

It's hard work to learn how to write a grant. But if you're reading this, you already know that. You are ready to do the hard work. You just want to know where to invest your energy and time.

The Grant Writing Guide is your road map for learning how to write more fundable grants. Excellent books on grant writing already exist. This book is unique in two important ways. First, this book is written for scholars. I focus on guiding scholars from all disciplines. Likely that means you have or are earning a terminal degree (e.g., PhD, EdD, MD, or DSc). As scholars, we are trying to gain support for our ideas. This distinct goal shapes how scholars write grants.

Second, this book focuses on career choice and freedom. Instead of learning how to write one specific type of grant (e.g., an Australian Research Council grant), you will learn fundamental skills so you can choose which grants to write. (As an analogy, you won't learn one pattern for sewing a tweed jacket. You will learn the fundamentals of sewing so you can choose to make a tweed jacket, throw pillow, or more.)

In sum, this book concentrates on universal grant writing skills that will help you write better grants for any funder. Every chapter in this book revolves around developing specific grant writing skills. Each chapter describes motivating examples of scholars using a skill, an action plan for developing the skill, and exercises and cases showing how to use the skill. And each chapter ends with tips and responses to frequently asked questions. The chapters are organized around four tasks:

A. **Develop an idea** (chapters 1–4). How do you know what grants are available? How are grants funded? How do you generate ideas? How can you use grants to further your career goals? How do you pitch a grant idea?

B. **Target a funder** (chapters 5–8). How do you know if a funder will like your idea? What can you do to sound like you belong in the coveted group of "funded investigators"? How do you figure out what you need to write for a grant? How do you create a timeline for your grant writing? Why do you need reviewers to advocate for you?

Task A: Develop an Idea	Task B: Target a Funder
Chapter 1. The Landscape: Find Available Grants	**Chapter 5. Talk to a Program Officer: Fit with a Funder**
• Define types of grants	• Describe program officer roles
• Road map of the grant process	• Examine what you learn from program officers
• Identify your usual suspects	• Reach out to program officers
• Dig deeper: Find abstracts	• Study the program and operation of the funder
Chapter 2. Your Values: Generate Ideas	• Meet with a program officer
• Ikigai: Examine your values	• Debrief after your meeting
• Develop exciting ideas	**Chapter 6. Get Samples: Signal That You Belong**
• Create a short list of ideas	• Recognize samples that fast-track your intuition
• Identify potential funders and mechanisms	• Find general samples
Chapter 3. External Values: Further Your Career Goals	• Find specific samples
• Understand external values	• Request samples: How to email
• Uncover external values	• Read samples for signals
• Meeting 1: Aspirational peer	• Try to serve on a review panel
• Meeting 2: Mentor or potential mentor	**Chapter 7. A Grant's Anatomy: Outline and Timeline**
• Meeting 3: Senior administrator	• Understand application instructions
• Select a grant idea	• Outline using application instructions
Chapter 4. The One Pager: Create Phenomenal Pitches	• Partner with research administrators
• Understand the one pager	• Plan your writing timeline
• Evaluate a structure for one pagers	**Chapter 8. Evaluation Criteria and the Mission: Make It Easy to Advocate for You**
• Build your pitch: Be a prosecuting attorney	• Understand how evaluation criteria drive the review process
• Construct your one pager	• Develop sound bites: Use good headings and emphasis words
• Avoid common mistakes	• Test your sound-bite skills
	• Address the mission

FIGURE 1. A Framework for Developing Grant Writing Skills

C. **Draft your grant** (chapters 9–12). What story does your grant need to tell? How do you design your research plan? How should you structure your grant? How can you strategically use figures in your grant?

D. **Polish your grant** (chapters 13–15). What style strategies make reviewers say, "This is a well-written grant." How do you convince reviewers to pick you and your team? What types of feedback help you polish a grant?

Task C: Draft Your Grant

Chapter 9. The Literature Review: Clear and Simple Communication

- Bust myths that create confusion
- Explain a mindset shift: From peer to guide
- Become a guide
- Understand literature reviews
- Evaluate a literature review template and sample
- Draft your literature review outline
- Refine your literature review outline

Chapter 10. Your Research Plan: Living up to the Hype

- Understand research plans
- Brainstorm your research plan
- Craft a project timeline
- Offense: Build your case
- Defense: Anticipate reviewer questions
- Craft your research plan

Chapter 11. Structure Your Draft: Consistency Is Comforting

- Describe the inverted pyramid approach
- Evaluate a sample that uses the inverted pyramid approach
- Flesh out your full proposal
- Avoid common mistakes
- Create consistency across your full grant

Chapter 12. Go Figure: Images That Deliver Value

- Understand ways to use figures
- Brainstorm how you want to use figures
- Create compelling figures

Task D: Polish Your Grant

Chapter 13. Style Strategies: Increase Readability

- Understand what makes grants readable
- Practice style strategies

Chapter 14. The Pick Me Factor: Sell Your Expertise and Team

- Understand how to excite reviewers
- Brainstorm what you bring to the table
- Build your dream team
- Reframe weaknesses
- Analyze a sample

Chapter 15. Critical Critiques: Identify Weaknesses

- Learn about red teams
- Form your red team
- Form a discussion circle
- Toss out weaknesses
- Pay attention to detail

Notice that we won't dive into a lot of writing until the last half of the book. This is intentional. The prep work you do before writing a grant is critical to your success. A significant idea (task A) and the right funder (task B) are the building blocks you need to draft and polish your next fundable grant (tasks C and D, respectively).

Your experience with grant writing will probably shape how you use this book. If you're new to grant writing, you may want to read the whole book first to understand the grant writing process. Then circle back to the beginning to dive into exercises. If you've submitted grants, use the book to strengthen your skills. The chapters are designed to sharpen your skills sequentially. But each chapter can stand alone if you want to jump ahead to specific skills. You may find it helpful to grab a colleague to share ideas with as you work through the book.

This book includes organizing tools to help you. A framework lists all the skills in this book (figure 1). It's a lot of information to look at now. Earmark the framework as a reference tool for later use. The end of this book includes a list of tips and frequently asked questions (organized by chapter), submission checklist, and glossary. All terms in the glossary are **bolded** the first time they appear in the book.

I hope this book empowers you to do the work you love. The job market is tight for scholars. Many people who are passionate about scholarship end up leaving their fields because they cannot find jobs. But grants create opportunities and open doors for you. At the end of the day, grant writing is a skill that can fund your dream work.

TASK A

Develop an Idea

1

The Landscape

FIND AVAILABLE GRANTS

Getting a grant is validating. Someone who doesn't know you at all believes in you as a researcher.

—JULIE SCHNEIDER

MENTORS WILL tell you, "You should write a CAREER grant or K grant." Or they'll say something like, "Start with an R03." They mean well and want to help you. They give this advice because focusing on one type of grant worked for them or someone they mentored.

But you don't have to limit yourself to one type of grant. Around the world, more than sixteen million grants have been awarded since 2003.[25] Currently, more than \$83 billion in grant funding is available.[26] That's a galaxy of possibilities waiting for your incredible ideas.

Having a narrow focus on just one type of grant is costly. Here's an example from Kate Guastaferro. Kate was in an outstanding training program that coached researchers in how to write R03 grants, a type of grant funded by the National Institutes of Health. "But I don't do secondary data analysis, which is what R03 grants are for. I spent three months writing an R03 before I needed to walk away from that project. It just wasn't right for me."

On the other hand, taking a broad viewpoint can help you create the career you want. Mary Beth Grimley Prieur's work has been funded by the National Institutes of Health and the Cystic Fibrosis Foundation, among others. She says, "People often don't realize there are many kinds of grants. Get creative in looking for funding because this is how you get to do the work you care about."

Mary Beth was passionate about starting a palliative care team at her hospital. But she needed money to do this work. The palliative care team she wanted to create wasn't a great fit for a traditional research grant. She got scrappy and found a funder, an institutional fundraising drive, that was excited about her work. It funded her palliative care team for the first three years while her team searched for additional funding sources. Keeping an eye out for opportunities allowed Mary Beth to move her career in directions she cares about.

And here's an inside tip. You get better at finding opportunities when you start looking for them. Not only that, but as soon as you receive some grants, your ideas become more fundable as well. This is because of the **social proof principle**. When funders see the social proof that others believe in your ideas and want to fund them, funders see that you're a proven quantity who can deliver on great ideas.

The **goal of this chapter** is to help you understand the grants landscape so that you know what grants are available to you. By the end of this chapter, you'll home in on funders that are likely to love your grant ideas.

Action Plan

Each chapter in this book has an action plan that outlines material in the chapter. If you're a checklist person, use the action plan to track your progress as you work through the chapters.

- ☐ Define types of grants
- ☐ Road map of the grant process
- ☐ Identify your usual suspects
- ☐ Dig deeper: Find abstracts

Define Types of Grants

There are three main types of grants for researchers: **federal**, **foundation**, and **internal grants**. Each type is named after the funder or the entity that awards the grant. Funders usually award grants through different types of **mechanisms**, or grants that target specific purposes, activities, or audiences.[27] Examples of mechanisms include career development or training grants (e.g., CAREER grants at the National Science Foundation or K grants at the National Institutes of Health), research project grants (e.g., Research Grants on Education: Large at the Spencer Foundation, or R01 or R03 grants at the National Institutes of Health), or workshop grants.

1. **Federal grants**. This is a term used in the United States to refer to government-funded grants. Federal grants are held in high esteem by institutions and colleagues. Outside the United States, the closest equivalent to federal grants are government-funded grants (e.g., Tri-Agency grants in Canada or Australian Research Council grants).

   Examples. There are twenty-six federal agencies in the United States, including the National Science Foundation, National Institutes of Health, and Environmental Protection Agency.[28]

   Mechanisms. There are over a thousand federal grant mechanisms in the United States that award more than $500 billion each year.[28-29] Federal grants come in many sizes, from less than $10,000 to more than $1 million. Federal grant mechanisms are searchable online (grants.gov). In addition, the National Institutes of Health has a Matchmaker portal online. You can enter an abstract into Matchmaker, and the program will give you a list of related funded projects.

2. **Foundation grants**. These are nonfederal grants. The foundations may be public or private. Examples of these funders include the Spencer Foundation, Jacobs Foundation, and William T. Grant Foundation.

   Mechanisms. There are more than a hundred thousand foundations worldwide.[30] Every funder and mechanism has different priorities and award amounts, so it's important to find a good match. We'll walk through that match process in chapter 5 of this book. Foundation grants are searchable through candid.org or the Pivot database (pivot.proquest.com). Your institution needs to have a subscription to Pivot in order for you to access it.

3. **Internal grants**. These are grants from your institution. They range in size and competitiveness depending on your institution. For internal grants, it's especially important to talk with someone who knows your institution well. They'll have inside information on how competitive internal grants are and how to pitch your ideas successfully. I'll show you how to tap into their knowledge in chapter 3.

   Mechanisms. Internal grants usually fund pilot studies, meaning work that lays the groundwork for securing federal or foundation grants. Internal grants may also be dedicated to topics that are of special interest to your institution (e.g., building local partnerships, purchasing technology at your institution, or bringing in external speakers). Your institution will list internal grants on its website or in email newsletters.

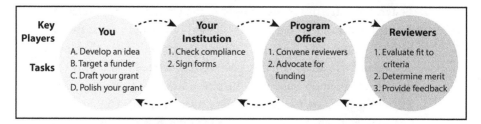

FIGURE 2. Road Map of the Grant Process

Road Map of the Grant Process

Almost all grants go through the same funding process. Above is a road map (figure 2) for how the grant process generally works. In a nutshell, there are four key players you need to pay attention to while writing grants: you, your institution, a **program officer**, and reviewers.

To illustrate the process, you submit your grant to your institution. Your institution then checks the compliance of your materials, signs forms, and submits your grant to the funder. The funder routes your grant to a program officer. The program officer invites reviewers to evaluate the submitted grants, and then the program officer sends your grant (and others) out to those invited reviewers. Reviewers evaluate the grant. They give their reviews to the program officer. The program officer advocates for funding decisions based on reviewers' comments. Finally, this decision comes back to your institution and then to you.

A Closer Look at the Tasks of Each Key Player

You. You develop an idea, target a funder, and then draft and polish your grant. This book covers all of these tasks, in this order. When you finish your grant, you submit your grant to your institution.

Your institution. Here's an important fact that often surprises people: grants are usually awarded to your institution, not to you. That's because your institution is in charge of managing and vouching for the funds.* For example, when I moved from Georgia State University

---

* There are special cases where grants are awarded directly to you. Those grants tend to be smaller, so I don't focus on them in this book.

to Boston College, my grants didn't automatically follow me. That's because the grants were not "mine." Instead, Georgia State was the "recipient" of the grants. Georgia State had to agree to transfer the grants to a new "recipient," Boston College. Even then, the funders had to approve this change. Ultimately, your institution is responsible for the grant. So you need to submit your grant to your institution before the grant deadline. Your institution needs that extra time to check the compliance of the forms and sign required ones. These required forms indicate that your institution will abide by the rules of the funder if the grant is awarded. After completing these tasks, your institution will submit your grant to the funder.

Program officers. When your institution submits your grant to a funder, your grant gets routed to a program officer. Program officers are employees of the funder. A program officer's job is to build a portfolio of grants for a **program**, which is a specific area of focus for the funder. For instance, my program at the National Science Foundation is Humans, Disasters, and the Built Environment. This program focuses on research related to hazards and disasters. My program officer seeks to create a portfolio of hazard and disaster grants that includes cutting-edge research and represents a range of ideas. When program officers receive your grant, they will convene reviewers to evaluate the grant. Then, program officers typically advocate for grants that get outstanding reviews and/or balance out the portfolio of the program.

Reviewers. Reviewers are people that the funder invites to review submitted grants. They are experts in your field. Usually they've received grant funding from the funder in the past. Their job is to evaluate how well a grant fits the funder's evaluation criteria (I'll cover what evaluation criteria are in chapter 8), determine the merit of your idea in relation to the field, and provide feedback. For many funders, reviewers will also serve on a **review panel** to discuss comments with other reviewers. If reviewers think your idea has promise, your grant will be discussed during the panel.

In later chapters, I will break down the motivations of each of these key players so that you know how to write in a way that speaks to their needs. For now, let's do a simple exercise to help you better understand the grants landscape for your field.

Identify Your Usual Suspects

Navigating the grants landscape is easier when you have a list of what photojournalist Daniella Zalcman calls the "usual suspects," or funders that like your ideas.[31] Scholars can spend years figuring out their list of usual suspects. But if you're like most scholars, you don't have years to waste trying to find this information. You need funding now, not in ten years.

To identify your usual suspects now, leverage the knowledge of scholars who went before you. They've had time to navigate and find success in the grants galaxy. They've left bread crumbs behind (i.e., their curriculum vitaes [CVs]) to tell you who their usual suspects are.

First, pull the CVs of three aspirational peers and three leaders in your field. Save these CVs in a file, as we will return to them later in this book.

- **Aspirational peers** should be people in your field who do work you admire. They should be people who've received grant funding. They should be three to five years ahead of you, and be in positions that you consider to be the "next step" in your career. They should also be doing work in your field that you think is exciting and you would love to do.
- **Leaders** should be people who are at the top of your field. To be helpful to you for this exercise, they need to have received grant funding. These should be "big names" that you know and cite in your work. Leaders should be the people who seem to be everywhere you want to be. Their jobs should be what you consider to be your ultimate dream job.

Next, check out the bread crumbs they left behind. What grants have they secured? If you're lucky, they listed the grants they applied to and received, but also the grants they did *not* receive. There are many lessons to learn from grants that were not awarded. In this light, no grant is a failure. Many people, however, don't include "failures" on their CVs.

Looking at the CVs, fill out this chart (figure 3):

- **Type of grant (federal, foundation, or internal)**. Did their grants change over their career from when they were at your stage versus where they are now?
- **Mechanism (e.g., CAREER, K award, R01, or R03)**. What types of mechanisms were they able to leverage for success?
- **Award amounts**. What amounts of money were they able to secure? That gives you a sense of what's typical for your field. Pay attention to how amounts may have changed as they advanced in their careers.

Researcher	Type of Grant (federal, foundation, or internal)	Mechanism (CAREER, K award R01, or R03)	Award Amount
_____	_____	_____	_____
_____	_____	_____	_____
_____	_____	_____	_____

FIGURE 3. The Usual Suspects Chart

- **Also note awards or fellowships they've secured.** People often list these separately from grants. Study CVs to understand how to be competitive for these awards and fellowships. What publications or presentations did the researchers have when they secured these awards and fellowships? What was their career stage? Securing awards and fellowships adds to the social proof factor I discussed earlier in this chapter. I'll capitalize on social proof later in this book, in chapter 14 on the pick me factor.

Dig Deeper: Find Abstracts

You now have a starter list of your usual suspects (i.e., possible grants and mechanisms that you can target in your career). Dig deeper to find abstracts for the grants that seem most interesting to you. Federal grant abstracts are published online. For example, the National Institutes of Health and National Science Foundation websites allow you to search for abstracts of funded grants. Foundation grants and internal grants frequently, but not always, publish abstracts for grants. Keep a file of all of these abstracts because they will help you understand the language that was compelling to funders.

Tips and Frequently Asked Questions

Am I too early in my career to begin applying for grants? No. Applying for grants is an important way to build your CV. Imposter syndrome can make you think you need to graduate first or that you need ten more publications before you can apply. It's not true. Use the usual suspects exercise to find funders that want to support people at your career stage. As medical doctor Crystal Zheng shares, "I wish I'd known to apply for training grants for residents even before junior faculty grants. Grants can get you started much earlier; you don't have to delay."

What do I do if I have trouble finding CVs? CVs are usually available on institutional websites. If you can't find CVs after searching, email people on your list to ask if they wouldn't mind sharing their CVs. These are people you want to build relationships with, so it doesn't hurt to start forming connections now. If you're struggling to find good "target" scholars, that's OK. It takes time to figure out who has carved a path you want to follow. Keep searching and keep your eyes out for these scholars. Your usual suspects chart is one you will continue to build over your career.

The usual suspects exercise lets us track the careers of a few people. How else do people hear about grants? Researcher Katie Edwards shares these ideas: join listservs, talk to colleagues, network, and read papers. Published papers list funders under acknowledgments. Also, look for fellowship opportunities. Fellowships are a great way to hear about funding opportunities. And most of the grant writing skills in this book translate directly to writing competitive fellowship applications.

I work in an area that isn't a high priority for funding. How do I find people who might support my work? Look at your CV. See which organizations have already supported your career with travel grants, poster awards, and so on. Those organizations are good targets for your future work and ideas.[32]

What are the success rates of grants? It varies by funder and mechanism. Check the funder's website to see the most up-to-date information. A 2018 survey of grant practices across twenty-one countries found that success rates vary, but most funders support between 10 to 20 percent of the applications.[33]

How long does it take to write a grant? This also varies. Similar to paper writing or planning a party, grant writing can take a little or a lot of time. Successful grant writers agree, however, that a compelling grant takes a long time to write (we'll cover outlines and writing timelines in chapter 7). For example, Ya-Hui Yu cowrote a grant with her postdoctoral mentor to the Canadian Institutes of Health Research. It took Ya-Hui about six months to develop the idea, and about one month of full-time writing to draft the grant. Rachel Pizzie's first R01 grant to the National

Institutes of Health took six months of preplanning plus active writing for twenty-five hours a week for two months. Bottom line, start early and use as much time as you are able to spare.

What are the differences between funders? For instance, how do I figure out the difference between the National Science Foundation and National Institutes of Health? The main difference is that every funder has a unique mission. To succeed in grant writing, find a match between your ideas and a funder's mission. The usual suspects exercise helps you fast-track this match process. In later chapters, I'll help you better understand different funders along with their missions and programs by talking to program officers (chapter 5) as well as examining evaluation criteria (chapter 8).

Are there other ways besides grants for researchers to support their work? Yes. Scholars are able to support their work in many ways such as contracts, donations to their institutions, or crowdsourcing. I don't focus on those types of funds in this book, but they can be a powerful possibility for your work. Chairs and mentors will have advice on how to find those opportunities.

The Takeaway

You've now created your own list of usual suspects. This is a working document you'll want to update throughout your career. The value of this list is that you know which funders and mechanisms like the types of work you want to do. That means if you can craft a well-written grant, your ideas will be exciting to the funder.

But how do you generate those ideas? Keep reading to find out.

2

Your Values

GENERATE IDEAS

Connecting your work to your purpose gives me the energy to keep going.

—KYLE HART[34]

IT'S EASY TO GET LOST in chasing funding as the goal in grant writing. But chasing funding has no intrinsic value. Most kids don't grow up saying to themselves, "I really want funding when I grow up." (That is, unless you grow up with a mom who is a researcher like my two poor kids.)

For this skill, we're focused on understanding your values. When you know what you value, you'll be able to home in on grant ideas that help you stay close to them. If you skip this step, you run the risk of working on grants that move you away from doing work you care about. This is the point at which researchers say grant writing is emotionally draining. What's more, half-hearted grants are unconvincing to reviewers. That's a losing combination: a grant proposal *you* don't want to write and that *reviewers* don't like.

Here are three examples of how values can help you focus your grant writing energy. Raquel Muñiz started writing grants because it was important to her that her work contributed to her community. "Being able to give $40 gift cards to participants was really important to me. That $40 made a big difference for the first-generation students in my work who were helping us by sharing their time and experiences."

If your focus is mainly on paying participants, you don't need a six-figure grant to do this. You can begin with smaller foundation grants that will cover participant costs. Raquel did this for one of her first grants—a $49,978 grant from AccessLex.

Here's another illustration. Becca Lowenhaupt started writing grants because she's a "radical extrovert." She enjoys and thrives on interacting with others. When she began as an assistant professor, however, she found that all of a sudden, her work required her to sit alone at a computer. This wasn't the work she wanted to be doing. Becca used grants to forge connections to researchers whose work she found exciting and with whom she wanted to spend more time thinking critically.

But note, collaborations are expensive. You have to "**buy out**" your collaborator's time. This means that the grant pays your collaborator's salary so they are able to dedicate time to working on the grant project. For instance, you might buy someone out of a course. That frees up the time your collaborator would normally spend teaching one course. Buying out of a course typically costs 12.5 to 18 percent of someone's salary, depending on the institution. That adds up really quickly. So if collaborations are your goal, know that you will need to aim for larger grants. Case in point, Becca's National Science Foundation grant with Katherine McNeil was for $449,839.

Finally, here's an example from Donna Wu Roybal. Donna is an MD who wanted to carve out a research path to help youths at high risk for bipolar illness. To develop as a researcher in this area, Donna wanted to train in emerging neuroimaging and neurocomputation skills.

If your main goals are carving out a research path or training in a new area, you'll need a grant that covers more than one year of your time. That's because a one-year grant isn't enough time to establish a new line of work or learn unfamiliar skills. Training or early career grants (e.g., CAREER grants from the National Science Foundation, K awards from the National Institutes of Health, or early career fellowship grants) are a good choice in this case. Training grants tend to fund you for more than one year and usually have protected time built in.

Protected time means that your time can only be used toward the activities related to the grant. Your chair or mentor is not allowed to ask you teach or cover a clinic during your protected time. The funder is paying for that time. Protected time acknowledges that your time is precious and finite. Donna secured a K award from the National Institutes of Health that protected 75 percent of her time for four years. This is not unusual for K awards. The total costs of Donna's grant for just one year was $190,072.[35]

You probably have many values. How do you find one grant idea that meets all of those values? The good news is that you don't. One grant can't do everything because money and your attention are limited. Instead, start with one or two values, and see what grants grow from those values.

The **goal of this chapter** is to help you generate a list of ideas that are aligned with your values. By the end of this chapter, you'll have a short list of grant ideas that you can vet with trusted mentors.

Action Plan

- ☐ Ikigai: Examine your values
- ☐ Develop exciting ideas
- ☐ Create a short list of ideas
- ☐ Identify potential funders and mechanisms

Ikigai: Examine Your Values

To give you a frame for understanding your values, we're going to focus on your **Ikigai**. Ikigai is a Japanese concept that translates to your "reason for being."[36-38] Western interpretations of Ikigai explore what gives your life meaning by posing questions around four pillars: What does the world need? What do you love? What are you good at? What could you be paid for?[39]

Below I'll walk through these four pillars to help you generate grant ideas. For each pillar, I'll present prompts to help you think through grant ideas that come from your values. The purpose of this exercise is to generate as many ideas as possible that are seeded by your values. You may not have ideas for every pillar. That's OK. We're just brainstorming right now.

Pillar 1: What Does the World Need?

This is the pillar that seeded Raquel's grant idea. Raquel felt the world needed information about first-generation students along with payment and acknowledgment to students for sharing their experiences.

You may already have a clear sense of burning questions that meet the needs of the world. But sometimes it takes digging to figure out what you think the world needs. Here are some prompts to help:

- **The next steps approach.** *Look back at the last paper you wrote. What did you list as the future directions?*

- **The jumping off point.** *Pull up the last paper that excited you. What did the authors say were the next directions in this line of work? What could be done better?*
- **The fresh perspective.** *Brainstorm a list of things you think are missing from the literature. Is it certain voices or populations? A location for the research? Ideas researchers missed or did not consider?* Researcher Claire Spears used this approach in her work. She builds and tests mindfulness apps that help people stop smoking. She noticed, however, that low-income populations were not included in the development of these applications. This is surprising because low-income populations are more likely to smoke. So she wrote a grant (now funded) to focus on low-income populations.
- **A problem.** *What is a problem that you encounter in your work? Or a problem others tell you they encounter?* Nicole Nugent was leading an R01 project (a type of National Institutes of Health grant) to help children hospitalized for suicidal thoughts and behaviors. During the project, the parents often struggled with how to handle their kids' social media use. The parents wondered if their kids should be allowed back on social media. Nicole wanted to understand how to best guide parents. So she wrote her next grant to address this problem.
- **Limitations approach.** *When you write or read limitations sections, what is the focus? Complete this phrase: I wonder if _____ could address this problem?* I used this technique in one of my grants. I noticed that disaster research tends to focus on a single disaster event. *I wondered if* we could find techniques that would help us generalize findings across disasters.
- **Where is it approach.** *Are you looking for research you cannot find?* This happened to Ginny Vitiello. As she noted, "Everyone says differential instruction matters in kindergarten. But when I tried to find articles to cite for this recommendation, I could not find empirical research that had actually tested this recommendation." She wrote a grant to do so, and her grant was funded by the Institute of Education Sciences.
- **Theories.** *What do theories tell us the mechanisms of change are? Have those mechanisms been tested? Are there places where theories fall short?*
- **The other fields approach.** *What is an insight from other fields that might address problems in your work?* Researcher Beth Auslander noticed that nonprofits always say stories are what move funders. She also noticed that when children in her schools shared stories, the narratives were

incredibly powerful. Beth wondered if storytelling could be applied to her research questions about increasing vaccine acceptance. Voilà! A grant was born.

Pillar 2: What Do You Love?

This is the pillar that seeded Becca's grant idea. As a radical extrovert, Becca wrote a grant because she wanted to work with collaborators and generate ideas. She followed her sense of what she loves in order to build a grant that excited her.

- **Follow the energy.** *What is work that you find really exciting right now? What are you pumped to read about? What talks do you attend at conferences?* Remember that grants can help you develop in areas you care about. And you'll spend a lot of time reading literature for your grant. It's fun only if you pick an area that you think is fun. Here's one example of following energy. Donald Chi notes that he enjoys "intellectual wandering," or the opportunity to explore areas that are slightly different from his core area of research. Donald allows himself to intellectually wander into one new area at a time. That strategy is fulfilling and strategic, as it keeps Donald from wandering into twenty new areas at a time.
- **Moving away approach.** *Are there areas in your work that you find draining? Why? What would you want to change?*
- **Discussion fuel.** *When you talk to colleagues and mentors, what are the areas that generate questions or insights? What are ideas or conversations that you are having?*

Pillar 3: What Are You Good At?

This is the pillar that seeded Donna's grant idea. She had extensive clinical and research experience with youths at risk for bipolar illness. That's where she wanted to focus more of her time.

- **Easy peasy approach.** *What is something that comes easily to you, but is hard for others?* You likely have innate talent in this area. It may take time for you to figure out what this area is, but keep your eye out for it.
- **Advice beacon.** *What do people call or email you for advice about? What do you give talks on? What have you received awards for?* These are all signs that you have expertise in an area. This is a great place to start

because in your grants, you need to convince reviewers and funders that you are an expert (this will come up again in chapter 14 about the pick me factor).

- **Unique position approach.** *Are you uniquely positioned to answer certain types of questions? Based on your institution? Your training? Your experiences? Your past work?* Joe Evans is a researcher who has been awarded over $24 million in grants and contracts. Joe observes that this strategy has been a winning approach for his work. "In Nebraska, half our state is rural. So that's one way we've been able to make our niche. We emphasize our expertise in rural environments. Conversely, our colleagues in Philadelphia emphasize their expertise on inner cities in their approach."

Pillar 4: What Could You Be Paid For?

I focus on this pillar last. I do so because when you start by asking what you could be paid for, you risk getting stuck in the trap of chasing funding as the goal. Funding can be a goal, and it's a good one. Yet as author Francis Chan once said, "Our greatest fear should not be of failure . . . but of succeeding at things in life that don't really matter."[40]

You probably became a researcher not to get funding but instead because you saw a need in the world (pillar 1), loved something about research (pillar 2), or had a lot of talent in an area (pillar 3). As you saw above, there are many ways to prioritize those needs first in your grant writing.

All of that being said, we live in a world where it's important to be practical, and the prompts below will help you identify practical grant ideas quickly.

- **Request for Applications.** *Start regularly reading and searching for requests for applications from your target funders.* Look back at your list of usual suspects from chapter 1. Keep tabs on all of these funders to see what calls for applications they are putting out. **Requests for applications** (also called requests for proposals or RFPs, or funding opportunity announcements or FOAs, pronounced "foh-ahs") are announcements from the funder about the areas they want to fund. Brainstorm ideas after reading requests for applications.
- **Grant mechanisms approach.** *Follow up on the grant mechanisms you identified in your usual suspects list. What ideas do you have that might fit specific mechanisms?* Pull up the abstracts you found in chapter 1. Consider their scope and size. Do you have ideas that fit within a similar scope and size?

- **Existing data.** *Do you have access to data that can answer exciting questions? Is there a way to leverage that data?* My mentor, Annette La Greca, had conducted seminal studies on children's responses to disasters. We wondered if new analytic techniques could help us ask new questions of this data. This became our R03 grant, which the National Institute of Mental Health funded.
- **Collaborators approach you**. Sometimes you will be lucky and a collaborator will approach you with an idea. Questions to ask yourself in these situations are: *How much of my time will this collaboration take? Is the idea exciting to me? Will I get an experience that I value from this collaboration? Do I like working with this person or could I like working with this person?* Collaborators can be especially helpful if they are experienced grant writers. Paula Strickland from the National Institute of Allergy and Infectious Diseases says that collaborators "will have a good idea about how to be successful in getting [a grant] or maybe tell you about the pitfalls that they had and challenges and what they then had to do to become successful."[41]

Congratulations. After working through these prompts, you'll have a list of seed ideas for potential grants. Keep reading to find out how to take those ideas from seeds to fully bloomed grant ideas.

Develop Exciting Ideas

A common concern I hear from people new to grant writing is, "But I have no original ideas. Someone scooped my idea."

First, if other people are getting funded for ideas you have, this is a good sign that you are on the right track. You are identifying important problems in the world that others want to fund.

Second, it is unlikely that you will come up with an idea that no one has ever thought of before. There are just too many scholars in the world and your field to make this likely. In fact, if no one has ever considered the issue you are puzzling through, it could be a sign that it's not important work. As scholars sometimes joke, "'It's never been done' is not a strong argument. If it's never been done before, it probably doesn't need to be done."

I say all of this to encourage you to persist when you are developing ideas. It's easy to get discouraged or dismiss your seed ideas. But your seed ideas are just seeds. Coax and work on your ideas. Help your ideas bloom to their full potential.

Here's one strategy for developing your ideas. Dan Whitaker advises, "Sometimes combining ideas can make something innovative."

For instance, Shannon Self-Brown has been working on a program to prevent child abuse, SafeCare. Testing SafeCare is not innovative because, thankfully, it works. Shannon, however, combined SafeCare with a program to prevent secondhand smoke. All of a sudden, she took a tried-and-true prevention program, SafeCare, and created a new application that was really exciting. The National Cancer Institute agreed and funded this work.

Here's another example from Nancy Kassam-Adams. Nancy had just finished a project on a web-based mental health game. She was talking with her web vendor about the next steps for this work. They had what Nancy calls an "aha" moment. They noted that in addition to mental health work, there needed to be work on web-based assessments. And they noticed that it was especially hard to assess children after they left the hospital and link this data back to follow-up care. Nancy and the team combined these seed ideas about *next steps* (what's next for their project) with a *fresh perspective* (pivoting to assessments) to address *a problem* (linking to follow-up care). Notice that these seed ideas are all related to our Ikigai prompts. Nancy and the team wrote a grant to create web-based assessments for children after they leave the hospital that would connect the data to follow-up care. That was a winning combination worth funding, which is exactly what the Eunice Kennedy Shriver National Institute of Child Health and Human Development did.

Look back at the seed ideas you generated above. Consider whether any of these seed ideas could be combined to create an exciting grant idea. Take some time to think through combinations you might like. For example, does an innovative approach from pillar 1 combine well with a mechanism you were looking at in pillar 4? The sum of your ideas is often greater than any individual idea alone.

Create a Short List of Ideas

Now it's time to generate a short list of your best ideas. Create a bulleted list of ideas. Each idea only needs to have two or three sentences. Write down the essential heart of the idea so that you could explain your grant idea quickly to someone else. You'll use this short list like an elevator pitch. Your elevator pitches will help you get feedback from experienced grant writers on which ideas to submit first. (Stay tuned for the next chapter, where we will actually do this.)

For instance, early in my faculty career I created a short list of grant ideas. Here's one those ideas:

> Track Texas academic performance before and after Hurricane Ike to understand hurricane impacts on schools. The Texas schools database has nineteen years of data. Compare the data with comparable districts that were not in the path of the hurricane.

This tiny idea became my first major grant, funded by the National Science Foundation. This idea grew from needing a *fresh perspective* (pillar 1: wanting to understand how disasters impact schools), *following energy* (pillar 2: as a former schoolteacher, I wanted to focus on working with schools and children), a *unique position* (pillar 3: I discovered a special data set that would help us address questions about school functioning), and the *easy peasy approach* (pillar 3: this idea requires a lot of statistical expertise, which is what I am good at).

Identify Potential Funders and Mechanisms

Now that you have a short list of ideas, go back and look at your usual suspects list of funders and mechanisms you identified in chapter 1. For each idea, identify which funder and mechanism might be a good fit for that idea.

To illustrate, here's what I did when I started my grant writing journey. I generated a short list of ideas I thought were important and innovative. Then I brainstormed which funders and mechanisms might be a good fit for the idea.

Betty's Short List of Ideas with Funders and Mechanisms

1. Track Texas academic performance before and after Hurricane Ike to understand hurricane impacts on schools. The Texas schools database has nineteen years of data. Compare the data with comparable districts that were not in the path of the hurricane. (Note that this is the idea you just read above.)
   Funder and mechanism. National Science Foundation. Regular grant submission to the Humans, Disasters, and the Built Environment program.
2. Test the feasibility of integrating complex data sets to understand factors that impact child mental health outcomes after disasters. Risk factors could include access, quality, delivery, and efficiency. This

would be a data synthesis project. Potential hurricane data sets: Hurricanes Ike and Katrina.

Funder and mechanism. The National Institute of Mental Health or the Eunice Kennedy Shriver National Institute of Child Health and Human Development. R03 grant.

3. It seems important to understand how the environment and access to play spaces, alongside child population density, changes over time pre- and postdisaster. A geographic information system mapping approach would be needed.

Funder and mechanism. National Science Foundation. CAREER grant submitted to the Humans, Disasters, and the Built Environment program.

Tips and Frequently Asked Questions

Find your North Star. Researcher Sam Brody shares that early in his career, a senior colleague told him to dream big. The colleague asked Sam to think about what his programmatic line of study would be, if Sam could start a center or institute with $100 million in funding. Sam said that beginning with that big vision first "guided me throughout my career. It helped me figure out where to focus. From thinking about individual papers, a National Science Foundation CAREER grant, tenure, to full professor." And the wonderful thing is, Sam now runs the center he dreamed about at the outset of his career.

Is it a problem if my ideas don't cover every pillar? No. The pillars are just a starting point for generating ideas. Fantastic grants usually grow from multiple pillars, but they don't have to. If you look at the web-based assessments grant idea under "Develop Exciting Ideas" above, that idea grew out of seeds from one pillar—pillar 1.

Avoid proposing ideas that are too big to be feasible. Your grant ideas are just one step in addressing a bigger problem in the world. Does your grant idea help you work toward where you hope your research program is in the next five to seven years? Answer the first and most important question you need to answer to do the work you care about.

At the same time, avoid proposing ideas that are too small. You may be feeling like Goldilocks here. How can ideas be too big and now too small? Well, if your idea is too small, it's probably not worth funding.

It's hard to develop this intuition for what's "just the right size." Don't worry, I'll help you figure out what's the right size in our next chapter.

Which comes first, the idea or the funding target? This is a true chicken-or-egg question. For some people one comes before the other, but usually this is an interactive process of finding ideas that fit your values and funders that like your ideas. You'll continue to develop your ideas as you learn more about the power of grants (chapter 3), start to pitch your idea (chapter 4), and talk to funders (chapter 5).

Should I start with "safe" or "risky" ideas? The beauty of grant writing is that this is up to you. Ultimately, you're the one who has to do the work when it's funded. Start with ideas you care about and are getting encouraged to pursue. But you'll want to weigh more than just the riskiness of your ideas. As researcher Aisha Dickerson shares, she also considers "whether a grant may only be available for one cycle or if she might have a limited window of eligibility for a grant." In addition, consider the value of different types of grants for your career (I'll discuss more on how to do this in our next chapter).

Is it harder to get funded for more controversial topics? Not necessarily. It's about making your case. Researcher Katie Edwards shares that she has had good success getting her work on social justice funded. She advises that you have a clear theoretical approach, show empirical data that supports your approach, and look at and cite the people who are likely to review your work.

The Takeaway

Remember that you are the most important player in the grant writing process. Put your values and needs first. I'll leave you with some words of encouragement from researcher Melissa Osborne. "Remember why you are doing the work." Melissa felt buoyed in her own work when a reviewer wrote, "I'm so glad you are doing this work. It's really needed." I know that if you stick close to your values, you'll get this feedback from reviewers too.

In the next chapter, you'll learn how to figure out which idea on your short list is likely to have the highest impact on your career and be most fundable.

3

External Values

FURTHER YOUR CAREER GOALS

Grants benefit everyone, not just the person who writes the grant.

—CAILLE TAYLOR OSTROLENCKI

DURING ONE OF MY FIRST WEEKS as an assistant professor, I had an important meeting with a senior administrator. They told me, "If you want to be promoted, you need to secure a federal grant. A foundation grant will not count."

This meeting was a wake-up call. I realized I couldn't focus solely on my values in grant writing. I also needed to pay attention to external values, or the values of the people and institutions around me. External values had ramifications for my career. In this case, my first institution highly valued federal grants. A federal grant would create leverage in my career. I could broker a federal grant into a promotion. Conversely, if I ignored these values about federal grants and concentrated only on foundation grants, I'd lose my job. I would not be promoted.

External values matter for your career too. You can only write a few outstanding grants at a time. Understanding external values helps you channel your writing energy. You may decide you don't want to focus on grants that matter to others. But you can only make that choice when you understand the external values at play.

The **goal of this chapter** is to help you understand external values so you make informed decisions about where to put your grant writing energy. I'll walk through examples of external values. Then I'll show you how to expand your network to uncover external values that matter for your career. Finally, you'll use the information you gather about external values to decide which grant idea from your short list you want to target first. By the end of this chapter, you'll understand how to use grants to further your career goals.

Action Plan

- ☐ Understand external values
- ☐ Uncover external values
- ☐ Meeting 1: Aspirational peer
- ☐ Meeting 2: Mentor or potential mentor
- ☐ Meeting 3: Senior administrator
- ☐ Select a grant idea

Understand External Values

It took me a long time to figure out why my first institution was so focused on federal grants. All institutions have a vested interest in getting you to bring in grant money. Grant money benefits the whole organization. Institutions, however, don't value all grant money equally.

Here's why.

Institutions often receive more money if you apply for federal grants. This is because for federal grants, institutions are able to charge **indirect costs** (also known as indirects or IDCs, overhead, or facilities and administration, or F&A). Indirect costs are the costs of the grant that go toward overhead (e.g., keeping the lights on, paying administrators, and running libraries). Indirect costs get charged to federal agencies at a set negotiated rate by each institution. Indirect costs are based on a percentage of your **direct costs**, which are the costs you budget for the work in the grant (e.g., for salaries, participants, and equipment).

To illustrate this, let's look at how indirect costs work at Harvard. Harvard's current federally negotiated indirect cost rate is 69 percent for on-campus research.[42] That means if a researcher secures a grant with direct costs of $100,000 from the National Science Foundation, Harvard will get an *additional* $69,000 in indirect costs ($100,000 multiplied by 0.69). In other words, Harvard will receive a total of $169,000 (i.e., $100,000 in direct costs plus $69,000 in indirect costs).

This one fact about indirect costs has huge implications. In 2019, Harvard received approximately $560 million in federal funding.[43] Based on Harvard's indirect cost rate, we can guess this breaks down into roughly $331 million in direct costs and $229 million in indirect costs (i.e., 69 percent of $331 million). This means indirect costs were worth an additional $229 million to Harvard. Put another way, Harvard would have missed out on $229 million if the same investigators had applied to foundations that didn't allow indirect costs. Hopefully you can see now why indirect costs are important to institutions.

But rules about indirect costs are complex. For example, some foundation grants allow institutions to charge indirect costs, similar to federal grants. Foundation indirect costs rates are often lower than indirect cost rates for federal agencies. Indirect cost rates for a foundation might be 15 or 20 percent of the direct costs, compared to the 69 percent we saw above for Harvard. And even federal grants have quirky rules about indirect costs.

Caring about indirect costs is just one instance of an external value, meaning a judgment that institutions have about the worth of grants. Institutions have different and conflicting external values. Some institutions care about indirect costs, while others do not. My first institution did not want me to seek out foundation grants, but my current one wants me to apply for foundation grants. (Many institutions highly value foundation grants. I don't want to give the wrong impression that foundation grants don't matter.)

Here's one more example to illustrate how complex external values can be. Recall Donna Wu Roybal's story from chapter 2. Donna wanted to help youths at high risk for bipolar illness. She secured a K award, a federal training grant from the National Institutes of Health. The direct costs of Donna's grant for 2020 were $175,993.[35] If Donna's grant was a typical federal grant at Harvard, you'd expect to see her institution receive an additional $121,435 (i.e., $175,993 in direct costs times Harvard's 69 percent indirect cost rate). But K awards don't allow large indirect charges. The indirect costs from Donna's grant in 2020 were $14,079. Remember too that K awards protect your research time— specifically, 75 percent of Donna's time. That means 75 percent of Donna's time could not go toward teaching, clinical work, and so on.

Some institutions will nudge you away from K awards. Those institutions might devalue K awards because the indirect costs are low and the built-in protected time takes researchers away from the work they were hired to do. Other institutions will push you toward K awards because K awards have high prestige and help develop faculty careers.

It's hard to navigate complex external values on your own. Here's how to get help.

Uncover External Values

Messages about external values are frequently subtle and not written down. As one assistant professor said to me, "My institution told me that grants aren't critical, but I learned really fast that when I did secure a grant, this was the thing people paid attention to, that got written up for publicity, and that got talked about in mentoring meetings. It took a while, but it became clear to me that grants were much more important than people were letting on." (Note, when key information is not written down or talked about openly, this is usually a sign that the hidden curriculum is at work.)

How do you navigate these subtle messages to get information about external values? I'm a psychologist, so I bet you can guess what my answer is. You have to talk it out and ask questions. What's more, you need to talk to different power brokers to develop a complete picture of external values.

For the exercises in this chapter, set up three important thirty-minute meetings. Talk to an aspirational peer, mentor or potential mentor, and senior administrator. These meetings are ordered from the least to most intimidating. If you're an introvert like me, it can help to work up to the most senior meeting last so that you feel well prepared for that final meeting. We're focused on thirty-minute meetings because even extremely busy people are typically able to clear a half hour for talented researchers like you.

For each meeting, bring copies of your:

- **Short list of ideas from chapter 2**. You are going to ask for feedback on which ideas are most fundable or would create the most leverage in your career.
- **Your CV**. The people you meet will be able to provide feedback on how competitive you are for certain grants and how to become more competitive.
- **A list of your questions**. I'll outline potential questions for each meeting below.

Meeting 1: Aspirational Peer

Ideal target. For your first meeting, this aspirational peer could be someone from the list you pulled in chapter 1, when you were evaluating CVs for the usual suspects exercise. An aspirational peer will be most helpful if they are already at your current or dream institution. Choose someone who has some grant experience. At a minimum, they should have submitted grants, even if those grants were not funded.

Why their perspective is helpful. This aspirational peer is well positioned to give you advice on the politics and administrative red tape of your institution or dream institution.

Questions to Ask Your Aspirational Peer

- How are grants viewed by the institution?
- Are there certain mechanisms that are viewed more highly?
- What resources have you been able to access here that you would recommend for an early career scholar?
  Example: Sometimes there are formal and informal resources you can access. Maggi Price, for instance, noted that she asked for copies of successful grants from colleagues and mentors, thereby aiding her own grant writing (e.g., the samples served as templates for grant writing mechanics and illustrated correct formatting).
- What challenges have you encountered in trying to submit grants here? How did you overcome those challenges?
  Example: Kim Ono learned she needed extra time to focus on internal paperwork because it needed to go through two offices for review.
- If there is time, ask about the ideas you included on your short list. What do they think is most fundable?
- If your aspirational peer has had success in your field, ask them, What funders have you had good experiences with? What made them good experiences? Were there certain program officers that you found particularly helpful?

Meeting 2: Mentor or Potential Mentor

Ideal target. You are looking for someone who has sat on a promotion or hiring committee for the job you want. You want someone who is highly regarded at your institution, has a job you might like to have one day, and has values similar to your own. It's hard to identify when someone holds similar values. Some signs could be a similar personal life, background, or whatever is meaningful to how you want to navigate your career. Many institutions have a formal mentoring system. Use this resource if it's available to you. If your institution does not have a formal mentoring system, ask your networks for suggestions for an ideal target.

Why their perspective is helpful. Funded senior mentors have intuition about what's fundable, understand the culture of funders, and can provide feedback on areas you need to develop to be competitive. For example, research dean Kirsten Davison shares that for an R01 grant application to the National Institutes of Health, she would advise that you start thinking about your publication record and pilot data, line up coauthored publications with your team, and more. Here's another illustration. Jon Wargo was puzzling through what the Spencer Foundation meant when it said it "fund[s] people not projects." His mentor helped him understand this phrase and how to make his grant (now funded) compelling to the Spencer Foundation.

In addition, talking to senior scholars matters because you're going to need a lot of letters in your career. Developing relationships now builds a foundation for when you need to ask for letters of support for fellowships, grants, tenure packets, and much more.

Questions to Ask a Mentor or Potential Mentor

- How are grants viewed by the institution?
- Are there certain mechanisms that are viewed more highly? How do people view **coinvestigator** status versus **principal investigator** status? (Coinvestigators are not the lead on grants, they are collaborators; the principal investigators lead the grant. Some institutions care about your role on a grant. For example, you may need to be a principal investigator on a grant, not a coinvestigator, to get promoted.)
- Would you mind looking at my short list of grant ideas? Which grant would you recommend I start with and why? Do you agree with how I'm thinking about funders and mechanisms?
- If my values are _____, do you have recommendations for how I can successfully pursue these values in this institution? (Pull from what you discovered in chapter 2's Ikigai exercise.)
- What funders have you had good experiences with? Why? How about particular program officers or programs that you've had good experiences with? Who are the reviewers typically reviewing for these programs? (I'll talk more about program officers and programs in chapter 5.)
- What resources (e.g., mentoring, grant writing training, and review of proposals) are available here to help me succeed?

Meeting 3: Senior Administrator

Ideal target. The best person to speak with is likely the dean of your school, someone in charge of research development at your institution, or your chair. You are looking for someone who interfaces with the larger organization and is in charge of promotion, hiring, and securing resources for your school or department. You may not be in the position you want to be in permanently (maybe you are a PhD student or postdoc, or maybe you are looking to make a career transition). In those cases, it's best to speak to someone who is an administrator for the job you want in the future.

Why their perspective is helpful. Senior administrators understand the bigger picture and politics at your institution. They will be able to guide you in how your success will catapult you into the position you want. They will also have insight into how those in even higher positions value contributions from individual researchers. And they may have tips for you. For example, if you are in a nine- or ten-month position, did you know that often grants can cover your **summer salary**, meaning the months you are not paid? This money is paid on top of your salary, which translates into a significant salary boost.

Questions to Ask a Senior Administrator

- Does our institution prefer certain types of grants? Why is that? (Again, external values are frequently not explicit. You have to ask people to gain this inside information.)
- What do you see as the key grant types for people in my position to go after? How do you view coinvestigator versus principal investigator status? Does it matter? How about internal versus foundation or federal funding?
- If my values are _____, do you have recommendations for how I can achieve these values at this institution? (Pull from what you discovered in chapter 2's Ikigai exercise.)
- What is your sense about how external senior colleagues (e.g., tenure reviewers) might value different types of grants?
- What resources (e.g., mentoring, grant writing training, and review of proposals) are available here to help me succeed?
- What should I be thinking about in terms of grants right now?
- Would you mind looking at my short list of grant ideas? Which grant would you recommend I start with and why?

Select a Grant Idea

When I was a new faculty member, I did the exercises in this chapter. One of the people I met with was Ann-Margaret Esnard, a senior scholar at my institution who is a longtime reviewer for the National Science Foundation and other funders. I showed Ann-Margaret my short list of ideas (the ones you saw in chapter 2). Ann-Margaret thought many of the ideas had promise, but she was most excited about idea 1 (examinations of Texas school data pre–and post–Hurricane Ike). She thought this work was missing from the field and what was being funded at the National Science Foundation. What's more, she had ideas about how this work could be expanded to include planning expertise.

Ann-Margaret's enthusiasm about this idea was the type of insight you are looking for in these meetings. When you submit your grant, you want reviewers (i.e., established scholars in your field) to be captivated by your ideas. If you are not able to generate excitement, your idea will not get funded. In addition, Ann-Margaret had intuition about gaps in research and funding built over years of experience. I did not have that intuition yet, but she was willing to share it with me.

What's more, you never know what may grow from your meetings. Ann-Margaret became one of the most influential people in my career. We cowrote grants and papers, cotaught a class, and comentored students. Ann-Margaret is still one of the first people I call about big career decisions, like moving to New England.

Take a moment to reflect on your meetings and values. Choose a grant idea based on what meets your values and career goals.

Tips and Frequently Asked Questions

Won't people steal my idea? A well-written grant proposal will convince reviewers that you are the one person in the world who needs to do this work. It will be hard for others to take your ideas because they come from your values and insights. But there are people who might try. Most scholars I spoke with advised speaking only with scholars you can trust. Researcher Ananda Amstadter offers this tip: "Do your homework. Ask peers and talk to the person's postdocs and graduate students to understand if they are responsive and create a culture of kindness and team science." An important point here is that these meetings are helping you build a network of trusted, helpful colleagues.

How do I get past feelings of intimidation in order to email experts? Remember that the worst possible outcome is usually just that scholars don't respond or don't have time to meet. That's OK. You still walk away with good information. You learn that the other person isn't able to support your career growth right now. And researcher Jessica Hamilton shares this advice: "When you're trying to schedule a time to meet, defer to the other person's schedule and times that might work for them. Be as flexible with timing as you can be. Oftentimes people are excited to meet with you, but they have limited availability."

Should I start with small or big grants? There is no correct path, and "small" is relative. A $100,000 grant is small in some fields yet large to other fields. Even within one field, a $50,000 grant could be highly valued by one institution and devalued by another. Use your meetings to learn what's small for your field/institution and how competitive you are for different grants. Small grants have many benefits. Michelle Pebole observes that small grants are important for building confidence.[44] Rebekah Levine Coley notes that small grants "show you can do grant-funded work, which is great evidence and reason for people to give you a larger-sized grant." And Lori Peek remarks that "when it comes to my graduate students, I encourage them to apply for everything they are reasonably qualified for. This ranges from $500 travel grants from our department to $1,000 university awards to $50,000 dissertation fellowships. This work does not go to waste as it helps students refine their ideas and research designs while pushing them to stay fresh with the literature. It also builds their CVs and gives students practice with lower-stakes award applications." I agree with all of these excellent points. Yet I will add that even small grants take a lot of effort. Compete for "big" grants too if they meet your values and you are getting feedback that you can write a competitive application. Aiming high is one way to ensure that talented Black, Indigenous, and people of color, women, and early career scholars aren't "sidelined."

How many grants should I be writing at one time? This depends on your bandwidth, values, and expectations in your job. To illustrate, I am in a **hard money position** (i.e., my salary does not depend on grants). I like to lead one grant writing project at a time, supporting other grants as a coinvestigator or consultant. I do not have a set goal for the number of grants I submit per year. As a counterpoint, when my colleague Stephanie Fitzpatrick was in a **soft money position** (i.e., her salary depended on grants), Stephanie would lead six to eight grant submissions a year, often working on two at a time. At the same time, researcher Susanne Brander urges you to consider how funding might wax and wane in your field. If you are in a field where investments vary widely, you may want to apply for multiple grants during times where investments in your field are high.

Should I focus on leading my own grant or being a collaborator? Weigh your values against your career goals. Some institutions will only promote you when you receive funding to lead a grant (i.e., you are the principal investigator). But there are many advantages to working with collaborators. Nicole Errett shares that working with one of her graduate advisers helped her get experience and feedback on grant writing. Use the external values analysis from this chapter to figure out what direction is right for you. Also note that there are many other roles you can play on a grant. You may see these roles: coprincipal investigator, multiple principal investigator, project leader, other significant contributors. Check the application guidelines (covered in chapter 7) for what specific roles mean at the funder.

How do I find collaborators? Meet with people. Donald Chi shares this strategy. Early in his career, Donald set aside time each week to have thirty-minute meetings with people at his institution. At those meetings, he'd discuss research and get to know the other person. Donald says, "This helped me understand potential areas for collaboration, areas where a drift in my work could eventually lead to a collaboration, and what it might be like to work with that other person. This strategy had a low yield, perhaps only one in ten people from these meetings became collaborators. But I still collaborate with those colleagues ten years later."

How do I choose collaborators? Pick people with expertise needed to carry out the grant. You want to convince reviewers you have a dream team (for more on this, see chapter 14). For example, if I were writing a grant on disaster communications with schools, I don't have expertise in communications. I'd need to add a collaborator with this expertise. But don't just focus on expertise. Lori Peek adds that "you want people who are responsible, can meet deadlines, and share similar values to you. Just because you like someone or they are fun does not mean that you will work well with them. This is why emphasizing shared values when it comes to work and life feels especially important." Keep in mind that if your grant is funded, you will have to work with a collaborator for a long time.

Are there other ways to build out my network? Start by making small connections with people (like the meetings in this chapter). Researcher Jim Slotta says, "Get coffee with someone at a conference. Go to sessions led by people with whom you want to connect. Read their papers before you meet. Down the road, reach back out and ask that person to be on a symposium with you. Then do a great job of organizing the symposium; send out a working document a month before your symposium. This is a chance to shape knowledge in the field and make yourself more visible. And remember, listening always wins. The goal isn't to wow them with your work but rather to hear what they are saying and develop a relationship."

What advice do you have for people who've had success with small grants but haven't landed that big grant yet? Figure out how you want to shape your career. Do big grants matter for your institution? It may perfectly meet your goals and those of your institution to concentrate on small grants. If you want bigger grants, however, but haven't found success yet, keep reading. Every chapter will cover strategies for making your grants compelling to reviewers and funders. You may already know some of the information in these chapters if you've had success with smaller grants. But these chapters may deepen or extend your skills.

What advice do you have for people who are not citizens in the country where the funder is based? For example, what can you do if you are not a US citizen but still want to apply for US federal grants? Check the eligibility requirements for the funder and raise this issue when you conduct your meetings.

Are there other benefits to grant writing? Grants are a chance to dream and grow as a scholar. What would you do with your work if you had money and support? When you write grants, you develop new concepts, start collaborations, and read about advances in your field. Grants have material benefits too. They help you see what other people are paid and how institutions value those people's time. Grant writing also gives you chances to increase your salary. As I mentioned earlier, you may be able to ask for a summer salary if you are in a nine- or ten-month position. Again, a summer salary is when you "cover" your summer months, meaning you're paid up to 33 percent of your yearly salary on top of your regular one. Sometimes people use grant writing to negotiate higher salaries. Talk to people at your institution to understand how grant writing helped them navigate career growth.

The Takeaway

Talking to people gets you inside information, draws on the intuition of senior scholars, and builds your networks. But now it's time for you to make decisions based on all of this information you've collected. Which idea do you want to start with? Choose one idea. Sometimes people struggle with feeling like choosing one idea means leaving other ideas in the dust. You're not giving up on the other ideas, you just need a place to start. Once you choose your idea, it's time to run with it.

Next, how do you pitch your idea?

4

The One Pager

CREATE PHENOMENAL PITCHES

Grant writing is just part of a larger goal of articulating and selling your work. Everyone has to sell their work, whether you're trying to get funding from a provost or trying to make a good impression on someone at a cocktail party.

—JAMES SHULMAN

TEARS, BAND-AIDS, and the words "thank you science" appeared all over the internet when people started receiving COVID-19 vaccine shots. People weren't reacting to the shot itself. People were overwhelmed with emotion because of what the shot represented. Averting deaths. Seeing grandparents. Opening schools.

What happened naturally with the COVID-19 vaccine is an example of the work you need to do when you pitch your grant. Connect *what* you plan to do with *why* the work needs to be done.

Great pitches are based not on *whats* but rather *whys*. For instance, no one actually cares about buying a hammer (the *what*). Hammers in and of themselves are not that interesting. Instead, people go to the hardware store to buy a hammer because they want to put a treasured picture on the wall. Or because they want to build a treehouse to spend time with their kids. Those are their *whys*. People are motivated to act when you speak to their *whys*.

Speaking to *whys* is critical in grant writing. As Valerie Durrant from the Center for Scientific Review at the National Institutes of Health says, "If reviewers can't answer, 'Why should I care about this project?' you're going to have a hard time finding success in this process."[45]

You need reviewers to understand why your work matters because you need at least one reviewer to believe in your work so much that they champion your grant. Dan Cooper shares how a mentor described the importance of having a compelling pitch: "By the end of the page, you want the reviewer to be weeping. To say to themselves, 'If this proposal doesn't get funded, I'm going to fund it myself!'"

The **goal of this chapter** is to show you how to create a phenomenal pitch. By the end of this chapter, you'll know how to create a pitch that reviewers want to champion.

Action Plan

- ☐ Understand the one pager
- ☐ Evaluate a structure for one pagers
- ☐ Build your pitch: Be a prosecuting attorney
- ☐ Construct your one pager
- ☐ Avoid common mistakes

Understand the One Pager

In grant writing, you pitch your ideas with a **one pager**. The one pager is a brief summary of key ideas in your grant.

The one pager in the grant writing world goes by many different names. Sometimes it's called the **specific aims** page, which is how it's referred to at the National Institutes of Health. But sometimes the one pager goes by more covert or less formal names, such as the problem statement, aims page, prospectus, goals statement, rationale, purpose statement, relevance statement, and more. You'll know someone is talking about a one pager if they are asking you to submit a short pitch for your grant. Usually "short" means one page long, but a one pager could be two- or even three-pages long. The name is not literal. (Grant writing can be so confusing sometimes. Don't worry, I'm here to guide you.)

The one pager is the most important part of your whole grant. It's your first (and sometimes your only) opportunity to convince reviewers and funders that your work matters. Reviewers who aren't assigned to read your grant are more likely to read your one pager than any other part of your grant. And program officers often use one pagers to "shop around" your grant to look for ways to fund it. For example, program officer Daniel Singleton at the National

Institutes of Health says he distributes the one pager "to my colleagues if I think that another program might be interested in this application or to complement one of our other programs, or if I want to nominate it for outside of Payline Bridge or Select Pay Award."[46]

Unfortunately, it's not always clear what information should go in a one pager. Instructions will have vague statements like "introduce your topic," write in "nontechnical terms," or write for a "literate lay audience."

These are coded ways of saying, tell the story of why reviewers should care and why the funder should invest in your work. As Mathew Kiang shares, "Everyone thinks their own work is important. Your job as a grant writer is to convince other people that your work is important."

Let's begin telling your story.

Evaluate a Structure for One Pagers

There are a million different, perfectly good ways to write your one pager. There is no one correct way. But when you're starting out, it's easier to have a structure.

Here's a sample structure for your one pager. Use this as a starting point and riff on it as you get comfortable with grant writing. I've added prompts and some examples to the structure to give you an idea of how to think through these core elements. Afterward, I'll show you two fully worked out (and funded) samples so you can see this structure in action.

1. **Significant area**. Grab your reviewers with the first two sentences. This is how you generate excitement for your work. Answer questions for your reviewers such as, *What's the big question you're trying to answer? Why this group? This population? What's under threat? Why should we be alarmed? What's the controversy? What's the importance? Why should any person care? Why should taxpayers care? How does this area affect us?*
   Example from Lori Peek illustrating a big question. In an era of climate change, where will people displaced by disaster live?
   Example illustrating a "what's under threat" case. In the United States, 36.5 percent of adults are obese. Obesity is implicated in the development of cancers, type 2 diabetes, cardiovascular disease, and hypertension. (Notice that numbers and specific outcomes amplify the urgency in this case. Specifics are more compelling than a vague statement such as, "Obesity is a problem in the United States.")

Example showing alarm from Vernita Gordon's R01 grant to the National Institute of Allergy and Infectious Diseases. "Chronic infections caused by biofilms annually affect 17 million Americans, cause at least 550,000 American deaths, and cost the US healthcare system billions of dollars."[47]

2. **What's been done**. Describe significant scholarship and movements in the area to date. This isn't a deep dive into past scholarship. You are just giving a broad nod to what's already known to set the stage for what's missing.

3. **What's the problem**. Explain the issue or problem you see in the field. Be bold here. You are making an argument for a problem you believe we need to address. State the problem in one sentence. This needs to be short so that it's a "sound bite" reviewers can use to convince everyone to fund your work (I'll talk about sound bites again in chapter 8 when I cover evaluation criteria).

   Why the problem statement works. Problems create what copywriters call **curiosity gaps** in your writing. Curiosity gaps are spaces between what we know and what we need to know.[48] Curiosity gaps motivate people to keep reading because people want to discover what you will reveal. These feelings are exactly what we're trying to create for reviewers with the one pager.

4. **Best way to solve the problem.** *How do we solve this problem? Why hasn't anyone else seen it? How does it overcome barriers in your field? Why is it better than what's currently being done?*

5. **Feasible and innovative plan for solving the problem**. You've described *why* you need to do this work (parts 1–4 here). Now you're saying *what* you plan to do. Use aims here (for most fields) because aims help reviewers understand how you plan to deliver on your ideas.

   Tips for aims. Make your aims testable. Make it a question that can be answered. Research development specialist Alma Faust shares that "saying, 'The aim is to understand,' is not testable. How will anyone know when they understand?" Your aims need to connect directly with the questions and problems you posed above. They cannot depend on each other. If you fail in achieving one aim, you need to be able to work on your other aims. Reviewers do not like dependent aims because if one aims fails, all the other ones fail too and your project grinds to a halt. Note that your aims will continue to evolve as you work on your grant. Draft your aims now so you have a starting point.

6. **Outcomes of this work.** *What can we expect if you complete this work? What are the long-term goals of this work? Who will this help? What difference will this work make in the world? Does this work help seed future work?*

Sample 1: National Institute of Mental Health Grant on Posttraumatic Stress

Note: This is a grant I wrote with my mentor, Annette La Greca. Eagle-eyed readers will notice this grant is idea 2 from my short list in chapter 2. In brackets, I show where I used elements from the structure above. The references in these samples don't appear in the chapter notes. I left references in samples throughout the book so you could see how references affect the writing. I made minor edits to samples when edits improved readability.

[**Significant area.**] Every year, more than 100 million children worldwide are exposed to natural disasters, including hurricanes, floods, earthquakes, tornadoes, and wildfires.[1-2] As climate change is expected to exacerbate the intensity and frequency of natural disasters, mental health policy planners anticipate that the need for mental health services for children will outstrip resources. [**What's been done.**] Disaster management experts universally advocate implementing *stepped care models of intervention* immediately after a disaster—the goal of which is to stratify children so that those at highest risk for persistent distress (e.g., clinically elevated posttraumatic stress symptoms [PTSS] that endure beyond three to six months postdisaster) receive the most intense level of intervention.[3-4]

[**What's the problem.**] To date, a critical barrier to implementing postdisaster stepped care models is the paucity of information about how and why children differ in their patterns of PTSS (i.e., trajectories). After disasters, there is a formidable range of child outcomes due to structural as well as individual risk factors for PTSS. Many children (some estimates say as high as 72 percent) initially report clinically elevated PTSS postdisaster, while longitudinal studies indicate that only a moderate minority of children, roughly 4 to 23 percent, report persistent PTSS after six months.[5-9] Information about PTSS trajectories following disasters that are related to climate change per se is needed to answer key questions related to mental health policy. Using a robust set of four studies that followed over 1,500 children after severe hurricanes, we seek to answer these questions: What proportion of children with initially elevated

PTSS are at risk for persistent distress? What proportion of those with minimal initial PTSS go on to develop clinically elevated PTSS? And what risk factors increase the likelihood of experiencing persistent PTSS?

[**Best way to solve the problem.**] We propose a novel methodological approach, Integrative Data Analysis (IDA), to overcome the limitations of drawing conclusions from the myriad individual studies of children's mental health outcomes after disasters. Specifically, existing published studies, while highly valuable in informing future directions for research, are limited in terms of the sample size and diversity, period of child development examined, postdisaster time frame, frequency of assessments, and risk factors studied. IDA methods integrate individual-level data from multiple studies, creating a pooled source of data that is more powerful and diverse than any individual study; IDA is also more powerful and flexible than meta-analysis.[10] Using IDA with four landmark studies that longitudinally assessed children's reactions to four of the most costly disasters in the United States (Hurricanes Andrew, Charley, Katrina, and Ike), we will increase our sample size to 3,245 observations of 1,653 children aged six to sixteen years, assessed from three to twenty-five months postdisaster. These studies represent some of the few existing longitudinal studies of children's postdisaster reactions.[11-12] The studies utilized similar methodology and measures, necessary for data harmonization in IDA, and assessed a range of risk factors relevant to the development of PTSS.

[**Feasible and innovative plan for solving the problem.**] The objective of this proposal is to use IDA to build an empirical knowledge base of data to understand which factors characterize varying trajectories of PTSS. This proposal addresses the *National Institutes of Health's goals for rigorous and reproducible science* by integrating data to generate robust estimates of the proportions of children falling into PTSS trajectories and identifying risk factors for these trajectories. The specific aims of this R03 application are:

1. **Develop an IDA methods framework to synthesize data across four studies of children's mental health outcomes after devastating hurricanes.** We will harmonize individual data for PTSS and risk factors in the domains of child characteristics, exposure, loss/disruption events, stressors, social support, parenting, and coping at time points up to twenty-five months postdisaster. We will test measurement invariance across trials. Next, we will create commensurate measures that adjust for between-study heterogeneity in item responses. IDA methods will limit biases and maximize comparability across disaster studies.

2. **Determine trajectories and associated risk factors of PTSS following the hurricanes**. We will apply growth mixture modeling to the integrated data set to evaluate an empirically informed model of trajectories of PTSS among children exposed to hurricanes. Testing the risk factors identified from theoretical models on the development of PTSS in children, we will statistically determine risk factors that influence the likelihood of children reporting persistent PTSS after a hurricane.[13-15]

[**Outcomes of this work.**] The study's long-term goal is to develop risk models to more effectively use scarce postdisaster resources in stepped care models. Evidence-based PTSS treatments for children exist, but it is not clear which children are at higher risk for persistent PTSS after disasters.[16] The results will be directly applicable to clinical practice by providing guidance for the early identification and treatment of children at higher risk for persistent PTSS postdisaster. IDA methods used in this proposal may be used as a model for understanding children's reactions after other types of trauma.

Sample 2: National Science Foundation Grant on School Recovery

Note: This is a grant I wrote with my mentor and colleague, Ann-Margaret Esnard. You may notice it's grant idea 1 from my short list in chapter 2. The National Science Foundation doesn't specify that your one pager should be one-page long. This means your one pager for a National Science Foundation grant could be two- or even three-pages long (remember, the term "one pager" is not literal). Just make sure to keep your one pager brief. In this sample, we took advantage of not having to limit ourselves to just one page. Sample 2 is longer than sample 1. Notice that we used this extra space to flesh out our ideas. We wove in outcomes of this work earlier in the one pager.

[**Significant area.**] Schools are an epicenter of recovery after disasters. They provide an important point of access to households (Robinson 2012, 65), as approximately 98,500 public schools in the United States educate 50.1 million schoolchildren on any given day (National Center for Education Statistics 2015). Further, during and immediately after disasters, schools provide residents with access to shelter, food, medical resources, and psychological resources (Mutch 2015; Robinson 2011). [**What's been done.**] Schools have also been categorized as critical infrastructure, socioeconomic infrastructure, physical capital, and lifelines, given the significant impacts schools have on large sectors of the population when there is disruption, failure, or destruction (Cutter, Burton, and Emrich 2010; Peacock 2010; Rifai 2012; Bach et al. 2013). Schools contribute to community well-being in many ways. The reopening of schools after disasters reestablishes normalcy and routines for children and families. Returning children to daily routines is a primary recommendation for helping children recover from disasters (American Academy of Pediatrics 2015; American Psychological Association 2010). Emerging evidence further indicates that postdisaster mental health services for children may be more successful if they are based in schools versus clinics (Jaycox 2010). [**What's the problem.**] Despite the important role of schools in all aspects of daily life, little is known about how to *optimize the academic recovery of schools* after disasters.

For this proposal, we specifically focus on quantifiable levels of academic recovery after any kind of natural disaster as one proxy for "school recovery." We look at academic recovery in schools particularly because learning academic material is the primary purpose of schools. Schools that are successful in this regard are associated with better outcomes for children along with their families and communities in terms of educational attainment, income potential, and poverty alleviation (Altonji and Mansfield 2010; Dunn et al. 2015; French et al. 2014; Herd 2010; Miech and Hauser, 2001), all of which are crucial to the ability of a community to respond to future natural disasters, extreme events, and economic crises. This proposal also recognizes the importance of buildings, students, administration, teachers, and staff in school recovery. *This research seeks to describe in robust empirical fashion how and why schools differ in their postdisaster academic recovery.*

A central tenet of disaster research is that disasters do not affect all people or communities equally (Esnard and Sapat 2014; Fothergill and Peek 2015; Peacock et al. 2012; Thomas et al. 2013). Thus it is not surprising that schools in disaster-affected areas exhibit a multitude of responses, which can fall into empirically described and *potentially predictable patterns*. Some schools close immediately and permanently after disasters, usually due to devastating structural damage, while other schools repair, reopen, and return to (sometimes varying levels of) functioning quickly. Schools also close because of damage or disruption to interdependent critical infrastructure such as electricity, water, and transportation networks.

[**Best way to solve the problem.**] There is no body of literature that has examined patterns of school recovery in disaster-affected areas. Instead, studies have focused on examining *average* school academic performance pre- and postdisaster. These studies are limited in that they describe how schools *generally* respond to disasters (i.e., antithetical to a central tenet of disaster research that there is a plethora of responses), and interpretations clash with evidence describing the *multitude of responses* exhibited by schools postdisaster (e.g., Layton 2014; Texas Engineering Extension Service 2011). An important advantage of studying patterns, using appropriate statistical approaches, is that it will allow for examining the differential influence of vulnerability factors on patterns of school recovery.

[**Outcomes of this work.**] The *long-term goal* of this proposed research is to develop a novel approach to depict <u>profiles</u> of modifiable and immutable factors that identify schools at highest risk for academic decline after disasters. The richness and nuance of the information we can obtain from analyses that yield patterns will be important to prepare schools to mitigate the risks of disasters, and quickly identify and assist schools that are at risk for poor recovery after disasters. [**Feasible and innovative plan for solving the problem.**] The <u>research objective</u> here is to examine patterns of school recovery among Texas public schools after Hurricane Ike (2008). Given the dearth of research in this area, it is not possible to form a priori hypotheses about the exact nature of patterns of school recovery. Instead, we will conduct a discovery science examination leveraging advanced statistical techniques, namely growth mixture modeling, to empirically identify latent school recovery patterns. This kind of approach to school functioning is critically needed in order to provide information on the landscape of school functioning postdisaster.

We will explore well-characterized data collected from a cohort of Texas public schools in the path of Hurricane Ike in 2008, spanning the pre- to post-hurricane years of 2003 to 2011. The rich Texas data set will allow us to determine recovery patterns across a range of about 400 schools that vary in sociodemographic makeup, size, and predisaster school performance metrics. We will use a vulnerability perspective to examine the potential risk factors (e.g., institutional infrastructure, socioeconomic and demographic factors, location, and exposure) that distinguish schools that recover academically from those that do not.

SPECIFIC AIMS:

1. **Identify patterns of school recovery after Hurricane Ike**. We will model school performance (as measured by high stakes testing) of a cohort of 426 Texas public schools in 35 school districts that were in

the direct path of Hurricane Ike. We will apply growth mixture modeling and examine fit indexes (e.g., Bayesian information criteria, Lo Mendell Rubin likelihood ratio test, and bootstrap likelihood ratio tests) to ascertain patterns of school recovery.

2. **Examine the potential risk factors associated with school recovery patterns**. We will look at the potential risk factors and their associations with school recovery patterns, utilizing a vulnerability perspective. Specifically, we will test the relationship between school *institutional infrastructure* and *socioeconomic and demographic factors* and school recovery patterns. We will then examine the role of physical vulnerability in school recovery by mapping spatial clusters of school recovery patterns in relationship to *location* (e.g., school district and county location, coastal location, evacuation zone, and urbanized/nonurbanized area) and *exposure* (e.g., storm surge and flood-zone areas).

Build Your Pitch: Be a Prosecuting Attorney

Now that you understand a structure for one pagers, it's time to craft your own. Look back at the grant idea you landed on at the end of chapter 3. It is the *what*. Now you need to craft the *why* for this *what*.

Make your case. This idea comes from one of my grant writing mentors, Janet Gross. Pretend you are a prosecuting attorney, making opening remarks about why the funder should fund your work. Make your case out loud before you start writing. Talking out loud first helps you get to the point and be more compelling in your arguments. Remember that the goal is to generate excitement about your work. Here's a tip from Janet: "How would a group of educated people understand your grant? Bring it down from a very high level and make it clear."

Pitch your case to others. Once you've developed your case, pitch it to two or three colleagues. This could be someone directly in your field, but it doesn't have to be. You're looking for someone who will give you honest feedback about the urgency and significance of your case. This is not a large request because it will only take ten minutes of their time. Pitch your case to them out loud. (Later, in chapter 15, I'll walk you through how to get feedback on your written drafts.) For now, you're testing out the significance of your case and strength of your arguments (i.e., you're developing the *why* of your grant).

You'll know that your pitch is hitting the right marks when the other person is excited by it. This could look like fist pumps, clapping, and shouts of "hallelujah." Or if they are more reserved than I am, they'll give you this sort of feedback:

- This is an exciting idea. You've made a really strong case.
- The potential for this work is huge.
- We need this work. The outcomes are important and substantial. This will really benefit communities.
- This seems like a no-brainer. Why wouldn't we fund this?

Keep working on the significance of your one pager. If you aren't getting these types of statements every time you pitch, your *arguments* or *idea* need work.

- *Bolster your arguments.* Humility and cultural norms can make you feel uncomfortable selling the outcomes of your work. Researcher Emily Lattie offers this exercise for building the significance of your work. Emily says start small and ask, What is the outcome of this work? And if everything goes well, what's the biggest potential impact of that outcome? And if that outcome happened, what's the biggest impact of that outcome? Emily says this exercise helps her feel she is staying true to the work and not overreaching when pitching her ideas.

  Example of this bolstering arguments exercise. Researcher Mallika Nocco was working on a grant on deep root irrigation in California. Farmers told Mallika they were saving 20 to 50 percent of their water use when they adopted deep root irrigation. In brainstorming for her grant, Mallika thought about what it would mean if she were to get the best possible results? That would mean almond tree farms using half the amount of water they currently do. What does that look like at scale, when farms save 50 percent in terms of water usage? As Mallika says, "Grants are different from papers. In papers, I would focus on the lower end of the range, at 20 percent. But in grants, let reviewers dream with you about what your work could mean. You will get a chance to address the caveats of your work in a grant, but you don't have to start there."

  Additional example of this bolstering arguments exercise. Let's walk through the bolstering arguments exercise together, using this book as an illustration. *What is the outcome of this book?* Scholars learn how to write more fundable grants. *And if everything goes well, what's the biggest potential impact of that outcome?* Scholars get their grants funded. *What's the biggest impact of that outcome?* Scholars get to do work they're excited about. Scholars gain control over their careers, have more options on the job market, and have more negotiating power. *What's the biggest outcome if that happens?* If many scholars get their grants funded, we create system change. We hear from diverse voices missing in grant writing. We hear and fund the best ideas, not just ideas from scholars with better access to grant training. And voilà, these arguments are the introduction to this book. You owe it to your ideas to think through their potential. That's how ideas reach more people.

- *How to know when your idea needs work.* Spend twenty hours building your arguments. After that, if no one says to you, "This work matters," your idea needs work. Ask others, *What part of this idea feels weak?* Address those weaknesses. Go back to chapter 2. Could you add any of your seed ideas to enhance the importance or value of the work you are doing? It's normal for your original idea to need enhancements and refinements. For instance, the data synthesis grant idea (sample 1 in this chapter) wasn't strong enough in its original form (its original form appears in chapter 2 as idea 2 in the short list of ideas). I added important data sets and a theoretical framework as I built my case for the work.

Go back to the drawing board if needed. Building a strong case is essential. If your one pager isn't exciting enough, the rest of the application doesn't matter. As Eugene Wesley Ely says, "If you don't captivate their interest by the end of Page 1, you won't get funded. There's no page 2."[49] So keep sharing and refining your case until you get this type of feedback.

Construct Your One Pager

Once the feedback tells you that your pitch is strong, construct your one pager. Use the sample structure above to help you get started.

Avoid Common Mistakes

Not spending enough time on the one pager. The one pager is where you need to invest a large bulk of your grant writing time. Researcher Mathew Kiang shared a fascinating look at the time he spent writing his grant sections. He estimates that he spent 150 hours writing his K99/R00 grant (now funded). Of those 150 hours, 71.6 were spent on his one pager.[50] Revise, talk to others, and keep revising your one pager. Don't get stuck here, as you do need to write other sections. But remember to keep refining this part of your grant.

Your work is too ambitious. How is it possible for your work to be too ambitious when I just spent the whole chapter talking about how your work needs to address a grand challenge? Well, the problem is reviewers need to believe your work is feasible given your career stage as well as the money and time in the grant. Get feedback from mentors on feasibility. Ask mentors who are leaders in your field and have grant writing intuition for how big the scope should be. You are looking for the sweet spot of pushing boundaries in a feasible way. And remember that your grant is just one step in solving the bigger problem you care about.

Being a "me" grantee. Don Waters, who was a senior program officer for the Andrew W. Mellon Foundation for twenty years, relates that it's helpful to shift your mindset from being a "me" to a "we" grantee. "Me" grantees focus their grants on themselves, how much they've published, and how the grant furthers their career. You want to be a "we" grantee. Frame your grant around how it helps solve challenges we all care about and moves the mission of the funder forward. Another way to think of this is shift the frame from thinking about your past achievements to concentrating on the future potential for this work. This is true even of training grants.

Not simplifying enough. You are writing for a smart audience, but not every reviewer is an expert in your topic. Researcher Tom Cova shares that getting too technical too soon makes reviewers feel like they "stepped in a mud puddle up to the knee." So program officer Daniel Singleton urges you to create a one pager that "anyone in the broader field can easily read or immediately understand what the problem is, what the project is doing and how the project addresses the problem."[46] More tips on how to do this are coming in chapter 9.

Tips and Frequently Asked Questions

How many aims do I need? This depends on your field, but I like to stick with two or three. In chapter 6, I'll walk you through how to get samples so you can figure out the conventions in your field. But research development specialist Alma Faust offers this advice, "A key to grant writing is learning to be flexible in your writing. I used to like writing grants with three aims, but I often work on grants with two aims right now because that is what works for the questions being asked."

How big should the scope of my aims be? This is field dependent, so check with mentors, your research office, and colleagues. For a general guideline, researchers I spoke with said each aim should be big enough to turn into one paper. Program officer Valerie Maholmes notes your aim is probably too big if it contains "complex, compound sentences, includes multiple colons and semicolons, or requires two breaths to read." Valerie suggests mapping out your aims in a table. If you list your aims as the column labels, in the rows underneath write out: What expertise do you need? Approach? Time? Does that seem feasible for this amount of money and time?

Do I always need aims or hypotheses? No, not always, depending on the funder. But I recommend including aims because they help reviewers and funders understand what they can expect from your work.

What should I do if I'm overwhelmed and not sure where to start? Take some encouragement from experienced writers. Caroline Ashley says, "Don't stall on the intro. It will be rewritten anyway. Don't forget to rewrite it later when you have real clarity and can punch."[51] Mary Hertz offers this reminder: "The goal of the first draft is not to get it right, it is to get it written."[52] And finally, author Joan Didion once said, "I don't know what I think until I write it down."[53]

What should I do if my work differs from common practice or conventional wisdom? Make your case for why we need your innovative perspective. How are you solving a problem that traditional approaches cannot fix? And know that it's actually exciting when grants propose to do work that is better than the status quo.

Does the guidance here differ if I'm a bench scientist versus a clinical scientist versus a humanities scholar? No, not really. Your field guides your approach, but remember your approach is the *what* part of the equation. Much more important in the one pager is the *why*. Focus on why your work matters and why others should invest in it.

The Takeaway

Refining your one pager is the hardest part of grant writing. Don't be discouraged if you feel like you are struggling with this. Pitch, get feedback, draft your one pager, get more feedback, and keep going.

You've now developed an idea that meets your values and furthers your career goals (chapters 1–4). Congratulations. This is the first big task in writing more fundable grants.

Next I'll show you how to target a funder (chapters 5–8). Not just any funder, but the right funder for your ideas.

Target a Funder

5

Talk to a Program Officer

FIT WITH A FUNDER

If you judge a fish by its ability to climb a tree, it will live its whole life believing that it is stupid.

—OFTEN CREDITED TO PHYSICIST ALBERT EINSTEIN[54]

YOU'VE DEVELOPED a phenomenal idea. But here's the problem. Funders aren't looking for phenomenal ideas. Funders are looking for phenomenal ideas that *further their mission*.[55]

If you pitch your phenomenal idea to the wrong funder, you're a fish trying to climb a tree. The funder will never be interested in your idea because it doesn't further the mission. This is a worst-case scenario. You write an amazing grant that gets strong reviews, but the funder doesn't fund it because it doesn't match its program priorities. (This does happen, unfortunately. It's not a hypothetical scenario.)

It takes time to find the right fit. Here's an example from researcher Ryan Landoll. Ryan wrote a grant for treating anxiety in military children. He submitted his grant five times over five years to different funders until he found the right funder, the Military Operational Medicine Research Program at the Department of Defense Health Program. Ryan shares that he found the right funder through persistence. Talking to program officers at different agencies helped Ryan understand that this funder was concerned about military readiness. Once he understood this top-level concern, Ryan showcased how his work with children would contribute to military readiness.

Rebekah Levine Coley is another stellar researcher. Rebekah's work has been funded by the Australian Research Council, Russell Sage Foundation, National Science Foundation, and many others. Rebekah notes that "persistence matters. Keep trying. Some grants I've gotten after the fifth try. I've resubmitted to the same funder and then pitched to a different agency."

Bottom line, before you invest months (or years) writing a grant, talking to someone at the funder is a smart use of your time. And there is one perfect person to speak to: a program officer.

The **goal of this chapter** is to help you find the right funder for your grant idea. I'll explain why program officers are key experts you need to speak to after you've developed your one pager. By the end of this chapter, you'll have a game plan for helping your ideas find the right home.

Action Plan

- ☐ Describe program officer roles
- ☐ Examine what you learn from program officers
- ☐ Reach out to program officers
- ☐ Study the program and operation of the funder
- ☐ Meet with a program officer
- ☐ Debrief after your meeting

Describe Program Officer Roles

Who is this mythical human known as a program officer?[56] Let's read an official job description to find out. At the National Institutes of Health, a program officer "serves as a program expert for the research, education and training of individuals." The program officer is expected to "provide scientific and programmatic guidance and support to investigators in the early stages of their research careers who are conducting research" that advances the research mission.[57]

This job description tells us program officers choose their jobs because they want to guide scholarship. Program officers are often scholars themselves. This job description is not unique to the National Institutes of Health. Program officers at other funders often perform similar core roles, including articulating the goals for different funding mechanisms, defining criteria for applications, soliciting qualified applications, and supporting and monitoring the progress of awards. In other words, program officers can be an ally to you.

In fact, program officers are so helpful that during interviews for this book, the advice I heard over and over was, "Always talk to the program officer. Before and after you submit." That's a direct quote from Brian Smith, a former program officer for the National Science Foundation.

You don't have to wait until you have a full grant draft before contacting a program officer. Most program officers prefer that you contact them after you have your one pager, but before you've finished your full grant draft. In other words, the right time to reach out to a program officer is after you finish the one pager I just discussed in chapter 4.

Examine What You Learn from Program Officers

People often worry that they are bothering program officers by reaching out. But the opposite is usually true. Andrew Bremer from the Eunice Kennedy Shriver National Institute of Child Health and Human Development says developing relationships with program officers "is a bidirectional win. It allows the applicants to bounce ideas off the program officers scientifically and programmatically and operationally. And from the institute side, it affords the program officer the opportunity to really know the science that the investigator is trying to pursue."[58]

Let's break down what Andrew is saying. The purpose of speaking to a program officer is to get feedback on your idea scientifically, programmatically, and operationally. Below, I break down each of these core purposes.

1. **Scientifically**. It is appropriate to ask a program officer if they would be willing to review the one pager you wrote in chapter 4.
   A program officer can weigh in with a bird's-eye view of the science.
   For instance, a program officer can tell you whether your ideas are too ambitious or not ambitious enough. For one of my first grants, a program officer helped me understand that "proposing to explore" my topic was not exciting. They encouraged me to push harder to create a clear hypothesis. As another example, program officers can help you figure out how your science best maps onto the mechanisms at the funder. Michelle Desir planned to submit an F32 grant (a grant mechanism) to the Eunice Kennedy Shriver National Institute of Child Health and Human Development. Michelle spoke to program officer Valerie Maholmes about her grant idea and career goals. Valerie encouraged Michelle to

consider the K99/R00 mechanism over the F32 as a fit for Michelle's research and career goals. (And reviewers agreed. Michelle's K99/R00 is now funded.)

A program officer cannot *give an "on the ground" view of the science.* Program officers are not your collaborator. A program officer will not be able to give line edits on your one pager, debate whether you have the right experimental design, have recruited enough people, have a testable hypothesis, have found the best measure, or whether your findings conflict with a published article.

2. **Programmatically**. Program officers build and advance research in their program areas. They understand what has been or is funded by their program. And they frequently develop the funding opportunities.

A program officer can *weigh in on how your work fits with the program and how much of a priority it is.* Here's an example. James Shulman was looking for funding for Artstor, "the most extensive image resource for educational and scholarly use."[59] James thought the program on open education at the Hewlett Foundation could be a funder for a particular aspect of Artstor's work. But within five minutes of speaking with the program officer, James discovered that the foundation's new plan for the program was to concentrate on a particular strategy of deploying open online courses to community colleges. That short conversation saved James a lot of work, as he was not planning to focus on full courses for community colleges in Artstor's work. As another illustration, a program officer can help you understand if your line of research has already been funded several times and therefore may lack value to the program. Research administrator Rosemary Panza encourages you to ask about fit. "That's free information. They may be able to tell you, we are already funding four projects on inner-city teaching, so right now we're most interested in understanding teaching in rural settings. Or right now, we're interested in pilot projects." If your work isn't a good fit for the program, the program officer might be able to suggest other programs at the funder that could be a fit. Sometimes, program officers can also direct you to a better target funder for your work. It doesn't make sense to try to make ideas fit into a program if they don't.

A program officer cannot *share information that's not publicly available.*[60] Program officers usually won't tell you, "I think a request for applications is going to come out on this topic in nine months."

3. **Operationally**. Program officers are experts on their funding agency. Part of their job is to represent the agency and help scholars understand the mission and goals of the agency.

A program officer can *answer questions about policies and requirements.* That means they could tell you whether your work is aligned with a request for applications, also known as RFAs, RFPs, or FOAs (see glossary), answer questions about whether you or your institution are eligible for a funding opportunity, and help you understand the review process. For instance, researcher Andrés Castro Samayoa and his colleague applied for a grant that was jointly funded by the National Science Foundation and National Institutes of Health. Speaking with the program officer helped Andrés understand that the first reviewers for this work were National Science Foundation reviewers. Thus it was important for Andrés to make arguments that spoke to those reviewers first because the grant would not be passed onto National Institutes of Health reviewers until the grant cleared this initial bar of review.

A program officer cannot *answer questions about other agencies.* But they might be able to direct you to funders that have similar priorities.

Reach Out to Program Officers

Who is my program officer? Figuring out which program officer to reach out to is the first step. Look back at your one pager and the mechanism/funder you are targeting. Research who the program officer is. This is usually listed in the contact information on requests for applications. Remember that funders have a vested interest in getting program officers to speak with you. In fact, it's part of the program officer's job. If you aren't able to find the right contact, it's OK to reach out to the funder to ask.

Should you reach out via phone or email? Reach out via email first. There are some cases where program officers prefer to be contacted by phone, but these are few and far between. Email is better because you'll be able to attach your one pager, thereby cutting down on back-and-forth communication. Here's a sample email:

Sample Email

Subject Line: Meeting Request to Discuss Programmatic Fit of Future Grant Application

Dear [**Program Officer**]:

My name is [**your name**], and I am a [**your position**]. I am working on a proposal on [**your topic**], to be submitted for [**grant mechanism type; list a request for application number if you have one**]. Would you be willing to meet with me to discuss the extent to which [**my topic**] meets the mission of [**the program at the funder**]? I have attached my [**one pager; if your funder uses a specific term for one pagers, use that term here (e.g., specific aims or problem statement)**] to this email for your reference.

Sincerely,
[**your name**]

Study the Program and Operation of the Funder

Remember that the goal in meeting with a program officer is to understand the scientific, programmatic, and operational fit of your idea with the funder. You'll be better positioned to do that if you do your homework on the funder. You've already worked on the science part (chapter 4, your one pager). So the pieces you still need to understand are the program and operation of the funder. Here's the information you need to look up:

Program
- Read about the goals of the program
- See if you can find a list of priority areas or a strategic plan for the program
- Look up recent grants funded by the program

Operation of the funder
- Read up on the funder's mission. All funders have a mission, and every mission is unique. For example, the Australian Research Council's mission is "to deliver policy and programmes that advance Australian research and innovation globally and benefit the community."[61]
- Look up the strategic plan of the funder. Notice that this plan will be different from the strategic plan of the *program*. The funder is the umbrella body that oversees the program.

- If you are interested in a specific request for proposals, make sure you have thoroughly read and understood that call. Identify any questions you have about the specifics of the call.
- Look up how grants are reviewed at your funder. Is it a standing pool of reviewers? How many reviewers generally review your grant once it's submitted?

Meet with a Program Officer

When you meet with the program officer, have a copy of your one pager in front of you and be ready to take notes during your meeting. These meetings move quickly. You do not want to send a program officer an email after your meeting that says, "I forgot to take notes during our meeting. I know you mentioned I should follow up on XYZ important concept. Could you spell that out for me again?" This leaves the impression that you are unprepared, don't care about getting funding, don't respect the program officer's time, and you wouldn't be able to handle the much bigger responsibility of leading a grant on your own. None of these impressions are true for you. You've read this far because you have big ideas and care about securing funding. So take notes during your meeting.

You need to make a good impression on your program officer. It's important for your grant and career. Program officers have outsized influence on future directions for your field. I once heard a program officer joke that when they became a program officer, citations of their research skyrocketed. This is evidence that whole fields pay attention to program officers as power brokers. This anecdote also illustrates the hidden curriculum at play. Insiders use high-level strategies (citing articles) to forge stronger connections to program officers. You may not agree with insiders' citation strategy, but it's helpful to know this is happening in the background.

Here are some questions to ask during your meeting:

- **Science**: Would it be possible to give me feedback on the scope of this one pager and whether it seems appropriate for your program?
- **Program**: Does this work align with the mission of the funder and priorities of the program?
- **Operational** (if you are applying to a specific mechanism or in response to a request for applications): Would you be able to give me feedback on the fit of this work with the request for applications? (If applicable to

your funder): Are there specific review sections you would recommend for me?

- What are your tips for scholars in my position? (Meaning whatever is applicable to your current career, such as if you're an assistant professor, in a nontenure-track position, a postdoctoral fellow, a graduate student, have a career gap, or have an upcoming maternity/paternity leave.)
- Do you have any recommendations for resources that I should be aware of in order to prepare a strong application?
- How do you prefer to work with grant applicants? (Remember, program officers are human and therefore have different preferences. And funders have different cultures around working with grant applicants. At some funders, program officers do not work with the applicants. At others, program officers will sometimes conduct one or multiple rounds of review on proposals.)
- Are there any opportunities to serve as a reviewer?

For the last question, serving as a reviewer is one of the fastest ways to learn what makes grants more fundable (for more on this topic, see chapter 6). Some funders allow early career scholars or those who are new to the funder to serve as a reviewer. It is helpful to understand what the process is. For example, the Environmental Protection Agency often starts recruiting reviewers for a panel as soon as a funding announcement has been advertised.

Debrief After Your Meeting

Spend thirty minutes after your meeting writing down additional notes and impressions. It may seem like you will remember everything the program officer mentioned, but this information fades fast, and this meeting is probably the most important one you can have while you develop your grant. You want to remember information you received from the program officer.

After debriefing, make sure to write a thank you note to your program officer. This may seem obvious or old-fashioned, but it is a needed and appreciated extra step. Your program officer invested time to help you grow in your career. Send a thank you email after your call and again after you submit your grant. You are building a relationship with a program officer. Program officers can advocate for your grant if it's on the cusp of getting funded. Your program officer will hopefully play an integral role in your career over time.

Tips and Frequently Asked Questions

Should I feel bad when my work doesn't align with a funder's mission or priorities? You don't have to contort your ideas and values to fit a funder. At some point, you may be aligned. But for now, it's not the right funder for your idea.

How closely do ideas need to be aligned with the program or funder? Does it need to be an exact match? It doesn't need to be an exact match, but your ideas need to fit the mission or it will be hard for the program to fund your work.

Is it OK to speak to more than one program officer? Like mentors, you'll probably have many program officers who will help you at different stages in your career. When you meet with a program officer, ask them if they think it's appropriate for you to reach out to their colleague.

Are there other times I can speak with the program officer? Yes. So much of grant writing is networking (see the introduction, which illustrates how some networks are more well connected and more likely to be funded). We need you to have access to networks (hence the focus on networks in chapter 3). It's never too early to start building your network. Network with program officers at conferences by attending sessions where they are on the panel. Look for webinars from your funder and sign up for them. Hearing directly from program officers about priorities helps you make a better case for how your work fits with the funder.

What do program officers say is a common mistake from new grant writers? Trying to pack all of your ideas into one grant. You don't have to squeeze every good idea into one application. Grants are one step in a research career.

Will every program officer give feedback? No. Some funders like the National Institute of Justice or Centers for Disease Control and Prevention do not provide feedback.[32] But it is OK to find out who will give feedback because this information is so helpful in your career.

What if no one gets back to me? Program officers have different priorities and workloads. They might not respond to your emails or may say they don't have time. Keep searching. If they can't make time for you, they're not the program officer for you right now. Your networks can help you find program officers known to support career development.

Speak with your office of sponsored research (more on these offices in chapter 7) and your colleagues, and search on social media.

Are there other strategies for finding fit with a funder? Yes. Here's a strategy from Andrés, mentioned above. He has developed a set of "key words" for his research: inequality, race, and racial injustice. Andrés keeps an eye out for funders that use these key words in their strategic plans and mission statements.

The Takeaway

After speaking to a program officer, you may find that the program you were targeting is not the right fit. Repeat until you find the right program for your idea. The world is small in grant writing and funding. This is never time wasted, as you may find out information that is important for your next grant. Use the information you've gathered from your program officer meeting to continue to revise your one pager.

After you've found the right fit, it's time to figure out what your grant should look like. That's my next chapter.

6

Get Samples

SIGNAL THAT YOU BELONG

Take a data-driven approach to learning grant writing. See what's worked for others.

—MASON GARRISON

MY MOM MAKES the best Taiwanese beef noodle soup in the world. Here's her explanation of how to make it: "Add soy sauce until it looks right." "Cook the beef until it's a good color." Think you could make beef noodle soup based on those instructions? Probably not.

Expert grant writers talk about grants the same way: "You can tell when someone's asking for too much." "Make sure it sounds significant." "Write a compelling strategy."

My mom and expert grant writers aren't trying to be sneaky. Their explanations make sense to them because they have years of experience. They've developed intuition that helps them understand when something "looks right" or is "too much."

But you don't have years to develop intuition. You want support for your ideas now, when it can help you most in your career. You need grant samples (i.e., copies of successful grant proposals).

The **goal of this chapter** is to help you use grant samples to develop your grant writing intuition quickly. By the end of this chapter, you'll know how to signal that you belong in that coveted group of investigators supported by your target funder.

Action Plan

- ☐ Recognize samples that fast-track your intuition
- ☐ Find general samples
- ☐ Find specific samples
- ☐ Request samples: How to email
- ☐ Read samples for signals
- ☐ Try to serve on a review panel

Recognize Samples That Fast-track Your Intuition

Samples show how people made a persuasive pitch for their idea to a funder. Look for two kinds of samples: general and specific. General samples are any grants that your funder awarded, while specific samples are from the mechanism or program you are targeting.

> *Example 1.* Imagine you are writing a grant for the Robert Wood Johnson Foundation's (the funder) Research in Transforming Health and Health Care Systems grant (the mechanism):
> **General sample**. Any Robert Wood Johnson Foundation grant.
> **Specific sample**. A Transforming Health and Health Care Systems grant.
> *Example 2.* Consider you are writing a grant to the National Institutes of Health (the funder), targeting the National Institute of Mental Health (an institute within the National Institutes of Health) for an R21 grant (the mechanism):
> **General sample**. Any National Institutes of Health grant.
> **Specific sample**. Either a National Institute of Mental Health grant or R21 grant. Ideally, your specific sample would be both: a National Institute of Mental Health grant that is an R21.

Next, let's discuss why you want these two types of samples as well as strategies for obtaining them.

Find General Samples

General samples are a good place to start because they are easier to find than specific samples because they include grants funded by any program at the funder. There are simply more general grants out there for you to find. General samples will show you how investigators made a case for fit to the mission of the funder, and you'll see examples of grant writing skills in practice. For this strategy, search for samples that are available on the internet. Don't spend too much time finding general samples, as specific samples will be more helpful to you for developing intuition. It's worth spending one to two hours looking for general samples, however, as this is low-hanging fruit worth grabbing.

Where to find general samples. General samples are available on the internet. One of the important movements today is the push for making grant samples accessible. Sharing grant samples is one way to increase equity and access for all scholars. I've compiled a list of openly available grants on my website for you (www.bettylai.com/samples). I list them on my website so that I can keep the links up to date.

Find Specific Samples

Specific samples will help you understand how someone speaks clearly to reviewers for your target program. You want specific samples that were funded within the last five years because they better reflect current funding priorities and reviewer preferences.

Where to find specific samples. For this task, you'll need to ask principal investigators to share their grants with you. You are targeting principal investigators, not coinvestigators, because coinvestigators usually defer to the preferences of the principal investigators. To identify the principal investigators you should contact, search for grants funded in the last five years by your target program. You already identified many of these people during the usual suspects exercise in chapter 1. Then try these approaches (ordered from the easiest to hardest):

1. **Reach out to your existing networks**. Do you know any of the principal investigators you identified? Does anyone you know have a relationship with them? If so, reach out to them or see if your networks wouldn't mind connecting you. This is a good place to start because you've already developed the know, like, and trust factor with these principal investigators. Trust matters because people may have concerns about sharing their grants. They worry that you might take their ideas. Given that our main output as researchers is intellectual property, people need to feel safe sharing their intellectual property with you. Grants also contain sensitive information like salaries in grant budgets, plans for hiring future staff, and more. People need to trust that you will treat this material carefully.

2. **Reach out to leaders**. When you're looking at recent principal investigators funded by your target program, who are the leaders in the field (i.e., the more senior scholars)? Target these people next, even though you don't have connections with them. Leaders are a good target because this is an opportunity to build more connections in your field. In addition, target leaders over aspirational peers because leaders are further along in their careers. It is less of a risk for leaders to help you develop new ideas. In fact, it should be part of their job to help mentor a rising star like you. Leaders benefit from staying connected to the next generation of scholars. If you feel nervous about asking for a sample, Katie Edwards shares this tip: inquire about a thirty-minute meeting to ask for advice about applying to the program. Then if you feel comfortable after that, you could follow up by asking if they might be willing to share a sample.

3. **Reach out to aspirational peers**. Aspirational peers (i.e., people who are your peers, but are doing work you'd like to emulate) are a good target. But know that people in more tenuous positions (e.g., postdocs, nontenure-track professors, and untenured professors) may be less willing to share their work at this point in their careers. Overwhelmingly, though, I have not found that to be the case.

4. **Freedom of Information Act request**. This is not my favorite option. Yet this strategy comes up in grant trainings, so I want to mention it here. For grants funded by the US federal government, you can request a copy of that grant under the Freedom of Information Act. The paperwork will be routed to the submitter so that they can redact confidential information. At that point, the submitter will send their grant to an administrator, and then the grant is forwarded to you. This involves many people, is a long process, and is an indirect way of requesting a grant sample. While it's possible to use this method, it's not my first choice. As a psychologist, I know you have an opportunity to create a healthier relationship by speaking directly to the principal investigator. By emailing directly, you can learn if they do or don't want to share their grant. That's good information because this is someone whose work you really respect. Hopefully they will be a future collaborator, and at the very least they could be a future reviewer of your work. Direct conversations create opportunities to connect and understand intentions. All of this being said, people who use Freedom of Information Act requests have noted it's an important way to gain access to samples.

Request Samples: How to Email

Now that you know who your targets are, you have to reach out to them. People often feel nervous about this step. Here are some words of encouragement from researcher Nathan Kearns. Nathan says, "Sometimes imposter syndrome or feeling like you need to be the one who knows everything can keep you from reaching out to people. And it can be scary to think that no one is going to write back. But almost everyone I reached out to wrote back and shared their resources. It's a game changer."

Also keep in mind that a "no" response frequently has nothing to do with you as a scholar. A "no" usually reflects concerns about sensitive information or a bad past history with sharing.

Here's a sample email for requesting a grant sample. I suggest you blame me (i.e., this book and the training here) for making the sample request. Sometimes it's easier to ask for help when you externalize the reasons why you're doing so. In other words, here you're saying that a mentor told you to make the request.

Subject: Willingness to share a grant sample?

Dear Dr. [**their name**]:

My name is [**your name**], and I am a [**your position**]. I am submitting a grant to [**name of the program**] at [**the funder**]. I am in a grant training program that suggests that I reach out to esteemed colleagues in the field to ask if they might be willing to share a grant sample with me. I was wondering if you would be willing to share a copy of [**name their grant**]? Please do not feel any pressure to share your grant with me. I understand that there may be many reasons why people would not want to share a grant. Thank you so much for your consideration.

Sincerely,
[**your name**]

Wrapping up Your Sample Search

Repeat this email exercise until you have two to three specific samples. Searching for more samples than this has diminishing returns.

Next, let's talk about what to do with these samples you've collected.

Read Samples for Signals

The first time I watched the *Mandalorian*, the main villain in this television story was named Moth Gideon. I thought this was strange because "Moth" isn't a scary name for the most evil person in the universe. Many weeks later, I realized the character's name was *Moff* Gideon, not Moth Gideon.

I asked my dear husband, "Did you know his name was Moff?" He said, "Yes, of course it is." "How did you know that?" I asked. He said, "Because there are tons of evil people in *Star Wars* that are Moffs."

This is an example of a signal. Signals communicate belonging and social standing quickly. Moff is the signal here. It revealed both my lack of belonging to the *Star Wars* world and my husband's familiarity with it.

Signals matter. Signals are a cornerstone of the hidden curriculum in grant writing. If you don't know the signals for your funder, you inadvertently communicate to reviewers that you're an outsider. But if you learn the signals for your funder, you can use these signals to show that you belong in that coveted group of investigators funded by the program.

Signals for your program are likely different from writing conventions you've learned to date. Developmental psychologist Rebekah Levine Coley cautions that grant reviewers are often more multidisciplinary when compared to article reviewers, where reviewers are typically from your field. "In my work, economists and sociologists review grants at the private foundations and federal agencies I submit to. They use methods that are different from those in my discipline. Reviewers ask about things like model specification, causal inference, and weak descriptive designs."

Learn your program's signals. The best way to do this is to treat your grant samples as "mentor texts."[62] This term comes from Ale Babino. It means that your samples can show you the signals of your program. Study your grant samples for these signals:

A. **Buzzwords**. You probably won't find buzzwords like "Moff" in your grant samples. But most programs have buzzwords—either words that are exciting or a big "no" to the program. As you look at your samples, ask yourself, *Are there terms that are used often? Used across your samples?* Those are signal words that you can use in your grant. *Are there words you aren't seeing?* Avoid those, as they can make you stick out like a radio in a library.

Examples of buzzwords. Joe Evans notes that for a time, "interprofessional" was a buzzword for Health Resources and Services Administration grants. Nicole Nugent says that "capitalizes on infrastructure" was a phrase she saw often in National Institutes of Health grants.

Example of words to avoid. Understanding what words to avoid is critical, as this signals you understand the mission of the agency. Tom Cova relays a story about one of his first grants to the National Science Foundation. "I wrote that my grant was the 'next logical step' in the field. My mentor crossed this out immediately. He said, never say that because the National Science Foundation's tagline at the time was, 'We don't fund the next logical step, we fund the next possible leap.' Can you imagine starting a proposal with the line, 'This is the next logical step!'" It's always hard to identify what's missing in a situation (in fact, this is a test in IQ assessments). Check in with your mentors about words to avoid.

B. **Structure**. Grants for a program tend to develop a typical structure. That's because people funded by a program become reviewers for that program and mentor people who apply to it. Reviewers tend to expect certain information in certain places. Jen Heemstra encourages her mentees to use samples to reverse outline this structure. As you read, ask yourself, *What is the purpose of each sentence and figure? What are the common elements that you notice across your samples?*

Example. Lauren Clay was working on a National Science Foundation CAREER grant (now funded) for the Humans, Disasters, and the Built Environment program. She obtained two samples from researchers funded by the program. She noticed that "they looked exactly the same structurally. I realized there was a way reviewers were expecting these grants to look. This is a great example of insider/outsider networking. Make sure you tap into that insider knowledge."

C. **Approach to content**. Grants have limited space. *How much detail is there in the literature review? Methods? What key pieces of content are you seeing across your samples?*

Examples. Scott Seider notes that early in his career, reading successful grants helped him understand how much detail reviewers might want to see about hierarchical linear models in his grant. Michelle Desir says that samples helped her see how applicants crafted tables to make their timelines and training goals easy to digest.

D. **Mad libs**. Identify sentence patterns people use to make their case to a funder. Researcher Emily Gates calls these sentence patterns "mad libs." For instance, *What sentence patterns did writers use to pitch the* *significance of their work? How did writers introduce the scope of their project?*

Example. Here are two mad libs (more on this topic appears in chapter 9 on literature reviews):

Failure to understand _____ prevents us from being able to _____.

By examining _____, we will have information we need to _____.

Try to Serve on a Review Panel

I've said this before, but serving on a review panel will help you understand how to write better grants.

To get these opportunities, ask for them. Researcher Jen Heemstra recommends checking in with your networks and letting them know that this is your goal. People will keep an eye out for opportunities for you. Also ask your program officer about opportunities to serve when you speak with them (chapter 5). Program officers often diversify panels by including some early career scholars (e.g., postdoctoral fellows and assistant professors). If you are a graduate student, it's unlikely you would be included on a panel for a large funder. Yet as a graduate student, you are a candidate for serving on smaller award or fellowship panels for your field.

Serving as a reviewer will help you deepen all the skills in this chapter. You'll access specific samples and have a chance to read your samples for signals. You'll also gain insight into:

- **What reviewers see**. Do reviewers have a different portal than applicants? How is information presented to reviewers? How many applications do reviewers receive? How much lead time are reviewers given? How intense is the reporting procedure? What information is presented to reviewers first?

  Examples. The first time I served on a panel, my reviewer portal did not match the applicant one. Bolding and underlining was erased on the reviewer side of the portal. This insight changed how I wrote grants for that funder. I realized that the only emphasis technique that would appear for reviewers would be CAPITALIZATION. I could not rely on bolding or underlining. As another illustration, for some funders the one pager appears in the middle of the application packet. Understanding what information is presented to reviewers first helps you craft a better story for them.

- **Review culture for the funder**. How are reviewers trained (if at all)? What guidance do reviewers receive about what to look for as they review? Do reviewers follow that guidance? What do reviewers care about, and does this match evaluation criteria?
- **How the panel is run**. Which grants are discussed? How are they discussed? Who leads? Who runs the meeting? What's the role of the program officer in panels? How do reviewers resolve conflict? Is consensus reached? How are group ratings handled? How much time is spent discussing each proposal? Do all reviewers speak?
- **What makes writing effective**. What excites reviewers? What confuses them? Where do reviewers get stuck? How do reviewers decide what feels significant?

Tips and Frequently Asked Questions

Is an unfunded sample still helpful? Yes, although they are less helpful than funded samples. An unfunded sample will give you an idea of how to put together a proposal, but it's not going to help you develop intuition around how people made a compelling case to reviewers. Focus your time on studying funded grants.

What if I can't find a sample of a grant that was funded by my program? It's worth it to find at least one sample. Without one sample, you don't have a clear sense of the types of grants that have been funded by the program. Reach out to your networks to see if they are able to help you identify someone who might be willing to share with you. This has the added benefit of letting other people know your goals so that they can look out for opportunities for you. Another option is to apply for fellowship and training programs. Mentors in those programs will often also help you find samples because they are invested in your success.

Does my sample need to be from someone in my field? Not necessarily. Remember you are reading samples to look for signals. You are not reading to understand ideas, research, or science (i.e., field-specific information).

I'm intimidated by my samples. How am I supposed to live up to them? Your work isn't supposed to be as good as your samples yet. You're learning new skills. If you keep writing, editing, and practicing these skills, your work will one day be as good as the samples you are seeing. Remember that these samples are the best work scholars were able to create. That takes time.

Are there other ways to get access to samples? Attend grant writing and professional development workshops when you see them. Workshops help you expand your network. While there, ask about strategies for accessing grant samples.

Can program officers provide samples? They may be able to, but I don't typically hear of people asking program officers for samples. As a reviewer for this book wisely noted, funders usually are not able to release grants without the express permission of the applicants. Grants are the intellectual property of the applicants. I recommend trying the other strategies in this chapter first.

The Takeaway

When you get samples and treat them as mentor texts, you'll learn the signals that will help you demonstrate that you belong in the group of investigators funded by your program. Use these signals. Signals show you've put in the hard work of learning the culture of the program and funder. Your understanding of signals will continue to develop as you submit and get feedback from reviewers, get funded by the program, and become a reviewer yourself.

Next, let's create your plan for writing your grant before the deadline.

7

A Grant's Anatomy

OUTLINE AND TIMELINE

First drafts should never be last drafts.

—DR. TERRINIEKA W. POWELL[65]

A GOOD GRANT takes a long time to write. Researcher Tom Cova says he realized this fact early in his career when a senior investigator mentioned, "I'm in the final push of my grant. This final push is going to take me a hundred hours."

Let this sink in for a moment. A senior, well-funded investigator was planning to spend a hundred hours just on the final push of her grant.

You *will* hear stories of investigators who wrote $1 million grants in two days. But keep in mind, those investigators are usually seasoned grant writers. They have access to past grants to help draft new ones. Those two days of writing build on years of experience.

And for all of these success stories, you'll also hear stories of how working too quickly caused regrettable problems. For example, there's an urban legend of researchers who used an old grant on prostate cancer to write a new grant on breast cancer. They were working so quickly, they forgot to change the sex of their participants from male to female.

If you're new to grant writing, it's hard to know how long it will take to write your grant. It depends on the type of grant, your experience, how fast you write, your job requirements, your collaborators, and more.

Here are some researchers' experiences to help you get a sense of what your timeline might be. Mason Garrison wrote an R01 to the National Institutes of Health. Mason's writing time clocked in at 158 hours total. (Can you tell Mason is a quantitative psychologist? I love the precision here.) Emily Lattie wrote a K grant to the National Institutes of Health. Emily reached out to a program officer nine months before the deadline and spent three to four months "seriously focused" on writing. I had a similar timeline for my first National Science Foundation grant. I reached out to my program officer seven months before the deadline. I spent 50 percent of my time for one semester writing the grant.

Because writing timelines vary widely, my best advice is to start early and make time for writing. Submit the best grant possible. Sloppiness does you no favors. It is damaging to your reputation at any phase of your career. You need to impress reviewers. It matters not just for this grant but also for the work you hope to do in the future. Reviewers are esteemed colleagues that may be your tenure reviewers, sit on awards committees, and more. You will hopefully work with your program officer for many years to come. You want to impress reviewers and program officers—even if it means you have to wait for the next grant cycle to put in a grant you are proud of.

The **goal of this chapter** is to help you create your outline and writing timeline for your grant. I take the tortoise approach (as opposed to the hare one) to make slow and steady progress. By the end of this chapter, you'll have a sense of what you need to complete in order to submit your phenomenal grant.

Action Plan

☐ Understand application instructions
☐ Outline using application instructions
☐ Partner with research administrators
☐ Plan your writing timeline

Understand Application Instructions

When my partner and I moved to our first house, we decided we needed a leather ottoman. We wanted an ottoman you could put your feet on, but that looked fancy enough for company. I was pregnant with our first child, and we were strapped for time. We ordered the first decent ottoman we could find on the internet. When it arrived, it was four times the size we expected. In our haste, we hadn't bothered to check the measurements. Years later we still have this ottoman. But it's sitting unused in our basement because it's just too big.

Writing a grant without reading the application instructions is like ordering an ottoman without measuring. You're jumping in before you understand what you've committed to. Don't do this to yourself. You're going to spend weeks or months writing an amazing grant. A few hours of reading the instructions is time well spent.

Skipping the application instructions can cause a lot of stress. Grants consultant Janet Gross (one of my grant writing mentors) shares that she was working with a researcher who read application instructions incorrectly. They thought the budget was for $500,000 in direct costs. But it was for $500,000 total (direct plus indirect costs). The researcher discovered this right before the due date and had to redo 67 percent of the budget in two days.

And the worst-case scenario is that misreading instructions can lead to your grant being disqualified. There are horror stories of scholars whose grants were disqualified because they included hyperlinks in a National Institutes of Health grant—a funder that doesn't usually allow those links. Or scholars whose work was disqualified because they wrote about "merit" instead of "Intellectual Merit" for the National Science Foundation. When your grant is disqualified, you miss out on a whole application cycle. For some funders, this could mean that you have to wait six to twelve months before you can submit again. Or if you are submitting to a special call, you may not get another chance.

You may think it's someone else's job to know the rules. It's not. Your grant is going to have the biggest impact on your career. No one is more invested in getting your grant funded than you. Others want to support you, but remember that they are supporting *your* dream work. Invest the time to understand the rules and requirements for your grant.

Now I will say that when I interviewed people for this book, experts were mixed on whether you *needed* to read all the application guidelines. Some said that it was a time drain. Many, though, insisted it was necessary to get you acclimated to language and guidelines. Choose what makes sense to you. But if you don't have a strong research administration staff (more on this later), you need to read the application instructions.

Outline Using Application Instructions

Start by finding and carefully reading the grant application instructions. They are there to guide you. You are looking for:

1. **Required proposal elements**. Create a document that lists every proposal element you will need. This is your new outline for all the tasks you need to complete or get help with before the deadline. Note

that your grant samples may not be samples of a full grant. Often, grant samples show only a portion of the entire grant (e.g., the one pager and research plan). Full grants usually have many additional elements that are required for submission. Learn what these are, as they differ for each funder and mechanism.

Examples of required proposal elements. Specific aims, project summary, human subjects forms, facilities, data management plan, quality assurance plan, postdoctoral mentoring plan, CV or biosketch, budget, budget justification, and letters of support.

A researcher's story. Claire Spears shares that for her first grant, a K23 grant from the National Institutes of Health, she "forgot to think about the forms until later in the process. The amount of additional paperwork was overwhelming, and I didn't set aside enough time. I was able to finish the paperwork, but it created a great deal of stress during the final push for submission."

2. **Special requirements or disqualifying rules**. These differ for each funder and mechanism. You need to know these. Be sure you understand what items are required or not allowed.

Examples of requirements. For the Environmental Protection Agency's Science to Achieve Results program, you need to include a quality assurance approach. Reviewers are specifically asked to comment on this approach, and it needs to include a statement, project plan, and quality management plan. Many funders have rules about what information needs to appear in certain documents. (In addition, many universities and institutions have strict *internal* deadlines for grant submissions and will not allow late submissions.)

Examples of items not allowed. Some funders do not allow URL links. Some funders do not allow **letters of support**, while others require letters of support.

If you feel overwhelmed by the size of the application instructions, re-searcher Katie Edwards has a tip for you. There are often "cheat sheets" or summary sheets online to help you understand these long documents. "Search for them and see if they help you make sense of the instructions." Here's another strategy from researcher Mathew Kiang. Mathew made a copy of the application instructions and crossed out each line as he met each directive.

In this section, I focused on actions you need to take to submit a grant that meets the application criteria. Yet you don't have to work alone. Brian Smith shares that for his first grant, "I made the mistake of having the wrong starting date. Luckily, my Office of Sponsored Programs caught the mistake." Brian was fortunate to have people looking out for his success.

Let's help you create a team of people invested in your success.

Partner with Research Administrators

Your institution has people who are ready to help you: **research administrators**. Research administrators are experts who understand the rules of different funding agencies. They help you make sure you comply with those rules.

Sometimes principal investigators complain that they are fighting with research administrators. Principal investigators will say, "They're holding me up." This is a misunderstanding of the goal of research administrators. As a seasoned research administrator Michelle Gittens shares, "We are not the enemy. Our job is to protect the university and the principal investigator. Start early and ask questions. Last-minute proposals cause stress and can introduce mistakes."

Research administrators usually work in a central office at your institution that goes by a title like **Office of Sponsored Programs**, Grants Administration, or University Research Services and Administration. If you're lucky, you will also have research administrators who are staff members in your school or department.

Research administrator positions are sometimes split into **pre-** and **post-award** functions. Preaward refers to people who work with you before you submit your grant. Postaward means people who work with you after your grant is awarded. Postaward work involves things like helping you spend the grant, review budgets, or complete annual or final reports to the funder.

To figure out who your research administrators are, talk to your colleagues or mentors. Institutions vary widely in terms of how many research administrators are on staff (from one-person offices to whole departments). That's why you need to network. Networks will point you to which research administrators are most helpful at this stage of your career.

The best time to reach out to research administrators is as soon as you know you want to write a grant. Sam Westcott has twenty years of experience as a research administrator. Sam observes, "It's never too early to tell research administrators you are going to be working on a grant. It's like doing your taxes. Let us get started on the pieces we are experts at."

New investigators often think they should wait for a "slow season" before reaching out. Don't wait. Research administrators work with so many scholars that you help them plan better when you reach out early.

Plus, you want to develop a strong relationship with your research administrator. As Ido Rosenzweig comments, "Emails and phone calls cannot solve problems the way you are able to when you sit with someone one-on-one." Many experienced grant writers told me they are so grateful for their research administrators that they make it a priority to drop off donuts, cannoli, or other special treats as a thank you. If you're not a baked goods person, send a thank you note to your research administrator after grant submissions. This is how you show gratitude to research administrators for setting you up for career success. Many researchers forget to say "thanks." Treat this as a nonnegotiable step.

To work well with your research administrator, you need to email them information about the proposal, do your homework so you know what questions you have, and meet with them to discuss your grant proposal.

A. **Email information about the proposal**. Your research administrator likely has to track your grant proposal in an institutional tracking system. Emailing your research administrator information about your proposal helps them organize their workflow. Research administrators work on many grants at any given time. Anything you can do to make it easier for them to prioritize your grant helps. This is what your email could say:

> Subject: [**your last name**] [**funder**] Grant Proposal for [**funder and request for applications #**]
>
> Dear [**their name**]:
>
> Hello. My name is [**your name**], and I am a [**your position**]. I am submitting a grant to [**funder**] for [**due date**] in response to this [**request for applications; link to the request for applications and also attach a copy**].
>
> Would it be possible to meet with you to discuss procedures at [**institution name**] for submitting grants to [**funder**]? Thank you so much for your time. I am looking forward to meeting with you.
>
> Sincerely,
> [**your name**]

B. **Do your homework**. Before you meet with your research administrator, write down the questions you have after reading the application guidelines. Look up your institution's indirect cost rates, direct cost rates, **fringe rates** (i.e., costs for benefits like health insurance and retirement plans), and tuition coverage (i.e., your institution's policies for tuition expenses for students on the grant). Doing your homework lets you ask informed questions during your meeting.

C. **Meet with your research administrator**. Research administrators are experts on your institution and funders. Ask them about the best strategy for creating your writing timeline. Here are key questions to ask:

- *What are the deadlines for submission here?* All institutions have different norms for how far in advance of the deadline you need to submit to the institution (as represented by your research administrators). Remember that usually your institution submits your grant to the funder. Knowing and meeting deadlines makes it easier for everyone involved.
- *Are there any special rules for this funder and our institution that I should know?* For example, sometimes a funder will limit how many proposals the funder will accept from a single institution. In those cases, institutions create special processes to determine which scholars are allowed to apply to the funder.
- *What additional forms do I need to complete for our institution, and when will you need to receive those?* For instance, my institution has us complete conflict of interest forms in a special portal.
- *What signatures are needed in order to submit this grant to the funder?* For example, does your chair need to sign off on your grant in order for you to submit?
- *How do you prefer to work with principal investigators?* What is the process? Some research administrators like to have a four-week lead time on the budget, for example. Remember, your research administrators are human. You are building what will hopefully be a long and fruitful relationship.
- *What types of logins are needed?* For instance, you may need to ask them to create an account for you on eRA Commons, login.gov, or elsewhere. Here's a tip from researcher Mallika Nocco: sign into the grant submission portal early to test what application pieces are needed and what formats are required.
- *Show them your list of required proposal elements.* How do you like to work with principal investigators to complete these forms? Do you complete any of these forms in whole or in part?
- *Could you confirm indirect and fringe rates for this funder at our institution?* How about tuition coverage? Do you anticipate the rates will change?

- *What advice do you have for new investigators?*
- *What problems do you see new investigators encounter* (and how do you fix those problems)?
- *Do you have any completed samples of forms I need? Would you be willing to share those samples?*
- *Do you know anyone here who's been successful with this mechanism? Would it be possible to connect us?*
- *How do you prefer to work with the research administrators of my collaborators?* This question is only relevant if you have collaborators at other schools within your institution or external institutions. Cross-school and cross-institution collaborations typically involve more research administrators plus additional sign-offs (explained below).

Plan Your Writing Timeline

Now it's time to create your writing timeline. Create a timeline that works for you.

As you plan your writing timeline, pay attention to the three items below. New grant writers often don't know to plan extra time for these activities.

1. **Official sign-off and submission of your grant**. Remember that most grants are awarded to your institution, not directly to you (chapter 1). You are not the person who submits your grant. Instead, your research administrator will send your grant to the central office (e.g., Office of Sponsored Programs or University Research Services Administration). When everyone agrees your grant is compliant, an official person at your institution (e.g., your **authorized organization representative**) signs off on the grant and submits it for your institution. Learn what the deadlines are (from your research administrator) and stick to them. Submit your grant early so that there is enough time for this process. Don't wait until the last minute just in case something goes wrong. Things usually go wrong. You need your grant to be compliant, and you need your grant to be submitted. Otherwise, your grant won't be reviewed.

2. **Collaborators outside your school (even within the same institution) or at other institutions**. When you have collaborators that are not within your school, this adds extra layers of paperwork. For collaborators outside your school, but within your institution, your schools have to agree on how to split indirect costs. For collaborators at other institutions,

you usually need **subcontracts**. Subcontracts are official contracts between institutions. Your institution "contracts out" part of the grant work to another institution. This is how another institution will pay your collaborator to work on the grant. Subcontracts require many forms, including budgets and signatures (i.e., they take a lot of time).

3. **Community partners**. Partnerships take time to build. For grants, you may also need an official **letter of support** or a letter documenting that the partner wants to work with you if the grant is awarded.

   Tips for building partnerships. Researcher Melissa Osborne shares that a colleague was able to help make an introduction for her to a new organization, thereby making it easier for her to connect. Ask for introductions, make cold calls, and offer help to organizations with which you'd like to connect.

If you're feeling overwhelmed by this chapter, take some encouragement from Donald Chi's story. Donald's first R01 to the National Institutes of Health took him six months of full-time effort to write. This was after he'd written his specific aims (i.e., his one pager). That R01 wasn't funded. Yet Donald's advice to early career scholars is "persistence matters. This is a numbers game. It's exhausting in the beginning, but it gets easier over time. It's like if you went to a spin class for the first time. The first class is terrible. But if you keep going back, suddenly you realize you can keep up." Donald has more than kept up in his career. Donald's current funding portfolio includes grants from the William T. Grant Foundation, National Institute of Dental and Craniofacial Research, and Health Resources and Services Administration.

Tips and Frequently Asked Questions

What's the best place to begin in terms of writing? Researchers differ on this issue. Shannon Self-Brown advises, "I start with methods and budget. This helps me know what methods can fit within the grant mechanism and the amount of money available. But there is no right or wrong process. Figure out what works for you, and remember efficiency is key." The best way to figure out what works for you is to simply get started. Don't worry about perfection when you are getting going. As Amanda Aykanian suggests, "Write now. Edit later."[66]

Figure out what time of day is most productive for writing; guard that time. Some people call this your tiger time. It takes time to figure out your tiger time. For years I thought my tiger time was in the afternoon because I'm a night owl. But my tiger time is actually 9:30–10:30 a.m. Once you figure out your tiger time, schedule it in your calendar for yourself before other people take that time from you.

More on budgets, because they are tricky. As Deb Thomas counsels, "Your budget has to match up with what you're trying to do. Scope out what you want to do, work on your budget, and dance back and forth between the two. Be realistic and don't overpromise." Former program officer Don Waters advises, "At the Mellon Foundation, we asked applicants to provide job descriptions for budgeted positions. This question helped applicants to explore whether a person like they would need actually exists? Could they be recruited in the time frame of the proposed grant? Is the budget consistent with the salary range of the position?" In other words, a budget can showcase how feasible your grant is. When you're new to grant writing, it's hard to figure out how much it will cost to do your work. Ask mentors and research administrators for guidance on your budget. They will think of items you may forget (e.g., travel to present your work at conferences). Also look at award amounts for funded grants doing similar work. Federal grants publish award amounts. Studying published amounts will give you a sense of how experienced investigators scoped out the cost of their work.

What are fringe rates? Fringe rates are the costs for benefits like health insurance, retirement plans, tuition reimbursement, social security, and unemployment/worker's compensation. Fringe rates are usually a set charge applied to salaries or wages of anyone paid by the grant. But fringe rates are complex. To illustrate this, at Boston College, the fringe rates for fiscal year 2020–21 were 30.7, 48.3, and 7.65 percent for professional, nonprofessional, and part-time staff, respectively.[67] Check with your research administrator about rules for fringe rates for your institution and funder.

Divide and conquer. Ananda Amstadter has a tip for approaching grant writing. Divide tasks into those you will complete when you are focused (e.g., a research strategy) versus when you just need to feel productive and gain momentum (e.g., a facilities document or letters of support). "That way, you can work on the hard pieces when you have greatest clarity. When you are looking to knock out pieces, focus on the gaining momentum list." Here's an example of what this could look like. Researcher Youngjun Choe tracked his grant writing activities over his first and second year as an assistant professor. On average, he spent about 26 hours a week on grant writing activities. Youngjun says about 6.5 hours of those hours went toward "actual" writing.

Define roles early. This is true of working with anyone, but consider how many people you will interact with while writing your grant: research administrators, collaborators, community partners, and trainees. It helps if everyone knows what's expected. And this is true of mentors too. Grants consultant Janet Gross shares that mentoring can become a trouble spot for scholars. Bring up expectations early around what type of feedback you're expecting (for more on feedback, see chapter 15). And researcher Nicole Errett says, "Remember to bring your methodologist on board early. They have expertise essential for your study design."

Don't reinvent the wheel. As Matthew Fox jokes, "Writing the facilities and other resources section of a grant is the equivalent of when they made us run the mile in gym." Save time by getting samples of certain grant sections (e.g., facilities or data management) from people at your institution. Many of these additional documents are exercises to show you are able to follow directions. I don't cover these types of documents in depth in this book because they are specific to each funder. The best use of your time is to get samples from funded grants (ask your research administrator and colleagues), and model those successful forms. Notice I am saying *model*, not copy.

What is a letter of intent? Some funders will ask you to submit a **letter of intent** (sometimes referred to as an LOI). Letters of intent are usually short, one- to two-page documents indicating that you plan to apply for a grant. Funders often have specific rules about letters of intent. Read the application guidelines carefully. For example, sometimes you are only allowed to apply if you submit a letter of intent. Funders request letters of intent for various reasons, including to weed out applications, gauge interest, or provide feedback.

Read all instructions carefully. I know. I already said this. I really do mean it, though. I'm guilty of skipping this step sometimes, and it has huge ramifications. I worked on a $40,000 internal grant where we didn't realize we needed to include tuition support for graduate students in the budget. We received an email saying that there was a lot of excitement for our grant. But we had a shortfall of $13,000 in our budget because we didn't include tuition support. That meant we either needed to cut 33 percent of our budget or they were going to see if they could find extra money to cover this shortfall. Our mistake meant there was no guarantee that they could fund us.

The Takeaway

This chapter covered everything you need to create your outline and writing timeline. Use the application instructions to outline your grant. Partner with research administrators to understand how to get your grant to submission. Then plan your writing timeline. As you create your timeline, include "buffers" for unexpected problems and issues outside your control (e.g., subcontracts).

The information from this chapter is pretty straightforward. So why doesn't everyone get funded? What can you do to stand out in the crowd? That's my next chapter.

8

Evaluation Criteria and
the Mission

MAKE IT EASY TO ADVOCATE FOR YOU

You're not going to do well on a test if you don't figure out what's going to be
on the test.

—EMILY GATES

I LOVE the *Great British Baking Show* (Bake-Off, for my non-US colleagues).
But there is a section of the show called "technicals" that always feels extremely unfair. During technicals, the contestants receive a recipe that they
need to bake. The catch is that the show leaves out critical information about
what the judges are looking for in the final result. For example, in the cherry
cake technical, judges Mary Berry and Paul Hollywood wanted to see evenly
distributed cherries cut into quarters throughout the cake. No one tells the
bakers this key information. You cringe and watch as the bakers take their
best guess at what the recipe means. Inevitably, some of the bakers use whole
cherries instead of cutting their cherries into quarters. It's unfair because
those bakers would have quartered their cherries if they'd known it mattered
to the judges.

Writing grants is like going through technicals. Everyone has the recipe
(i.e., the grant application instructions discussed in the previous chapter).
Yet many people are missing key information about how they will be judged.
You need to know what the judges (i.e., reviewers and funder) are looking

for in the final product. To go back to our analogy, you need to know if people want to see quartered cherries in your grant. Let's break down how your grant will be judged.

Reviewers judge your grant based on evaluation criteria from the funder. They want to see that your grant has information on these criteria. Find and study these evaluation criteria. Then write with these criteria in mind. As Emily Gates advises, "Make sure you literally address the evaluation criteria. If you miss any of these criteria in your application, you get no credit for that area."

BreAnne Danzi discovered this principle when she was working on her F31 grant to the National Institute of Mental Health. In her first submission, she focused her attention on the science aspects of the grant. The feedback on her first submission made her realize the evaluation criteria asked reviewers to also rate her development and potential as a researcher. So when BreAnne worked on her revision, she expanded her frame. She focused on explaining her ability to do good research and spent a lot of time on her training plan. Once she spoke to these criteria, she was funded.

Funders are looking for outstanding grants that further their mission. They decide whether grants are outstanding based on reviewer ratings on the evaluation criteria we just discussed. Funders also examine whether your grant furthers their mission. Make it easy for funders to find this information. Write about how your grant advances their mission.

Here's an example of how one group did this. Andrés Castro Samayoa and colleagues applied for a Spencer Foundation COVID-19 grant. Andrés and colleagues studied the request for proposals, which noted that the Spencer Foundation was looking for grants that would create a lasting perspective on COVID-19, and so they spoke directly to this mission. They talked about how their work with archival data would provide the historical perspective needed for creating a lasting perspective and broader context for the moment. The Spencer Foundation agreed and funded this work.

The **goal of this chapter** is to help you design your grant so that it's easy for reviewers and funders to advocate for your work. I'll talk about how to ace the evaluation criteria and show that your work furthers the funder's mission.

Action Plan

- ☐ Understand how evaluation criteria drive the review process
- ☐ Develop sound bites: Use good headings and emphasis words
- ☐ Test your sound-bite skills
- ☐ Address the mission

Understand How Evaluation Criteria Drive the Review Process

Here's how the review process typically works. Funders usually ask at least three reviewers to judge your grant based on evaluation criteria.[33] Reviewers rate and critique your grant on these criteria. Then reviewers send their reviews back to the funder.

Then funders often convene a review panel (either virtual or in person) for reviewers to discuss their reviews. Funders usually **triage** grants. Triaging means that the lowest-scoring grants don't get discussed during the review panel because they are unlikely to be funded.

If your grant makes it past triage, one of your assigned reviewers will present your grant. The other assigned reviewers will chime in with their opinions. Everyone else on the panel was not assigned to read your grant. These other reviewers are skimming your grant as the assigned reviewers discuss it.

Only the top grants from review panel discussions are likely to be funded. Stand out by studying the evaluation criteria. Evaluation criteria shape how your assigned reviewers judge your work.

Example 1: National Science Foundation Evaluation Criteria

When I was first writing National Science Foundation grants, a seasoned National Science Foundation reviewer revealed to me that they use the search function to see where the words "Broader Impacts" are mentioned in a grant.

Why would they do that? I wondered. That seemed silly.

Here's why. The National Science Foundation asks all reviewers to rate proposals against two criteria.[68] Reviewers have to write their evaluations from the perspective of these criteria. Verbatim, these evaluation criteria are displayed here in figure 4:

> **Intellectual Merit:** The Intellectual Merit criterion encompasses the potential to advance knowledge; and
> **Broader Impacts:** The Broader Impacts criterion encompasses the potential to benefit society and contribute to the achievement of specific, desired societal outcomes.
>
> The following elements should be considered in the review for both criteria:
> 1. What is the potential for the proposed activity to
>   a. Advance knowledge and understanding within its own field or across different fields (Intellectual Merit); and
>   b. Benefit society or advance desires societal outcomes (Broader Impacts)?
> 2. To what extent do the proposed activities suggest and explore creative, original, or potentially transformative concepts?
> 3. Is the plan for carrying out the proposed activities well-reasoned, well-organized, and based on a sound rationale? Does the plan incorporate a mechanism to assess success?
> 4. How well qualified is the individual, team, or institution to conduct the proposed activities?
> 5. Are there adequate resources available to the PI (either at the home institution or through collaborations) to carry out the proposed activities?

FIGURE 4. National Science Foundation Evaluation Criteria

The reviewer was using the search function to look for "Broader Impacts" so that they could quickly locate this information in the grant because they needed to speak about how each grant addressed "Broader Impacts" to complete their reviews. Reviewers are often assigned hundreds of pages to read for review. (Funders differ with regard to how many grants reviewers are assigned. But it's safe to assume that your reviewers are tired and reading more than one grant.)

The lesson is: make evaluation criteria easy to find in your grant.

Develop Sound Bites: Use Good Headings and Emphasis Words

Sound bites are the secret to making evaluation criteria easy to find in your grant. Sound bites are short snippets of text that include language from the evaluation criteria. When you include evaluation criteria language, you signal to reviewers this is a section they can use to champion your work.[69] Jen Heemstra notes that you'll know you've done a good job with creating sound bites when "you start to see phrases from your grant copied in the review. That's powerful."

To develop sound bites, use good headings and emphasis words. For the National Science Foundation, for instance, you need a heading that says, "Broader Impacts." If you don't have this, reviewers using the search function will not find this information. As Emily said earlier, that means you get zero credit in this area.

Creating sound bites is easier to understand when you see it in action. Looking at the National Science Foundation evaluation criteria, here's how you shape sound bites for reviewers:

A. Good headings. In your grant, create headings based on the main evaluation criteria.

Example. I make sure that grants I submit to the National Science Foundation always have two headings, "INTELLECTUAL MERIT" and "BROADER IMPACTS." I want them to be so easy for reviewers to find that I write these headings in CAPS.

B. Emphasis words. Don't stop at creating headings. Look at the evaluation criteria and emphasize words the funder cares about. This is a cue for reviewers that this sentence or paragraph contains information they need to rate your grant.

Example. The National Science Foundation asks about Intellectual Merit and Broader Impacts, but it has much more detailed criteria in the points below these two broad categories. Use and stress that language in your grant. Put stems of the evaluation criteria throughout your proposal. This means, underline or italicize these words directly in your grant:

- This proposal will <u>advance knowledge</u> by
- This proposed activity will <u>benefit society</u> through
- These proposed activities are <u>potentially transformative</u>
- The <u>rationale for the proposed activities</u> is
- <u>Mechanisms for assessing success</u> include
- <u>Qualifications of the [individuals, team, or institution] to conduct the proposed activities</u>
- <u>Resources available to the principal investigator</u>

Good headings and emphasis words make it easy for reviewers to give you "credit" for these areas. They're starter language for sound bites in written reviews and panel discussions.

Follow up each emphasis word stem with strong evidence and arguments. Reviewers may not agree with the ways you support these sections. But if you have these emphasis words, there is no way reviewers can say, "They didn't talk about it at all." Instead of being annoyed with you for forgetting quartered cherries in your grant, they will grapple with your awesome ideas.

One objection I hear from scholars to this approach is, "Isn't that boring? To use the same language the funder used? Shouldn't I change it up?"

The answer is no. If a reviewer can't find the words "Broader Impacts" quickly in your proposal, they assume you didn't speak to Broader Impacts. You could have written beautiful paragraphs talking about the potential for your work to make a huge difference, shape society, and so on. You know you wrote about Broader Impacts. Yet the problem is, *reviewers* don't know you did.

Changing up wording makes it hard for reviewers to find the information they need. That's annoying to reviewers. They do not have time to unearth hidden ideas. Reviewers will start to question both the value of your ideas and your potential to carry them out. Use the exact words from the evaluation criteria. If you only write "Impacts," a reviewer using the search function for "Broader Impacts" won't see your heading. Remember, the goal is to make it easy for reviewers to find the information they need.

Let's try one more sound-bite sample.

Test Your Sound-bite Skills

Sometimes you may not find an explicit evaluation criteria ratings sheet. In these cases, search for any information about the review process. This information is your key to understanding how you will be evaluated.

Here's an example from the Spencer Foundation. The Spencer Foundation posted information about the "review process" for its Racial Equity Research Grants program. This is a clue to what evaluation criteria look like for these grants. On the review process page, the foundation notes that reviewers are "asked to rate and comment" on the following (figure 5):[70]

Significance of the Project: Reviewers will evaluate the centrality of racial equity and education in the research, the importance of the topic to transforming inequality, and the quality of the research question(s) and/or direction of inquiry.

Connection to Research and Theory: Reviewers will evaluate the adequacy of the description of how other researchers have treated the same topic and how well the proposal responds to prior work and theory.

Research Design: Reviewers will evaluate the overall quality, sophistication, and appropriateness of the research design as well as its alignment with the research question(s) and/or conceptual framing.

Budget and Timeline: Reviewers will evaluate the adequacy of the budget and timeline.

Project Team: Reviewers will comment on the potential of the investigator(s) to complete the study as described and share the results or other findings.

FIGURE 5. Spencer Foundation Review Process Information

Try it. If you were writing a grant for the Racial Equity Research Grants (the mechanism) at the Spencer Foundation (the funder), what good headings and emphasis words would you use in your proposal? Try it on your own and then see how your answers compare to mine below.

My Answer

A. **Good headings**. I would use these headings: SIGNIFICANCE OF THE PROJECT, CONNECTION TO RESEARCH AND THEORY, RESEARCH DESIGN, BUDGET AND TIMELINE, and PROJECT TEAM. I've probably overwhelmed you by putting these headings in all caps. Note that these headings would be spread out in the grant (so they'd be less overwhelming), but by putting them in CAPS, I'm ensuring that reviewers can't miss these sections.

B. **Emphasis words**. I would use these emphasis words:
   - Racial equity and education are central in this proposal
   - This topic has the potential to transform inequality through
   - This proposal responds to prior work and theory by
   - Research design alignment to research questions (swap in conceptual framing, if appropriate)

     For this section, I would also add subheadings to demonstrate that the research design is based on research questions or conceptual framing. For instance, if I had two research questions in the one pager, I would write:

     Research design alignment to research questions
     - Question 1: Evaluation of COVID-19 impacts
     - Question 2: Identification of risk factors

     Alternatively, if my project were based on a conceptual framework, I would list the framework in subheadings as follows:

     Research design alignment to conceptual framing
     - Framework part 1: Stressors
     - Framework part 2: Mediators

   - Timeline

     Notice how much the Spencer Foundation cares about research design alignment. Stand out in the review by using your timeline to show your alignment. In your timeline, list your research questions or the conceptual framework. For more tips on timeline design, see chapter 10.
   - Evidence of our teams' ability to complete the study as described
   - Our plan for sharing the results and findings includes

Wrapping up Sound Bites: How This Applies to Your Grant

You need the evaluation criteria for your grant. Most funders post these criteria. Sometimes the criteria are even listed at the end of the application guidelines. Funders are doing this to help you. They want you to write to those criteria. If you can't find the evaluation criteria, research online and check with your mentors. Evaluation criteria may be buried in online documents about the grant mechanism.

When you find the evaluation criteria, add good headings and emphasis words to the outline and timeline you created in chapter 7. Use language directly from the evaluation criteria so that it's easy for a reviewer to do a "find and search" for this information. It should be so easy to find that even someone who is just skimming your proposal would find it. Remember that many of the people on review panels are *only* skimming your work. They never read your full grant because it was not assigned to them.

Address the Mission

Seasoned grant writer Nicole Nugent offers this advice: "Some agencies pick and choose who they fund based on their priorities. That means if you are solidly in their priority area, then you're more likely to be funded. Make sure you communicate how and why you are solidly in that priority area!"

Here's researcher Dana Rose Garfin's suggestion for how to do this: find and make a copy of the funder's request for proposals and its mission statement or strategic plan. Then use these documents as reference points. Weave key terms from these documents into your grant.

Let's try one example together so you can see this strategy in action.

Address the Mission Example: The Jacobs Foundation

If you were to apply to the Jacobs Foundation Research Fellowship, the mission of the fellowship is to improve the "development, learning, and living conditions of children and youth."[71]

The Jacobs Foundation is interested in

"scholars who seek to combine *multiple levels of analysis* and engage in *interdisciplinary work*. A special focus lies on work to *understand and embrace variability in learning; promote the generation, transfer, and practical application of evidence on human learning and development* or increase the capacity to *scale up effective education policies and practices."*[71]

Try it. How would you show that your grant addresses the priorities of the Jacobs Foundation? Hint: researcher Mallika Nocco says that you should "mirror the funder's language" to show how your work is tied to its mission or the policies the funder cares about.

MY ANSWER

If I were writing a Jacobs Foundation Research Fellowship proposal, I would include some or all of these sentences and sentence stems in my proposal:

- This proposal <u>directly meets the mission</u> of the Jacobs Foundation Research Fellow through emphasis on questions to improve the "development, learning, and living conditions of children and youth."[71]
- This proposal integrates <u>multiple levels of analysis</u> by
- This <u>interdisciplinary approach</u>
- Evaluating <u>variability in learning</u>, I will
- This proposal will <u>promote the generation, transfer, and practical application of</u>
- Taken together, this work will address the Jacobs Foundation mission to "<u>increase the capacity to scale up effective education policies and practices</u>."[71]

APPLY THIS STRATEGY

Find copies of the request for applications, mission statement, and strategic plan for your program and/or funder. Look back at chapter 5 if you're not sure where to find this information. Use these documents as reference points. Include clear language in your outline that shows your grant meets the mission of your funder.

Tips and Frequently Asked Questions

Is it a problem if my work doesn't address all aspects of the funder's mission? You don't have to meet all aspects of a funder's mission. But if you don't meet any aspects, it's probably not the right funder for your work. Your meetings with colleagues (chapter 3) and the program officer (chapter 5) should provide insight on whether this funder is the right one for you as a first target. Spend time reflecting on how your work aligns with the mission of the funder. Put in all evidence of how this is true. Don't fake mission alignment, however, if it's not there. Reviewers are smart and will see through this.

Make sure you also directly address the solicitation or request for applications (discussed in chapter 2). Use emphasis words in your grant to show reviewers how you did this.

Who are my reviewers? Funders differ. Some funders have standing review panels, while some convene new panels each cycle. Research review panel information online and check in with your mentors (chapter 3) and program officer (chapter 5) to see what they can tell you about typical review panels at your target funder.

How do funders make sure reviewers don't have conflicts of interest? Funders work hard to identify **conflicts of interest**. When you submit your grant to a funder, the funder will first make sure your grant is compliant on application instructions (see chapter 7). As long as your grant is compliant, the funder will generally show reviewers the grants they may be assigned and ask if there are any conflicts of interest. Conflicts of interest include things like if the reviewer was your mentor, published with you, is at the same university, or has any relationship that could make it difficult for them to objectively review your grant.

The Takeaway

Reviewers and funders are more likely to love your work when you make their job easy. Give reviewers and funders what they need by preparing sound bites from evaluation criteria as well as addressing the funder's mission.

You may have noticed we're halfway through the book and haven't done much writing yet. That's about to change. Now that you've developed an important idea (chapters 1–4) and targeted the right funder for your idea (chapters 5–8), it's time to start writing in earnest.

Draft Your Grant

9

The Literature Review

CLEAR AND SIMPLE COMMUNICATION

You cannot disguise a weak idea with great grantsmanship . . . but bad grantsmanship can disguise a good idea.

—VALERIE DURRANT[45]

MY SON WENT to a baseball camp when he was six. Before it started, the camp sent a twenty-eight-page "handbook." I opened up the handbook to look for the drop-off times and locations. Instead, I found information about the camp's philosophy on innovation, discipline policy, and refund logistics. This extraneous information made it difficult to find the critical information I needed about what time and where I should drop off Mark. Apparently, other caregivers were equally frustrated. The camp sent an apology email and responded to questions it had received about the handbook.

Writing grants is like sending a handbook to reviewers. Your grant tells reviewers what they can expect from your project. And reviewers read your grant to look for critical information (i.e., the evaluation criteria from chapter 8).

This means you need to write clearly and simply. Avoid extraneous information so there is no chance for confusion. This matters for handbooks, but it's especially important for grants. Let me explain.

First, your writing needs to be simple and straightforward because reviewers don't have time to search for information. Unrelated information (e.g., camp philosophy on innovation) lowers the chance reviewers will see the information they need. Reviewers only spend about three to five hours on each grant they review.[72] As mentioned before, your grant is one of many grants that reviewers are assigned. They often receive five to fifteen grants to review.[63-64] And reviewing is service. That means reviewers are reading your grant while also trying to manage their regular job. Generally, reviewers are able to carve out about ten days per year to review, according to a survey of forty-seven hundred researchers across different funders.[19]

Second, your writing needs to be clear because reviewers can't call or email you when they're confused. There are usually no chances for you to interact with reviewers during a review cycle. You can't provide missing information or answer questions. This means confused reviewers have to guess what you mean to do and why your work matters.

Confused reviewers are a real problem for you. They usually decide they don't like your ideas. A general rule in marketing is, "A confused mind always says no.[73] In other words, when people don't understand what you're selling, they choose not to buy it.

The **goal of this chapter** is to show you how to write clearly and simply in your grant. You'll use these skills to create your literature review. This chapter is the most mentally challenging one in the book. That's because writing easy-to-read grants is hard work. As writer Ernest Hemingway said, "Easy reading is hard writing."[74] The hard work in this chapter includes letting go of writing myths, making mindset shifts, and building a new perspective. Let's get started.

Action Plan

- ☐ Bust myths that create confusion
- ☐ Explain a mindset shift: From peer to guide
- ☐ Become a guide
- ☐ Understand literature reviews
- ☐ Evaluate a literature review template and sample
- ☐ Draft your literature review outline
- ☐ Refine your literature review outline

Bust Myths That Create Confusion

1. **Myth: Your grant needs to show everything you know about a topic.**
   The purpose of a grant isn't to show off your knowledge. The real purpose is to give reviewers the information they need to evaluate your work. Unrelated details confuse reviewers. Keep it simple. This doesn't mean dumbing down. It means focusing on relevant information.

Example 1. The handbook above was twenty-eight pages of thoughtful work on camp philosophies. But I didn't care because that's not what I needed to know. It would have been more effective to send one page with drop-off times and locations.

Example 2. You could tell a story that involves points AGXBQRDFC. If you just tell me ABC, though, you are focusing my attention on these critical points.

2. **Myth: Your writing needs to be flowery**. Grant writing is not fiction writing. As one researcher commented, you're not trying to impress reviewers with unusual sentence structure and writing flair. You are trying to impress them with your ideas.

Flowery example. My pithy precis on this controversial topic is that there is a central core essential principle in the field that I must evaluate in this work in order to rapidly make huge changes in our emerging field.

Showcasing ideas example. I will evaluate a core principle in our field.

3. **Myth: Your grant is about your journey through a topic**. Grant writing is actually about leading the *reviewer* on a journey. It's not about you at all. As professor Donald Moynihan shares, "Don't confuse your journey in understanding a topic with what the reader needs to know." Don't tell reviewers every single thought you had as you landed on your final idea. Carefully consider what reviewers will and will not already understand. This is part of why you do your homework on who the reviewers are.

Example from the Center for Scientific Review at the National Institutes of Health. "Lots of people go too far describing routine laboratory methods, which just take up space and really distract reviewers. It gives the message that the applicant is not really as organized as they should be. New investigators, however, should make a little more effort to show that the techniques they proposed to use are within their capabilities.[75]

Example from Betty. When I write for my program at the National Science Foundation, reviewers are disaster experts. In those grants, I don't spend much time explaining what disasters are. But at the National Institutes of Health, most reviewers are not disaster experts. In those grants, I spend a lot of time making the case for what disasters are and why research in this area matters for public health.

Try It. Revise This Paragraph

How would you revise this example based on all the myths I busted above? Compare your answer to my answer below.

> Given numerous extenuating circumstances that hindered the productivity of our collaborative research group during a worldwide pandemic (i.e., COVID-19) that devastated hundreds of millions of people globally and closed our respective institutions, displacing numerous students, multiple permutations and considerations for potential assessments were evaluated across disciplines and silos, resulting in changes to our original plan.

BETTY'S ANSWER

We revised the timing of our assessments because of the COVID-19 pandemic.

CONCLUSION

In the exercise above, your answer may have been different from mine. This is what happens when writing is too complex. Reviewers make guesses about what you mean. That means reviewers may draw different conclusions.

In contrast, clear and simple messaging ensures reviewers understand your point. My short answer above doesn't leave any room for guesswork. Reviewers walk away with the same understanding of my point.

Explain a Mindset Shift: From Peer to Guide

You're writing a phenomenal grant. You now know that this means you need to lead reviewers on a journey through a topic. As you write, make sure you are actually taking the lead. New grant writers are often too timid about leading reviewers. New grant writers act like a peer on reviewers' journeys. This is a problem because reviewers don't want a peer. They want a guide.

Let's walk through an analogy to illustrate this concept. In the *Hunger Games*, protagonist Katniss could turn to Peeta or Haymitch for counsel.

Katniss doesn't want advice from a *peer*, Peeta. Peeta's new to the whole mess of the Hunger Games. Peeta can't give clear and simple advice because he's stumbling around learning information at the exact same time as Katniss. "Gosh those wasps are really deadly. Yikes! Another tribute. Gone."

Katniss seeks advice from a *guide*, Haymitch. Haymitch understands the terrain. He's been through the Hunger Games in the past. Haymitch has a good idea of how Katniss can navigate potential paths to success. That doesn't mean he knows what will work for Katniss, but Haymitch has a much better sense of what could work than Peeta does.

Don't be Peeta when you write your grants. Be Haymitch. Take the lead for reviewers. Write from the perspective of someone one step higher than reviewers on the expertise ladder. It's not that you have to be a leading expert in your field. You just want to make it clear you've spent a lot of time thinking deeply about an issue. You've carefully considered what isn't working now and how life could be better in the future. Give advice about paths forward for solving a problem in our world. Guide reviewers along those paths to a better future.

Become a Guide

To become a guide, stop making statements and start giving guidance. Instead of describing our present (i.e., statements), give recommendations about our future (i.e., guidance). This mindset shift between statements and guidance is abstract and subtle.

This mindset shift is based on the difference between paper and grant writing. Papers and grants have a different orientation to time. As research development specialist Alma Faust explains, "Papers are demonstrations of facts. The data already exist. Grants are about data to be collected in the future." This means that papers are about the present or recent past (i.e., existing data). Grants are about the future (i.e., data that doesn't exist yet).

Guide reviewers to a better future. Let's make this concrete. Here are examples that show the difference between statements and guidance. In the table (figure 6), watch for the mindset shift as you read the table from left to right. Notice that the difference between statements and guidance isn't about the length of a sentence. It's about how you are orienting yourself to reviewers, time, evidence, and direction of sentences.

Your Turn: Brainstorm Your Guidance

Brainstorm how you will guide reviewers. *Why does this work matter? What is the right method for addressing this problem in the world? What will this information tell us?* Create a bulleted list of points that reviewers need to understand, framed as guidance.

	Statements	Guidance
Orientation to Reviewer	**Peer** *It is hard to improve health behaviors in work settings.*	**Expert** *Improving health behaviors in work settings will require training managers on benefits and providing resources.*
Orientation to Time	**Paper mindset. Stuck in present or recent past.** *Post-disaster responses have been well studied among adults.*	**Grants mindset.** **Oriented to the future.** *Post-disaster research with adults is insufficient for understanding children's responses to disasters.*
Attitude to Evidence	**Observational. Fails to summarize meaning of evidence.** *Disaster exposure is associated with negative outcomes for children.*	**Evaluates what evidence means and lessons learned.** *Children are a vulnerable population after disasters.*
Direction of Sentences	**Neutral with no opinion or directions embedded.** *Integrative Data Analysis is a recently developed methodology.*	**Offers directions on next steps. Has momentum.** *Integrative Data Analysis is an innovative methodology that will help resolve inconsistent findings across child disaster studies.*

FIGURE 6. Statements versus Guidance

Hints: Each point should be one sentence, like the guidance in the table above. Notice that you are not presenting evidence yet (that is chapter 11). For now, you are mapping out how you'll guide the reviewer on their journey. If you are feeling stuck in brainstorming, here are some mad lib stems you can use to generate your guidance.

Guidance Mad Lib Stems

- A critical gap in the literature is a _____.
- Although important, this work fails to _____.
- Failure to understand _____ prevents us from being able to _____.
- By examining _____, we will have information we need to _____.
- _____ is a significant threat to _____.
- _____ to date has focused on _____.
- It is not clear how to _____.
- To address this critical gap in the literature, this proposal _____.

- Research to date tells us _____, but has _____ limitations.
- Therefore it is difficult to _____ recommendations in _____.
- _____ method is an innovative methodology to help _____ in order to_____
- _____ will allow us to _____.
- To summarize, understanding _____ will _____.

Understand Literature Reviews

The guidance you just brainstormed will become the backbone of your literature review. So let's turn our attention to what literature reviews are. The literature review goes by many names in grant writing. Depending on your funder, the literature review could be called the research strategy, project description, background section, rationale, or justification section.

In terms of how grants are organized, most grants have a one pager (chapter 4), followed by the literature review (this chapter), and then the research plan (that's the next chapter).

Literature reviews are a road map for reviewers. They have a different purpose than the one pagers I discussed in chapter 4. As researcher Jessica Schleider explains, "[The one pager] helps reviewers imagine what the world would be like if the problem you're focused on goes away. The literature review is the path to get to that future."

Your literature review should concentrate on the most direct paths to that future. There should be no detours. That's why experienced grant writers often call the literature review the "review of *relevant* literature."

Don't review all the literature in the world. Unrelated information is confusing. The camp handbook example illustrated this principle at the start of this chapter. You will know more than you share. That's normal and a sign you are streamlining your story to focus on information that matters for reviewers. Remember, the goal is to write clearly and simply.

Evaluate a Literature Review Template and Sample

Like all aspects of grant writing, there are many excellent ways to write a literature review. But it's not practical to explore every way right now. You just need one way to get started.

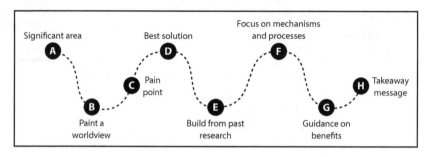

FIGURE 7. A Literature Review Template

Here's one template for a literature review (see figure 7). In the template, each point (A to H) is one guidance statement for your literature review.

Below, I walk you through each of these types of guidance statements, offering examples from publicly available grant samples. Remember, you are not adding evidence yet (I'll do that in chapter 11). After this literature review template, I show one fully worked out sample.

A. **Significant area**. State again why the problem area matters. It's true you already covered this in the first two to three lines of your one pager (for more examples, see chapter 4). Opening your literature review here helps reviewers remain oriented to why your work matters.

   Example from Yingru Liu's R44 grant to the National Institute of Allergy and Infectious Diseases. "Despite public health control measures, gonorrhea remains an all-too-common disease, and is the second most frequent reportable infectious disease in the US.[76]

   Example from Patricia Garrett's R44 grant to the National Institute of Allergy and Infectious Diseases. "Over three decades into the global HIV epidemic, identifying new HIV infections is critical to the evaluation of prevention and intervention strategies, because these must be specifically directed at interdicting new infections.[77]

B. **Paint a worldview**. Quickly narrow reviewers' focus to one way of understanding the significant area you just scoped out. This makes the large significant area you just described manageable. This worldview could be a specific topic, theory, model, or any lens you use to understand the significant area. In the examples here, see if you can identify the worldview. I put my answers in brackets.

Example from Toma Susi's Austrian Science Fund grant on graphene. "This grant proposal is based on the fundamental finding that a relatively low-energy electron beam in an atomic resolution scanning transmission electron microscope can be used to move silicon atoms embedded in the graphene lattice as heteroatoms."[78] **[Worldview: Low-energy electron beams are a way to understand graphene.]**

Example from Monica Gandhi's R01 to the National Institute of Allergy and Infectious Diseases on HIV prevention. "The PrEP clinical trials revealed the critical importance of evaluating adherence using pharmacologic measures: Massive advances in HIV prevention have been demonstrated over the past 5 years.[79] **[Worldview: Adherence matters for HIV prevention.]**

Example from Rosie Redfield's Canadian Institutes of Health Research grant on H. influenzae. "H. influenzae's only niche is the human body.[80] **[Worldview: The human body is a central organizing frame for understanding H. influenzae.]**

C. **Pain point**. Point out limiting factors in the worldview or ways we fall short of realizing our worldview. This guidance often includes the words "however," "yet," "despite," "but," "although," or "it is not clear."

Example from Jessica Burnett's US Geological Survey Grant. "Integrated Population Models (IPMs) have, however, not been adopted by the broader ecological research community, which may be stunting its development as a [decision support tool].[81]

Example from Arun Durvasula's National Science Foundation grant. "However, the state-of-the-art methods for pinpointing these regions of archaic ancestry are incomplete.[82]

D. **Best solution**. What is the best way to solve the pain point? This should match your one pager. It's usually your main research objective. I like this guidance to be an overarching summary of the full project.

E. **Build from past research**. Discuss why and how your solution builds from past work. State the connections clearly. Otherwise, it feels like you pulled your ideas out of thin air. Scholars frequently build the case for their best solution by discussing an analog situation or pointing out the limitations of past work. These strategies allow you to refute potential conflicting evidence and argue against alternative solutions. See if you can spot these strategies below. My notes are in brackets.

Example from Toma Susi's Austrian Science Fund grant. "Although electron microscopy is similar to optical microscopy in principle, the fact that electrons carry significant momentum is a crucial difference.[78] [**Analog situation in past research: electron microscopy and optical microscopy. Highlights that electrons are different.**]

Example from Chengwen Li's R01 grant to the National Institute of Allergy and Infectious Diseases. "[Adeno-associated virus] vectors purified from cesium chloride (CsCl) density gradients have been applied in clinical trials; however, this purification approach is not scalable.[83] [**Points out limitations of past work. Argues against alternative solution (purification) because it lacks scalability.**]

F. **Focus on mechanisms and processes**. Show why you expect certain outcomes. State what steps are missing to resolve the problems you've identified. How are your findings focused on a change that is reproducible? What will we learn about a process if your grant is funded? What would this prevent?

G. **Guidance on benefits**. Explicitly state the benefits of your work. Don't make reviewers guess what these benefits are. Usually the benefits are how your work solves the pain points and reveals processes we don't understand.

H. **Takeaway message**. Summarize your work and key message.

Sample Literature Review Outline: National Institute of Mental Health Grant on Posttraumatic Stress

Here's a sample literature review outline. Eagle-eyed readers will notice this literature review outline pairs with grant idea 2 in chapter 2 and the one pager you read in chapter 4 (sample 1, the grant I wrote with Annette La Greca). That one pager started the grant, and this literature review appeared immediately after the one pager. In the sample below, the left-hand side shows the literature review outline. Each part of the outline is one guidance statement. On the right-hand side, I've labeled each type of guidance statement (see guidance statement types in figure 7).

Literature Review Outline	Guidance Statement Type
Natural disasters present a significant threat to children's mental health.	**A. Significant area**
Disaster management experts universally advocate that <u>stepped care models</u> of intervention are needed to effectively address children's postdisaster mental health needs.	**B. Paint a worldview** *The stepped care model narrows reviewers' focus.*
It is <u>not clear how to stratify children</u> based on their risk for persistent posttraumatic stress symptoms after disasters.	**C. Pain point**
To address this <u>critical gap</u> in the literature, this proposal uses modern methods (integrative data analysis and growth mixture modeling) to develop risk models for how to stratify children based on the risk for persistent posttraumatic stress symptoms.	**D. Best solution**
Person-centered research conducted among <u>adults</u> provides robust evidence for <u>four prototypical adult trajectories of postdisaster responses.</u>	**E. Build from past research** *Pointing out an analog situation with adults shows this approach works well.*
Person-centered approaches have begun to be utilized in child disaster research, but the findings to date are inconsistent.	**E. Build from past research** *Pointing out a limitation of past work is inconsistency. Notice that I used two of this type of guidance statement (build from past research). You often want more than one guidance statement about how you build from past research. This feels "meaty" to reviewers because you are digging into the literature.*
Therefore it is difficult to generate clinical recommendations for future disasters from this research.	**F. Focus on mechanisms and processes** *I'm arguing we need consistent findings to generate recommendations.*
Integrative data analysis is an innovative methodology that will help resolve inconsistent findings across child disaster studies in order to meet the NIH's goals for rigorous and reproducible science.	**G. Guidance on benefits**

Literature Review Outline	Guidance Statement Type
The whole is greater than the sum of its parts: integrative data analysis allows for addressing questions that may not be addressed through individual studies alone.	**G. Guidance on benefits** *Notice that I used two of this type of guidance statement (guidance on benefits). This template is not a lockstep approach. Riff on the template in whatever way best tells a story for reviewers.*
To summarize, understanding how and why youths differ in their postdisaster, posttraumatic stress symptom trajectories requires integrative data analysis to integrate the findings across studies.	**H. Takeaway message**

Draft Your Literature Review Outline

If you were drawing a road map for a trip between Miami and Atlanta, you'd draw the big picture first (states and highways) to outline the route. Later, you'd fill in details like gas stations and Pollo Tropicals. (Pollo Tropicals are a fast-food restaurant. Try their curry mustard sauce if you ever get a chance to visit.)

Use the same approach when you draft your literature review. Outline the structure first and fill in the details later. You create a better road map for reviewers when you have a clear outline of the route.

To draft your outline, leverage the skills from this chapter. Pull the guidance statements you brainstormed under the "Become a Guide" skill. Next, look at the literature review template (figure 7). Figure out where each of the guidance statements you brainstormed fits on the template. Some people find it helps to write guidance statements on sticky notes or paper. That way, you can move guidance statements around to see where they fit on the template.

Once you've mapped your guidance onto the template, you have a rough outline for your literature review.

Refine Your Literature Review Outline

Keep revising your outline until you create a coherent journey for reviewers. As novelist Truman Capote said, "Good writing is rewriting."[84]

Remember, more is not better in grant writing. When you add in too much information, reviewers lose the thread of where you are taking them. That's when reviewers get confused and ask questions. Our goal here is clarity. Researcher

Nicole Nugent says, "Reviewers should be able to just read your headings and know what your grant is about." The headings Nicole is talking about are the guidance statements you just created for your literature review outline.

Here are tips for refining your literature review outline.

1. **Justify every paragraph**. Is there any information in your outline that doesn't need to be there? Is it clear why this argument is showing up? Make sure that each guidance statement has a purpose. Being clear doesn't mean you can't introduce complex concepts. It means you need to know when and why you want reviewers to understand complex concepts.

    Exercise. Cut any guidance statement that does not create clarity. Be relentless. This can sometimes feel like you are having to "murder your darlings," as writer Sir Arthur Quiller-Couch once said.[85] If it helps, create a "graveyard" or "parking lot" document for guidance sentences that don't fit in your literature review. You may be able to use them later, and it helps soften the blow of cutting a treasured sentence.

2. **Logic is critical**. As Shannon Self-Brown relays, "In a great grant, everything builds logically. There are no gaps and holes in the application." Researcher Olga Onuch elaborates on this point, noting, "You're taking the reader on a journey to your chosen destination. Make sure each word is taking them to where you want to go. No one enjoys unexpected road closures & several hour detours."[86]

    Test your outline. Walk through each point you're making. Have you covered all the information that reviewers need to understand what you mean? Does the structure make sense? Is there a simpler way to help reviewers get to your main point?

3. **Make explicit connections**. Your argument may be clear to you in your outline. But have you made the connection clear to a reviewer? Walk reviewers through all the connections you want them to understand.

    Example 1: This is a high priority area for (funder) because of X, Y, and Z.

    Example 2. Research development specialist Alma Faust shares this illustration: "A may imply C, but you need to tell reviewer sentence B that shows how A leads to C."

    Exercise. Look at your outline. Have you explicitly stated why you have information in the literature review? Have you explained why your approach improves on what's already being done? Is there any information the reviewer needs in order to understand your guidance? If so, explain it.

4. **Choose clear terms**. Pay attention to even the smallest details. Every word you choose should be clear on first reading. That means reviewers don't have to search to figure out what the word means. Choose words that reviewers will understand immediately *or* define the term the first time you use it.

Aims, an example of a way reviewers get confused. Don't say, "As we said in aim 3." "Aim 3" is not a clear word because reviewers have to flip backward in your grant to know what it means. Remember, reviewers only spend three to five hours with your grant. They have not memorized your aims. Instead, spell out what aim 3 is, or at a minimum, summarize the gist of it. This could mean writing, "Aim 3: Evaluating causal relationships."

Names, another instance of words that confuse reviewers. You may think it's clear when you casually name team members. That's because you know each person's expertise. Reviewers don't. They won't remember that page 2 said Person X was an expert in volcanic rocks when they reach page 10. Instead of saying, "Snape will train the graduate assistant," make the expertise of the team member clear by saying, "Snape (co-PI, potions expert) will train the graduate assistant."

Define ambiguous terms. A word as simple as "youths" means different things to different reviewers. Some people use "youths" to mean those under eighteen years of age, but the World Health Organization defines youths as those fifteen to twenty-four years old. To avoid confusion, the first time I use the word "youths" in a grant I will define how I am using the term. For instance, "Youths (i.e., those fifteen to twenty-four years old)."

Tips and Frequently Asked Questions

Evaluate the literature reviews in your samples. I gave you one literature review template (figure 7). But you could also model your literature review outline on the samples you pulled in chapter 6. Model doesn't mean copying ideas or words. You are looking at samples to understand how writers laid out effective guidance. *How many paragraphs do they have in their literature review? What guidance are they using to drive reviewers forward in their journey?*

How long should a literature review be? Every funder is different with regard to expectations, so check your samples (chapter 6) and the application guidelines (chapter 7) for guidance on this issue. Lori Peek notes that even considering how much funders vary with regard to grant length, "The literature review should be long enough to accomplish the goals established in this chapter, while still leaving plenty of space to describe your research design. As a general guide, it probably should not be more than 20 to 25 percent of your proposal, so you reserve space for the other key elements."

Make sure you include foundational works from your field in your grant. The National Institute of Allergy and Infectious Diseases offers this reminder: "References show your breadth of knowledge of the field. If you leave out an important work, reviewers may assume you're not aware of it."[87]

No sentence in your literature review should span more than three lines. Long sentences open the door to confusion. Cut words or split the sentence.

I'm feeling stuck. How can I get started? As researcher Raul Pacheco-Vega says, set small goals. That could be, "Today I am going to OPEN THE DOCUMENT I am supposed to be working on."[88] Further, Daniel Gould advises, "Fuss about refining it later. Just get some words down first."[89] Samuel Perry offers two more related pieces of advice. "Don't 'find' time to write. Make time." And, "You can always edit a bad page. You can't edit a blank page."[90]

When can I begin to get feedback? After you finish your literature review, it's a good time to start getting feedback. As researcher Christine Weirich relates, "Show your first draft to people long before you think you're ready. By the time you are ready, you can get stuck on the structure—when most grants need to go through a major structural rearrangement."

How would you modify this advice for people working on training grants? Training grants are a little different in that you often make a case for both your training and research. Make sure your training plans and research plans match. Make a clear case for why the training grant will help you develop as a scholar beyond what you could already do without the grant. This includes courses, relationships you've already established, and existing research your mentors are doing. Explain why your team will help you develop in your training. Propose important work, but make sure it's also feasible in the time frame.

The Takeaway

Creating a clear and simple literature review is hard work. In this chapter, I talked about how you have to put reviewers' needs first, shift from being a peer to being a guide, generate guidance statements, understand the purpose of literature reviews, and then organize guidance into a coherent outline. And you can't stop at drafting an outline. You have to refine your outline over and over until the logic sparkles.

But the hard work is worth it. A clear outline guides reviewers to seeing your vision for a better future. Reviewers engage with your ideas instead of struggling through your writing.

Next up, what work will you actually do with your grant?

10

Your Research Plan

LIVING UP TO THE HYPE

Resist the temptation to try to use dazzling style to conceal weakness
of substance.

—STANLEY SCHMIDT[91]

THE LEGO® catalog is a big hit at my house. There are so many options. You
can buy a model of the Millennium Falcon™ spaceship and the apartments
from the television show *Friends* (Central Perk sold separately).

The point of the LEGO® catalog is to sell dazzling ideas. It's fun to imagine
being a rebel fighter or chirpy New Yorker. It doesn't matter that the spaceship
can't fly. Or that the *Friends* apartments are unlivable even by New York City
standards. The ideas aren't supposed to work.

Grants have a bigger purpose than the LEGO® catalog. Winning grants
sell dazzling ideas that could actually work. To get funded, you can't just
talk about your cool idea for a spaceship. You also have to show your plan
for making the spaceship work (e.g., how the spaceship would fly and
where the engine goes). Similarly, you can't just write a grant about your
idea to cure cancer. You have to delineate a plan for implementing your
idea too (e.g., the needed materials, technology, team, and deployment
strategy).

In grant writing, you sell your dazzling ideas with the one pager and literature review. The one pager says *why* a problem matters. The literature review
explains *why* you've chosen the right path to a better future.

You convince reviewers your dazzling ideas could actually work with a **research plan**. A research plan explains *what* you will do with the grant. It is the work you will carry out if your grant is funded.

Your research plan is the substance and heart of your grant. To get funded, you must convince reviewers and funders that you have a workable plan. You need to share detailed information about your plan and anticipate questions from reviewers.

A weak research plan is where many grants fail during reviews. Reviewers will complain that "the methods are unclear or lack specificity," or "it's not clear what the team will actually do." Or even worse, reviewers will say, "It's too bad. The idea has promise, but I'm not convinced the work can deliver on it."

The **goal of this chapter** is to show you how to draft a strong research plan. I'll walk you through every step of the process, from outlining, brainstorming, and crafting a project timeline, to building your case, anticipating reviewer questions, and pulling everything together into a draft. By the end of the chapter, you'll understand how to create a research plan that makes reviewers say, "This is a solid plan. This scholar can deliver on their promises."

Action Plan

- ☐ Understand research plans
- ☐ Brainstorm your research plan
- ☐ Craft a project timeline
- ☐ Offense: Build your case
- ☐ Defense: Anticipate reviewer questions
- ☐ Draft your research plan

Understand Research Plans

A research plan is a blueprint for how you will address your research questions. It describes the details of what you will do if your project is funded: the methods and rationale, data collection plan, instruments, data type and structure, analysis plan, expertise, leadership on tasks, plans for failure, assessments of success, timeline, feasibility, and more.

Research plans go by many names in grant writing. Sometimes they are called the research strategy, project description, project plan, methods section, research narrative, or research design. You'll know a funder is asking for a research plan if they ask for your plan for carrying out the work of the grant.

Your research plan should take up the largest portion of space in your grant because it is the substance of it. Learn about expectations for length, content, and organization by studying your samples (chapter 6) and the application guidelines (chapter 7).

Beyond these guidelines, there is no standard way to write a research plan. Research plans look different for every field and funder. This probably sounds like a familiar refrain. The one pager and literature review also have no one correct structure. This means there are an infinite number of ways to write a research plan.

But don't worry. You don't need to learn every way to write a research plan. You just need to learn what information to present in your research plan based on your field of study. As Lori Peek explains, a strong research plan in the social sciences describes *who, how many, what, when, where, and how*.

Let's make this concept of presenting information concrete. Read the sample research plan below. As you read, look for answers to the following questions:

- **Who** is the subject of the study?
- **How many** will be assessed?
- **What** methods will be used?
- **When** will activities happen?
- **Where** will the study be conducted?
- **How** will data be analyzed?

Sample Research Plan

This sample research plan is from a grant I wrote on institutions of higher education (IHEs) and disasters. I'm showing the portion of the research plan that describes how I will carry out aim 2 of the grant. Earlier in the grant, I explained why I'm focusing on three disaster events. This is a lot of text. I wanted you to have a detailed sample.

AIM 2: OBJECTIVES, RESEARCH PLAN, AND EXPECTED OUTCOMES.

The *objective* of aim 2 is to characterize the experiences of advisers who have assisted students after disasters in order to develop strategies for addressing student recovery before the next disasters strike. Our *approach* is to qualitatively interview advisers employed at affected IHEs at the time of the three comparison disasters. I seek to answer these *overarching questions*: What disaster-related barriers do students face in completing their degrees postdisaster? Which of these barriers are advisers positioned to address? What do advisers need in order to be able to help students affected by disasters? What challenges and supports do advisers encounter when assisting students postdisaster?

Research Plan for Aim 2

1. *Purposive interviewing of advisers*. During year two, I will conduct onetime interviews with forty advisers from affected IHEs, focusing greater attention on more recent disasters (i.e., fifteen advisers from Hurricane Harvey, fifteen advisers from the 2017 California wildfires, and ten advisers from the 2013 Colorado Front Range floods). I will recruit advisers based on the principle of maximum variation. Maximum variation involves selecting cases to vary the outcome of interest to capture the maximum variation in the sample.[92] In this case, the goal is to obtain a diverse sample with regard to employment experience and IHE sector type (e.g., four-year, two-year, and public IHEs). I will also target advisers from "high-performing IHEs" that had better than expected student recovery outcomes based on the analyses described in aim 1 (section 7.1.2). High-performing IHEs will meet these criteria: the IHE's student outcomes improved postdisaster (i.e., a significantly larger positive postdisaster slope compared to the predisaster slope), or the IHE reported a smaller disaster impact on student outcomes than peer IHEs from the same sector (i.e., the change in slope was significantly smaller than those of the peer IHEs). Participants will receive incentives for participation ($20 per hour).

2. *Interview question development*. Interview questions will be developed in partnership with my community advisory board (described later in section 12 on Advisory Board and Project Timeline). To address our overarching questions, preliminary interview questions include: What do advisers identify as the gaps in their knowledge about helping college students affected by disasters? What lessons would they like to impart to other advisers who may work with students impacted by disasters? What resources do advisers need to be able to better function in their roles helping students affected by disaster? What is the interplay between student and adviser needs after disasters? How do advisers learn about resources for students postdisaster?

3. *Interview content analysis*. The interviews will take place online. They will be audio recoded, transcribed, inductively coded, and thematically analyzed. Interview notes and transcripts will be read in their entirety. A preliminary codebook of primary and subcodes based on the research questions and data familiarization process will be developed. NVivo 12 software will be used to apply the codes to the data.[93] The text in each thematic index (i.e., code) will be read and synthesized into key points. A visual map of the themes will be developed to ensure robust analysis. Analytic memos will be written to record the discovery of patterns and relationships within and across the interviews.[94]

Feasibility. The primary risk to completion of aim 2 is low recruitment for qualitative interviews. This risk is minimal, as I have structured incentives for participation ($20 per hour), my team will make in-person trips to the study areas for additional interviewing and recruitment, and recruitment will build on existing professional networks. To illustrate using Hurricane Harvey as the context, my professional networks include extensive collaborations in the Houston/Galveston region. I conducted my dissertation work on the impact of Hurricane Ike in the Houston/Galveston area, I collaborate with researchers at the University of Houston Clear Lake and University of Texas Medical Branch, and my current National Science Foundation–funded project on K–12 schools examines the Houston/Galveston area (see section 11, Results from Prior NSF Support).[95] Further, I will draw on my disaster research networks to help identify connections at IHEs in the study areas. My research networks include colleagues from sixty-three different IHEs:

- **Enabling the Next Generation of Hazards and Disaster Researchers Program** (NSF funded). Role: Fourth Round Fellow. Network includes eleven mentors and twenty-two mentees.
- **Gulf Research Program Early Career Research Fellowship**. Role: 2018 Fellow. Network includes ten fellows from 2017, twenty from 2018, and a soon-to-be-named 2019 cohort.
- **Bill Anderson Fund Foundation**. Role: Mentor. Network currently includes twenty-nine fellows.

Expected Outcomes for Aim 2
  Research deliverables
- **Manuscript** on adviser experiences along with IHE barriers and supports that enabled advisers to act meaningfully in their roles to support college student recovery postdisaster.

Education deliverables

- **Adviser case studies** will be developed based on composites from adviser interviews in order to protect the anonymity of the original sources. Case studies are stories based on events and circumstances that help learners develop critical thinking skills and create convincing arguments.[96] Case studies in the disaster context are important because they capture the complexities of particular situations and appeal to a broad audience. They leverage knowledge from previous disasters by making "the most of each single case."[97] Case studies will be designed in order to help advisers develop professional skills, a solution-oriented approach to disasters, and the ability to generate solutions to real-world experiences.

Stakeholder engagement activities

- **Student advising challenge**. I will use the case studies just described in a new academic advising course (see section 9.2, Education Deliverables) to engage advisers to develop strategies for assisting students postdisaster (feedback loop C in figure 1 on disaster student recovery theory), based on the circumstances within the cases. As part of the challenge, students (many of whom are already employed at IHEs) will interview an IHE administrator at their current IHE, practicum placement IHE, or IHE of their choice. They will present their strategies to IHE administrators, and interview administrators regarding anticipated supports and barriers to implementing strategies in that IHE, considering both pre- and postdisaster time periods (feedback loop B in figure 1 on disaster student recovery theory). *Assessments* of this activity will ask: What content is most important for preparing advisers to effectively problem solve and role-play to help students affected by disasters? How and why should content vary based on adviser roles?

Betty's answers. Figure 8 shows my answers for how the sample research plan explains *who, how many, what, when, where, and how*. My answers appear in the middle of the text blocks.

Notice that my sample research plan didn't explain the answers to these questions in this exact order. In research plans, it's not the order of presentation that matters. Clarity is what matters. Present all the information that reviewers need to understand your plan for the grant project.

Next, let's brainstorm what information you want to present to reviewers.

1. Who	Advisers from affected institutions of higher education (IHEs).
Who is the subject of the study?	What will you focus on? What is the level of focus?

2. How Many	Forty advisers, using purposive targeting following three comparison disasters.
How many will you assess?	How much data do you need? Why did you decide on this number? How do you protect people and data?

3. What	Qualitative interviews. Questions developed with community advisory board. Sample questions provided.
What methods will you use?	What is the best method for addressing your questions? Why? What format will data take? What materials do you need? How will you access data? How will you share data?

4. When	One time during Year 2.
When will activities happen?	How long will it take to answer your research questions? Who will oversee each of the activities in the grant? How will team members be involved? What's your project timeline?

5. Where	Online interviews, with follow-up interview trips and recruitment as needed.
Where will you conduct the study?	Will you need to work at another location, institution, or office? Will the study require travel? What will meetings look like?

6. How	Thematic analysis and analytic memos.
How will you analyze data?	How will you know when you've addressed your aims? What is your analytic plan? What will you have achieved if you are sussessful? How will you know if you've made an impact?

FIGURE 8. Develop Your Research Plan

Brainstorm Your Research Plan

When I was a postdoc, I attended a dinner with a famous statistician. They said, "Listen. If an ANOVA [analysis of variance] answers your question, run an ANOVA." This statistician had invented cutting-edge methodologies that changed psychological science. Yet over pasta, they told me to run one of the simplest statistical tests possible, if that's what would answer my research question.

Ever since that dinner, I've put a framed motto in my office. The motto says, "What is your research question?" It reminds me that our goal as researchers is to answer questions. Cutting-edge techniques and shiny equipment can lure you away from this purpose. Don't fall into this trap. That path leads you to putting style over substance.

When you're developing your research plan, put your research questions first. Focus on the best and most feasible approach to executing your ideas.

Here are prompts to help you brainstorm how to best answer your research questions. They are organized around the prompts in figure 8. For now, just concentrate on generating ideas. I'll show you how to present your ideas later in this chapter.

1. ***Who* is the subject of the study?** In the research plan sample above, the subjects were people (advisers). But your subject may not be a person. It is whatever you need to focus on to answer your research questions. Your subject could be building strength, cell lines, the corpus of Toni Morrison's work, and so on. As you consider your subject, also ask at what level you will focus (individuals, schools, building frames, gene function, books published between 1980–90, etc.).

2. ***How many* will you assess?** How much data do you need (e.g., a certain number of scans, participants, or interviews)? Why did you decide on this number (power calculations, theories, past approaches, etc.)? How will you protect people and data? Research should always be secondary to the needs of people we hope to serve. Hints of ethical failures are an absolute no-go in review. What are standard ethical practices in your field? Have you followed those practices? Do you have extra ways of providing protection? Have team members participated in research responsibility workshops/trainings? Have you already obtained an institutional review board approval for your study? Could you create an advisory ethics board?

3. ***What* methods will you use?** What is the "best" method for addressing your questions? "Best" method doesn't mean newest per se. You make a judgment call about what's best. Reviewers are more likely to agree with your judgment if you can explain your reasoning. What have other researchers done? What approach do other researchers recommend? What were the limits of other approaches? What format will data take (e.g., questionnaires, public data, archival data, scale or subscale, quantitative, or qualitative)? What materials do you need (e.g., equipment, software, assays, analyses, or techniques)? Do you need an agreement in place to access data? How will data or outcomes be shared with participants and communities after the study?

4. *When* **will activities happen?** How long will it take to answer your research questions? What activities will you oversee? What will team members oversee? What will student involvement look like? Do you need an advisory board? Stakeholder involvement? How does each step of your project relate to your research questions? What's your project timeline?

5. *Where* **will you conduct the study?** Will you need to work at another location, institution, or office? Will your team or participants need to travel? What will meetings look like? Will you have meetings with collaborators, participants, advisers, and so on? When will they take place?

6. *How* **will you analyze data?** How will you know when you've addressed your aims? What is your analytic plan? Why is your analytic approach the best? Are you well powered for your approach? How will you test your hypotheses, if you have them? How will you interpret the data you collect? What will the results look like? What will you have achieved if you are successful? What outcomes do you expect from this grant? What are the deliverables (e.g., the products that reviewers and funders can expect, such as papers, presentations, or webinars)? Why is this information meaningful or worth funding? How will you know if you've made an impact?

The brainstorming phase of grant writing is exciting and overwhelming. You have a chance to dream about how you'd like to conduct your work. But every choice you make generates new concerns. Lori Peek offers this insight: "Proposal writing is iterative rather than linear.* You might start by answering one question such as, "Who am I going to study?" But then you may have to rethink your approach after you establish, "Where will I conduct the study?" or "What methods will I use?"

Don't be discouraged if you cycle through many ideas as you brainstorm the best approach to answering your research questions. Multiple iterations are a sign you're doing the hard work of creating a well-developed research plan.

---

* Lori and her colleagues developed resources for designing and carrying out research studies (through CONVERGE, funded by National Science Foundation Award #1841338, https://converge.colorado.edu/resources/check-sheets/). The brief check sheets focus on extreme events, but they are applicable to many fields and worth checking out. For example, this is a checklist on research design: https://doi.org/10.17603/ds2-txry-v075. Lori's feedback on this chapter (and the book) deeply shaped how I presented ideas. I am grateful to Lori for her continued guidance and mentorship in my career.

Before you start writing, there's one more activity that will help you understand how to lay out your research plan: crafting a timeline.

Craft a Project Timeline

Timelines are often included in research plans. Sometimes timelines are presented as a **Gantt chart** (for an example, see figure 9).

Timelines help you (and reviewers) understand how you will carry out the work of the grant. For example, look at figure 9. This Gantt chart illustrates the timeline for my grant on IHEs and disasters. The sample research plan above is the research plan for aim 2 of this grant. The project timeline shows you how aim 2 fits into the larger grant. Aim 2 is just one piece of the grant, which has several overlapping aims and activities over five years.

For this activity, craft a project timeline for your grant. Consider the information you just brainstormed. Ask yourself: *How many discrete steps will be involved in each part of my plan, and where should those pieces be placed on the timeline? What pieces of the project will overlap in time? How does this time frame match up with the scope of the project? Does this feel realistic, given the budget and time possible? How can I highlight the information that reviewers need to see in my research plan, based on the evaluation criteria?*

You may be wondering how to lay out your project timeline. There are many ways. I'll cover how to think through designs in chapter 12 when I discuss figures. For now, focus on the content of your timeline.

I've never regretted drafting a timeline. If your grant is funded, your timeline gives you a clear visual for where to start and how to assess your progress.

Next, let's look at how to present your plan so that reviewers understand you can deliver on your big ideas.

Offense: Build Your Case

I wanted a stellar cake for my wedding. Most bakers had "standard" cake tasting days for the public. Sitting in crowds, eating tiny rectangles of cake, I had trouble picturing if I'd like the cake these bakers would deliver. I didn't feel comfortable making a bet on them.

But one baker stood out. They sat down personally with my now husband and me. The baker built a case for their approach. They sketched a picture of our potential cake (a white lace pattern on white frosting), walked us through flavor options, and showed us past cakes they'd made. We could picture what

Project Timeline	Year 1	Year 2	Year 3	Year 4	Year 5
Aim 1: IHE contexts					
RP: Dataset Creation and Integration					
RP: Modeling and Disaster Comparison					
D: Manuscript, Data sets and Dictionaries, Annotated Syntax					
SEA: Communication Brief Design Challenge					
Aim 2: Adviser experiences					
RP: Advisor Qualitative Interviews and Analysis					
D: Manuscript, Advisor Case Studies					
SEA: Student Advising Challenge					
Aim 3: Student needs					
RP: Student Qualitative Interviews and Analysis					
RP: Archival Data Collection and Analysis					
D: Manuscripts (2), New Course, Student Case Studies					
SEA: Student Recovery Art Walk					
Assessment and Additional Stakeholder Engagement and Dissemination Plans					
Advisory Committee Meetings					
Conferences (e.g., Natural Hazards Workshop)					
Pedagogy Assessments					

Notes: RP = research plan tasks; D = deliverables; SEA = stakeholder engagement activity.

FIGURE 9. A Project Timeline: Gantt Chart for Institutions
of Higher Education (IHEs) Grant

our cake would look like. We were confident this baker would deliver a stellar cake. They got our business.

In grant writing, channel winning baker energy. Build your case for your approach. Walk reviewers through a solid plan (cake sketches), strong methods (cake flavor options), and feasibility evidence (pictures of previous cakes).

Losing bakers and grant writers often don't realize they need to build a case for their plan. They simply move from brainstorming and crafting a timeline to drafting their plan. They believe good work speaks for itself. In reality, this approach shifts the hard work to reviewers. Reviewers exhaust themselves trying to picture your work and whether you've chosen the right approach. Exhausted reviewers will not champion your work.

Do the hard work for them. Show reviewers:

1. **You have a solid plan**. Present detailed information about your plan. Help reviewers picture what you will do. Vague information is passive and makes reviewers uncomfortable. Reviewers have to imagine what your work will eventually look like. Vague information makes reviewers say, "I'm confused," or "The connection is unclear." Vague

information makes reviewers focus on what's missing instead of concentrating on your plan.

Vague plan example. We will collaborate on data interpretation. [Because the information is unclear, reviewers will ask, Who is "we?" How many people? Collaborate how? When? How will data be interpreted?]

Solid plan with concrete details example. To facilitate data interpretation, Dr. Aibileen Clark (principal investigator) and Dr. Minny Jackson (coinvestigator) will conduct four joint lab meetings (ten trainees total) each year. The joint lab meetings will be three hours long, covering data review, data analysis, and data interpretation. Three of the four joint lab meetings will be virtual. One joint lab meeting will take place at Harper University in Mississippi, the location of the principal investigator's lab.

Troubleshooting. If you write for an interdisciplinary audience, your plan can feel vague because your methods are unfamiliar to reviewers. To make your plan feel solid, walk reviewers through an "explanatory example." For instance, I worked on a grant that involved complex statistical analyses. Reviewers were not statisticians. To help them picture the statistical analyses, I drew a graph illustrating potential outcomes and what the analyses would look like in those cases. As another example, say you plan to conduct ethnographic research in Kuala Lumpur. Your reviewers are not ethnographers. You could walk reviewers through an "explanatory example," demonstrating the types of data you'd collect and how data would be analyzed.

2. **You chose the right methods**. For every method or design choice, explain to reviewers why you made that choice. Explain the advantages of your choices. Otherwise reviewers will say, "I can't figure out why they're doing this," "Why didn't they consider this alternate technique," or "Why are they bringing this up here."

Failing to explain why example. Dr. Boba Fett will breed one sarlacc to adulthood.

Explaining why example. To evaluate the composition of sarlacc digestive enzymes (aim 1), Dr. Boba Fett will breed one sarlacc to adulthood. Although industry practice has focused on enzyme analysis from deceased sarlaccs (Hutt 1977), the emerging evidence indicates that live sarlaccs provide more accurate data on enzyme composition (Shand 2022).

This skill in action. In my grant on IHEs and disasters (you read the research plan and timeline for this grant above), I focused on three disasters. I knew reviewers would need to understand why I made this choice. To explain my rationale, I wrote:

To increase the generalizability of findings, I will compare student recovery experiences following three disasters: 1) *Hurricane Harvey* (incident period August 23–September 15, 2017); 2) *2017 California wildfires* (incident period October 8–31, 2017); 3) *2013 Colorado Front Range floods* (incident period September 11–30, 2013). These disasters were chosen because they occurred within the last ten years, are diverse with regard to disaster type and geographic location, occurred during the fall semester, were declared as Major Disaster Declarations, and caused over $1 billion in damages (FEMA 2019; NOAA National Centers for Environmental Information 2019). [Notice that I said up front that my goal is to increase generalizability. This is how I signal to reviewers I have the right methods. Reviewers can follow my thought process, even if they do not agree with my choices.]

3. **You'll be able to do the work**. Give reviewers evidence they can use to advocate for you. Draw on the information you brainstormed above. Give facts, figures, pilot data, past history, or lessons learned that tell the story of why you will be able to carry out the work. Failing to give this information requires reviewers to have faith. Reviewers have to trust you with no evidence. That's a big leap for reviewers who likely don't know you personally.

Example where it's not clear you can do the work. We will use the Royco method.

Example that showcases feasibility. We will use the Royco method. Coinvestigator Tom Wambsgans (media expert) was trained on the Royco method by their mentor and the inventor of the technique, Dr. Siobhan Roy. Coinvestigator Tom Wambsgans has published two studies using the Royco method (Roy and Wambsgans 2021; Wambsgans 2022).

This skill in action. In a recent grant, I was making the case that I would be able to communicate my findings to a broad audience. I wrote:

I will increase the reach of these activities by leveraging my active social and traditional media platform. My Twitter account generated 1.3 million impressions in the past three months. This past year I have been quoted in the *New York Times, Washington Post,* and *Huffington Post,* and on *NBC News* and *Vox.* [Notice that I use the word "leverage" to show how the activities will build on my past history. This is a subtle way of indicating I've learned lessons in the past that will help me in the proposed future work. I give evidence (1.3 million) and also name specific media outlets to make it more concrete for reviewers.]

4. **Good outcomes can be expected from your work**. Paint a clear picture of the outcomes for reviewers. Help reviewers understand what will be possible because of this work. Vague outcomes are not convincing to reviewers.

  Example of vague outcomes. We will present findings to key stakeholders. [Reviewers will wonder, who is "we"? What are the "findings"? Who are the "key stakeholders"?]

  Example that helps reviewers picture good outcomes. Findings from this study will be incorporated into my master's course for academic advisers in training. Through this course, I will be able to disseminate information quickly to future advising professionals. My school's program on higher education has awarded more than 400 master's degrees and 150 doctoral degrees in higher education, and is currently ranked twenty-sixth among programs for education administration (Higher Education 2020).

  Sentence starters to indicate good outcomes. Signal to reviewers that you are about to discuss the outcomes of your work. Here are some sentence starter mad libs for your research plan:

  - The following significant outcomes may be expected from this work _____.
  - Successful completion of this project will result in _____.
  - By the end of research question 1, _____.
  - This project will result in the following deliverables _____.

Defense: Anticipate Reviewer Questions

It takes practice to write convincing research plans. As researcher Andrew Rumbach notes, "Grants help you become a clearer communicator. The writing needs to be accessible. Learning how to make convincing arguments is an additive process."

Part of this additive process is learning to write your research plan offensively *and* defensively. I just discussed the offensive strategy: building a case for your research plan. The defensive strategy is to anticipate reviewer questions. When you anticipate questions (or problems) that reviewers will raise, you can address those defensively by adding related information to your research plan.

To help you anticipate reviewer questions, try these exercises. In each exercise, I give you part of a research plan. Pretend you are a reviewer. What information would you expect to see next in the research plan, based on the text provided?

Exercise 1

Research plan text. The principal investigator (Spatafora) and coinvestigator (Pirozzi) will use data from the Youth Risk Behavior Surveillance System and Behavioral Risk Factor Surveillance System.

You're the reviewer! If you were a reviewer, what information would you expect to see in the research plan? Notice that I've only given you a small snippet of a research plan. Even small snippets start to generate questions for reviewers.

Betty's answer. Note, [**brackets**] show how questions relate to the previous skill: "Offense: Build Your Case." I anticipate reviewers will want to know: What are these two data sets, and why did the investigators choose them? [**right methods**]; How will the investigators access these data [**solid plan**]; Have investigators ever used this data in the past? Do investigators have the relevant expertise and equipment to use this data? [**able to do the work**]; and, Why is it better for the world that the investigators chose these data sets? [**good outcomes**].

Exercise 2

Research plan text. Drs. Spatafora and Pirozzi will share findings from the study with schools.

You're the reviewer! If you were a reviewer, what information would you look for in the research plan, based on this description?

Betty's answer. I anticipate reviewers will want to know: How will the investigators share findings [**solid plan**]; What method will investigators use to share findings? [**right methods**]; Will investigators actually be able to share findings? Do schools want investigators to visit? Is there a letter from schools showing support for the project? [**able to do the work**]; and, Is it helpful for investigators to share findings with the school? How will investigators know they've been helpful? Have investigators ever shared findings before with a school? Did that help? Do investigators have a way of testing whether feedback makes an impact? [**good outcomes**].

Exercise 3

Research plan text. Drs. Luna and Allison will obtain archival data on the 1918 flu from the historical image gallery at Acme Labs. On obtaining access, Drs. Luna and Allison will catalog and digitize archival prints.

You're the reviewer! As a reviewer, what information would you expect to see in the research plan, based on this description?

Betty's answer. I anticipate reviewers will want to know: How will Drs. Luna and Allison gain access to Acme Labs? [**solid plan**]; Why are they digitizing the prints? [**right methods**]; Will they be allowed to digitize the prints? Could the study still run if they aren't able to gain access to and/or digitize the prints? [**able to do the work**]; and, What will happen at the end of this study? [**good outcomes**].

When you anticipate what reviewers will ask, you get valuable information about what information to place in your research plan. So let's try it. It's time to draft your research plan.

Draft Your Research Plan

Combine the skills from this chapter. Consider all the information you brainstormed. Look at your timeline. Play offense, and then play defense as you write. Your goal is to present a clear game plan for reviewers about what they can expect if you are awarded your grant.

Now draft your research plan.

You're probably thinking you have too much information to fit into a short space. You're correct. But when you're drafting, don't worry about running out of room. In the drafting phase, your goal is to gather any information that helps build your case. Having too much information in the drafting phase is a sign you're building compelling arguments for why you have a strong research plan.

You will pare down to your most compelling arguments when we get to the polishing phase of grant writing (chapters 13–15).

But for now, focus on drafting. Here's how writer Shannon Hale explains the difference between the drafting and polishing process: "When writing a first draft, I have to remind myself constantly that I'm only shoveling sand into a box so later I can build castles."[98]

Concentrate on shoveling interesting ideas into your research plan. You will shape your ideas into castles later.

Tips and Frequently Asked Questions

Why do you recommend drafting the one pager and literature review before the research plan? If you cannot build a case for why a problem matters (one pager) and why you've found the right solution for the problem (literature review), it doesn't matter how strong your methods are. Reviewers need to know that you're asking the right questions to begin with.

How long should my research plan be? This varies for every funder, so there is no general guideline. Look at your application guidelines (chapter 7) for detailed instructions on page or word limits. Study your sample grant applications (chapter 6) to understand the culture of your funder and how long reviewers expect your research plan to be. Your research plan needs to be long enough to convince reviewers you have a solid plan, the right methods, you'll be able to do the work, and your work will lead to good outcomes.

Does my final research plan need to cover every single question from the activity about brainstorming your research plan? No. Grants have limited space. You will know much more about your research plan than you will be able to present in your grant. For example, the sample research plan in this chapter did not cover all the brainstorming questions. But remember you are in drafting mode for now. Marshal evidence to build your case. You will streamline this information later when you polish your grant (task D of this book).

How do I know if I've chosen the best methods? Remember, you aren't looking for best methods. You are looking for the best methods *for addressing your research questions*. If you think back to the baker analogy, the losing bakers may have had better methods. But we weren't looking for best methods. We wanted to know if they could address our problem (i.e., getting a stellar cake on our wedding day). Don't get stuck in the search for best. Take a stab at drafting your research plan. Your first draft will likely not be strong enough for funding. Keep revising to make your plan stronger. In chapter 15, you'll learn how to get feedback from colleagues and mentors to improve your grant. And after you submit, reviewers will also give you feedback. That's why it's important to submit. Putting your ideas out into the world is the best way to get feedback.

What do I do if my methods go against conventional wisdom? Many scholars fear their thinking is too "out of the box" to be fundable. Let me reassure you. It's often refreshing to hear ideas that disrupt the status quo. Yet your job as a grant writer is to build a case for your plan. If you go against conventional wisdom, explain why conventional methods fall short. Thinking defensively, reviewers will wonder why you didn't choose the standard way. Anticipate and address those questions. *For example: Although current standard practice is to offer two child tributes per district per year, this standard practice is unethical. Standard practice violates the principles of respect and rights for children (United Nation Convention on the Rights of the Child 1989; Collins 2008). Thus in this study, we propose that no tributes be offered in any year.*

What can I do if I don't have much pilot data? Scholars frequently think pilot data has to be perfectly aligned data from their own studies. But this is not the point of pilot data. The point is to build a strong case that you chose the right methods or you can do the work. There are many ways to make these arguments. For instance, have past scholars used the methods you're proposing? Can you show how the methods were used, and how you're leveraging that work in your plan? Have you or a collaborator done work in a related area that helps make the case for your proposed work? Could you apply for seed funding to gather initial data (and also show that your institution or field is invested in your work)? Search for any evidence that helps you build your case.

If I introduce ways my plan can fail, won't reviewers hyperfocus on problems with my work? Reviewers are already searching for problems with your work. That's their job. Your job is to instill confidence in reviewers that you can resolve foreseeable problems. Reviewers will worry if you write, "It's highly likely that we will encounter this unresolvable problem that will derail the project." In contrast, you instill confidence when you write, "We anticipate this terrible problem could occur. This terrible problem is unlikely because our team has five years of experience running this protocol. If this terrible problem occurs, however, we will implement the following protocol to overcome it." Here's another example showing how to instill confidence. *We are confident we will be able to recruit our target goal of a hundred students from the Hogwarts school. We focus on Hogwarts because it remains the world's premier school of wizardry (Bagshot 1997). We will invite the thousand actively enrolled Hogwarts students to participate in our study. Our team's past school-based studies have achieved an 80 percent participation rate from the invited students (Order of the Phoenix 2022). In the unlikely event we are not able to recruit a hundred students, we have engaged two additional community schools, Beauxbatons and Durmstrang, which have indicated their excitement and willingness to assist with recruitment. Please see our appendix for letters of support from Hogwarts, Beauxbatons, and Durmstrang.*

What if there isn't enough money in the budget to do the work I want to do? This is the hard dance between the budget and your research plan. Work closely with your research administrator (chapter 7) and mentors. They will help you understand what's possible with the budget and how much it will cost to conduct the research you're imagining. Remember, all grant writing is iterative. Pieces will change as you waltz between the budget and research plan. Are you able to sacrifice some of the work you hope to do in order to move closer to being able to do that work in a future grant? If you end up having to sacrifice a research component, move it to a "future ideas" document. Save it for your next fundable grant.

Wouldn't the optimal strategy be to add tons of experts to my grant? No. More is not more when it comes to experts. If you have too many experts, reviewers will think your grant is bloated and that collaborators will do no real work. I'll cover how to handle experts in chapter 14, but I mention this issue now in case you are wanting to "collect" experts for your grant. Be wary of asking too many people to join your team because you may have to ask them to leave if they don't have a clear role.

Don't hoard your data. Many funders promote open science. Sharing data is important for reproducibility and advancing our fields. In your research plan, discuss how you will share data at the conclusion of your project so that others will be able to benefit. Even better, look for what your funder says about the importance of sharing data. Cite this language in your research plan alongside your plan for sharing data. If there are ethical reasons for not sharing, explain these reasons. And one last tip from a colleague: build publishing fees for open-access journals into your budgets when possible.

Are research plans set in stone? Meaning, could a research plan be flexible if I run into problems later? Yes, research plans can change. Funders know changes happen. (Imagine all the changes that had to happen at the start of the COVID-19 pandemic, for example.) A reviewer for this book underscored this point: funders recognize that a grant proposal is not a guarantee. That's why most funders have policies for reporting changes to a grant (e.g., to timelines, recruitment, budget, etc.) after a grant is awarded.

The Takeaway

In this chapter, I covered all the elements you need to create a strong research plan draft: brainstorming, crafting a project timeline, building a case, anticipating reviewer questions, and sitting down to draft your research plan. A research plan is the substance of your grant. Use your research plan to show reviewers you can live up to the hype of your dazzling ideas.

At this point, you're probably wondering how to flesh out your full draft. You're in luck, because that's my next chapter.

11

Structure Your Draft

CONSISTENCY IS COMFORTING

In grantsmanship, there is value in not surprising the reader.
—ALMA FAUST[99]

AFTER COLLEGE, I was a math and science teacher. My first year was hard. So hard I'd daydream about breaking a leg to get a week off from teaching. I had no classroom management. I worried every minute that my middle schoolers would hurt themselves running around the classroom. I yelled my lessons over the racket and lost my voice three times. I didn't know how to fix my problems.

Observing master teachers didn't help. They had my same students, but none of my problems. The students stayed in their seats and moved seamlessly from activity to activity. These classrooms were well-oiled machines where everyone seemed to know what would happen next.

That was the secret. Everyone *did* know what would happen next. Master teachers are consistent. They structure classes so students know what to expect. Students feel supported and focus their energy on grappling with ideas.

I was not a consistent novice teacher. The students were shocked by every transition and new piece of information. They screamed, "Oooh, Ms. Lai. Why are we getting our books out now." Or, "Why are we talking about pasta? This is math class." (That was actually a cool lesson about the shapes of triangles. But as you can see, my lesson was lost in the chaos I created.)

Be a master teacher when you write. Create the comfort of consistency in your grant. Consistency makes it easy for reviewers to find the information they need to evaluate your grant (see chapter 8 on evaluation criteria). As researcher Mathew Kiang shares, "My goal is that a reviewer should be able to look at any one sentence and know exactly what should come next. For example, my K99/R00 opens with a comparison of the opioid crisis between Black and white Americans. That makes it clear that the next line should be about addressing racial/ethnic disparities in opioid-related deaths. Don't surprise reviewers. They are tired, overworked, and underpaid. I aim for a grant where reviewers should be able to read every other sentence and still know what the grant is about."

Researcher Nancy Kassam-Adams elaborates on this point: "You need a really compelling and consistent story so someone who reads your grant knows there's not a mismatch between your aims and what happens later on. This makes it easy for reviewers to know what you plan to do."

The **goal of this chapter** is to help you develop a consistent grant that makes your reviewers say, "Wow. This was so easy to understand."

Action Plan

- ☐ Describe the inverted pyramid approach
- ☐ Evaluate a sample that uses the inverted pyramid approach
- ☐ Flesh out your full proposal
- ☐ Avoid common mistakes
- ☐ Create consistency across your full grant

Describe the Inverted Pyramid Approach

I'm adapting the inverted pyramid strategy from journalism to create consistency in your grant. Journalists know how to communicate complex information quickly to readers with limited attention spans.

The inverted pyramid strategy is an approach to structuring paragraphs. The most important information leads the paragraph. Related but less important information appears in the body of the paragraph. This structure makes it clear to reviewers what your point is (i.e., it's the first line) and where to find the supporting evidence (i.e., always in the body of the paragraph). This is true even if reviewers only read the first line of every paragraph.

Front-load your point in every paragraph because reviewers don't have time to search for it. If your point is in the middle or bottom of a paragraph, you've hidden it from reviewers. Don't be coy.

A common objection I hear is, "But isn't it more fun to let reviewers make up their mind about the evidence? Don't reviewers prefer mystery and cliffhangers?" No. Reviewers don't have time for games. They need to quickly locate information in order to evaluate your grant. Any roadblocks to this mission are exhausting. Exhausted reviewers usually decide the problem is your idea, expertise, or organizational skills. Remember, your goal is to show reviewers the most direct path to a better future (chapter 9).

Now that I've described the inverted pyramid approach, here's what it looks like, as depicted in figure 10:

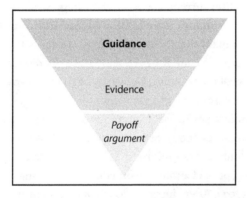

FIGURE 10. The Inverted Pyramid Approach

- **Guidance**. This is the main point you want reviewers to understand as they move on their journey to championing your work. These are the guidance statements you put into your literature review outline in chapter 9. Every guidance statement from your outline should now become the first line of one paragraph in your literature review.
- **Evidence**. Evidence should be references to the literature, data points, or concrete examples. Every piece of evidence is there to support the guidance argument. You can decide how many pieces of evidence are necessary to support your guidance.
- **Payoff argument**. The payoff argument is your chance to tell reviewers what you think the takeaway is to rapidly move the field forward. A payoff argument creates momentum to your next piece of guidance (i.e., the next paragraph). Not every paragraph needs a payoff argument. Use payoff arguments when you want to emphasize how your work will resolve a pain point in the field (for more on pain points, see chapter 9).

Evaluate a Sample That Uses the Inverted Pyramid Approach

Here's a short sample from a grant I wrote on IHEs and disasters (you saw the research plan and project timeline for this grant in chapter 10). I **bolded the guidance statements** and put the *payoff arguments in italics* to make it easy for you and the reviewers to see them. I left citations in the text so you could see how they look in a sample. But citation references are not listed in the chapter notes (to save space and publication costs).

> **No empirical literature has examined college student recovery after disasters, but abundant anecdotal evidence indicates that disasters may gravely impact the ability of college students to complete their degrees.** After Hurricane Katrina, 1,663 students did not return for the spring semester at the Southern University of New Orleans. This represents a 45 percent loss from the 3,700 students who had originally matriculated for the academic year (Special Committee on Hurricane Katrina and New Orleans Universities 2007). Similarly, although less severe, 12 percent of full-time students did not return to Tulane's uptown campus after Hurricane Katrina (Special Committee on Hurricane Katrina and New Orleans Universities 2007). After Hurricane Maria, 860 students withdrew from the University of Puerto Rico, while hundreds more applied to transfer to colleges on the US mainland (Korn 2017). As another example, during the California wildfires of 2018, classes were suspended for approximately two weeks at California State University at Chico, Pepperdine University, and the University of California at Davis (Dateline Staff and UC Davis News Service 2018; Pepperdine University 2018; Whitford 2018). Two weeks of lost classes equates to roughly 13 percent of a semester-long course.
>
> **A small but growing literature on schools and disasters, however, provides some insight into factors that may influence college student recovery; yet this work is limited to K–12 settings.** I am the principal investigator on a study evaluating the impact of Hurricane Ike on school academic functioning (see section 11, Results from Prior NSF Support). We analyzed academic outcomes among 462 Texas K–12 public schools. In our study, 9.4 percent of K–12 schools did not return students to their predisaster levels of academic functioning. School context factors (i.e., attendance and the percent economically disadvantaged youths) were significantly associated with falling in this subset of schools (Lai et al. 2018, 2019).

Sacerdote (2008) examined data from children in K–12 schools after Hurricanes Katrina and Rita. Sacerdote found that in some cases, <u>transferring to a new school</u> after the disasters *benefited* students with regard to their academic outcomes. Tobin's (2019) dissertation work evaluated educational continuity among K–12 schools in Lyons after the 2013 Colorado Front Range floods. Tobin found that dedicated <u>support from multiple levels of student ecology</u> was critical to student recovery. Overall, the evidence on supporting students after disasters is limited to K–12 settings and is in the context of primarily mandatory education, *which does not translate to college students and IHE settings.*

The broader disaster literature provides some insight into factors that may influence college student recovery, however this work is limited because it focuses on "children" and "adults." As noted earlier, disasters are associated with high levels of financial, social, and psychological stressors (Bonanno et al. 2006; Roussos et al. 2005; Self-Brown et al. 2013). These stressors differ in their form and meaning for children and adults (Lai et al., 2015), but it is not clear what form or meaning these stressors take for college students. This is because child studies <u>exclude</u> college students by definition, as they focus on those under eighteen years of age (Natural Hazards Center 2019). At the same time, studies of adults generally <u>overlook</u> college students because they do not purposefully sample from this group. For example, Bourque (2014) conducted a seminal study on public preparedness, mitigation, and avoidance related to disasters. Less than 1 percent of the 3,300 US participants in that study fell between the ages of eighteen and twenty-five (Bourque 2014), the age of most college students (US Department of Education 2018a). *In summary, the broader disaster literature has excluded or overlooked college students.*

These paragraphs are lifted from the middle of my literature review. Notice that these paragraphs still make sense even when cut from a larger grant. That's the power of the inverted pyramid approach.

Flesh out Your Full Proposal

Try the inverted pyramid approach on your grant. Let's walk through the three major documents you've created so far.

One pager (chapter 4). Look at each paragraph you've written. Apply the inverted pyramid approach to each paragraph except the first one. Exclude the first paragraph because it doesn't usually follow this structure (see samples 1 and 2 in chapter 4). Look carefully at each paragraph. Could you read just the first line and know what the paragraph is about? If not, rewrite the first line to make it a guidance statement. Next, look at the middle of each paragraph. Are the middle sentences evidence for the guidance statement? If not, they need to be cut or rewritten. Finally, do you have a payoff sentence at the end of each paragraph? Do you want one?

Literature review (chapter 9). Pull up your literature review outline. Each guidance statement in your outline is now the first line of a paragraph in your literature review. Brainstorm evidence and payoff arguments for each paragraph. I recommend sticking to an outline format with bullet points under each piece of guidance for now. That gives you the flexibility to rearrange evidence and payoff statements as needed. Keep rearranging until you get the best story flow.

Research plan (chapter 10). Pull up your research plan rough draft. Apply the inverted pyramid structure to each paragraph.

Avoid Common Mistakes

Here are common mistakes people run into when using the inverted pyramid approach.

1. **The evidence doesn't fit the guidance statement.** As scholars, we like to cram in evidence and share interesting facts. But researcher Jon Wargo notes that when evidence doesn't fit the topic, "the reviewer will stop and wonder why evidence is there and get confused." The inverted pyramid strategy only works well if you "chunk" related information together for your reviewers so they know what to expect. See if you can spot this mistake below:

   Example of evidence not fitting. **Disasters lead to the development of mental health distress.** Disasters are associated with posttraumatic stress, anxiety, and depression symptoms. Exposure to stressors during disaster events increases the risk for mental health problems. These risk factors include perceptions of your life being in danger, witnessing events (e.g., fires or windows breaking), and being harmed.

   What's wrong with the example. The back half of the paragraph talks about risk factors for distress. Risk factors are not mentioned in the guidance statement, so it's not clear why that evidence appears here.

Troubleshoot. You could split the example paragraph into two paragraphs on distress and risk factors, respectively. This is a fine strategy if you feel the two arguments are important for the reviewer's journey. Alternatively, sharpen your guidance statement. Here you could try, **"Key risk factors lead to the development of mental health distress after disasters."** This sharpened guidance statement covers all the evidence in the paragraph. The sharpening strategy saves space because you can stick with one paragraph.

2. **Sweeping conflicting evidence under the rug**. When the evidence doesn't fit your argument, you need to talk about it. Reviewers are smart. It's Murphy's Law that reviewers will always think of the evidence you really hope they won't think about. In fact, reviewers are usually most interested in this conflicting evidence. They want to know that you've considered all the evidence and are making a logical argument.

    Troubleshoot. Be honest. Engage with all sides of an argument. After you troubleshoot, you may decide that your argument is too strong and needs to be rewritten.

3. **Not revising enough**. Your grant needs a logical flow and momentum. In the course of writing your grant, new information will probably conflict with what you've already written. Revise to tell a compelling and consistent story.

    Example of why revision works. Kirsten Davison wrote a grant building the case that social workers are ideal champions for vaccine acceptance. As the grant developed, Kirsten realized the research would take place in Latinx mental health settings. Kirsten revised her initial case to focus on how Latinx populations use behavioral health services. If Kirsten had stuck with her initial plan to focus just on the case for social workers, she would have missed an opportunity to amplify the unique and important aspects of her work.

    Troubleshoot. Cut paragraphs you don't need. Revise and build your case as you learn new information. To write a fundable grant, you almost always need to rewrite the beginning to end several times. That's normal and a sign you're writing a compelling grant.

4. **Too much filler instead of evidence**. Filler statements are like cotton candy. They are empty calories that add no value. (No offense to those who love cotton candy.)

    Filler statement example. This extremely important information leverages knowledge and catapults our learning in new directions.

Troubleshoot. Cut the entire filler statement. As a good guideline, a line is filler if it's so general it could be dropped into any grant and make sense. Provide specific information to bolster your arguments. This means provide data, numbers, statistics, or examples. Specific evidence is more compelling than filler.

Create Consistency across Your Full Grant

Once you have a solid one pager, literature review, and research plan in place, outline and write the other sections of your grant (e.g., data management plan, facilities document, human subjects, and project summary). In this book, I don't go into detail on what information should go in these additional sections. That's because your funder's application instructions will dictate what information needs to be included in the additional grant sections. You're smart, so I'm confident you will read and follow those application instructions carefully.

Instead, here's an approach to writing your additional sections. All you need to do is stick to what I've discussed so far. Be consistent.

This answer is simple to say and hard to implement. Here are concrete strategies for creating consistency across your full grant.

A. **Signposts**. Signposts are words you use to tell reviewers what they can expect in a section.
   Examples. I do a lot of signposting in this book. Throughout the book, I bold the signposts. For instance, the introduction to every chapter ends with a paragraph that says, "The **goal of this chapter**." Then I highlight the "Action Plan" for each chapter. I end every chapter with another signpost, "The Takeaway."
   Strategies. You've outlined the required proposal elements (chapter 7) and evaluation criteria (chapter 8) for your grant. These are signposts you need to use in your grant. You can also use signposts like first, second, third, last, or ABC if you are making an argument that has many points (e.g., like in this section on skills and techniques, I've used A, B, C, D, and E to tell you these are all skills that fall under a similar idea). Beware of using too many of these signposts within text, as reviewers quickly get lost when you give them too many to track.
B. **Mirroring**. Mirroring means all sections of your grant appear in the same order and style. Mirroring helps reviewers focus on your ideas because they always know what will come next.

Mirroring example with aims. If your aims are 1, 2, and 3, then every section of your grant should describe information in that exact order, 1, 2, and 3. This is true across any section (e.g., approach, measures, timeline, and significance). Present information related to aim 1 before aims 2 or 3.

Mirroring examples from this book. I've used mirroring in this book. You always see an introduction, set of skills, exercises, tips and frequently asked questions, and then a takeaway paragraph. This is a combination of signposts and mirroring because I've also mirrored the signposts across the book.

Where people go wrong. People usually aren't consistent enough when using mirroring. Mirror everywhere you can because it makes it easy for reviewers to know when to expect information. For instance, sometimes people will talk about anxiety and depression. But in the next line, they will talk about depression and anxiety. That's inconsistent.

C. Repetition. Always use the exact same word or words to talk about a concept. This is different from teaching, where you want to introduce all the ways an idea may come up. When you change words, reviewers wonder if you are using different words for a reason. You're forcing reviewers to guess what you mean.

Example. You talk about "hazards" in one section and "disasters" in another section. Or you mention "posttraumatic stress symptoms" in aim 1 and "posttraumatic stress syndrome" in aim 2. You may be trying to differentiate concepts. If that's the case, tell reviewers this is your intention (e.g., hazards are different from disasters because of _____). Otherwise, use the same word every single time.

D. Use emphasis techniques. Highlight what reviewers need to know by using formatting or punctuation consistently. Don't overdo it.

"Overdoing it" example. Anything you can do to <u>underscore the main point</u> helps. But avoid **using too many emphasis techniques at once**, or the techniques will ***lose their power***.

Revision of "overdoing it" example. Anything you can do to <u>underscore the main point</u> helps. But <u>don't use too many emphasis techniques</u> at once or they will lose their power.

Star student tip: Mirror your emphasis techniques. This consistency helps reviewers understand why you are using an emphasis technique, which reduces distraction. In the literature review sample above, all the **guidance was bolded** and all the *payoff arguments were itali-cized*. Similarly, all the alphabetized lists in this book (like this current A–E section) start with bolded words followed by a period. Be this nitpicky in your grant too.

E. **Front-load your point**. State what you mean up front to communicate clearly to reviewers. This applies to paragraphs and individual sentences. Below, I'm showing instances where the information is not front-loaded and then I revise the examples to front-load the point. Notice the same information appears in the examples and their revisions. But the revisions are more clear.

Paragraph that isn't front-loaded. Sometimes A is associated with B. Sometimes B is associated with X. Therefore it is possible A may be associated with X.

Paragraph revised to be front-loaded. A may be associated with X. Here's the evidence. Sometimes A is associated with B. Sometimes B is associated with X.

Sentence that isn't front-loaded. Eight studies identified risk factors for tuberculosis.

Sentence revised to be front-loaded. Risk factors for tuberculosis were identified in eight studies. [Assuming that you are trying to highlight risk factors as your point in this sentence.]

Tips and Frequently Asked Questions

Where should I invest the greatest amount of time: the one pager, literature review, or research plan? The one pager is the "highest-impact" section of your proposal. The one pager is read more than any other section and sets the tone for your proposal. For that reason, the one pager often takes the longest time to refine. Yet you have to focus on all sections of your proposal to write a strong grant. Instead of thinking about drafting these pieces sequentially, many grant writers draft them in tandem. As you refine each section, they create "ripple effects" that will force you to rethink and rewrite the other sections.

How do I come up with a good title for my grant? I do not believe titles are a make-or-break issue. Titles are often generated early in the grant writing process, before the grant is even developed. I prefer titles that are descriptive rather than "sexy" (as you can see from this book's title). I have seen titles that are arresting (in the good way), however. Check past awards at your funder to see what types of titles the funder prefers. And most important, before you submit make sure that your title matches your final grant. Because grants change so much as you revise, this is a critical step you don't want to miss.

How do I handle the different writing styles of my collaborators? "You don't want to have a disjointed submission," cautions researcher Ashwini Tiwari. Ashwini recommends talking early on about the collaborative relationship and how people prefer to receive feedback. Decide how you want to divide the tasks of proposal writing. The principal investigator on the proposal usually takes on the largest share of writing and frequently has final say on style. That's because the principal investigator will lead the project if it's funded. But sometimes you'll be on a large or interdisciplinary team where you may need to have meetings or votes about decisions. Talk early and openly about preferred processes.

What reference style should my references be in? Always defer to the grant application instructions and follow those. If you are allowed to choose, follow the style of your sample grants. (This is an example of using signals to your advantage. For a refresher on signals, see chapter 6.) I've used different referencing styles in grants (as shown in the grant samples in this book). I don't think this is a make-or-break issue. Yet experts are split in their preferences. Some people prefer styles where citations are written in the text, like the American Psychological Association referencing. Proponents of these styles prefer them because reviewers are able to immediately see who is being cited and how old the research is. This helps reviewers know how much they trust your judgment on landmark research in your field. Some people prefer numbered styles, though, like the American Medical Association referencing. Numbered styles save a lot of space. Proponents of numbered styles say they allow reviewers to focus on your text rather than references. But numbered styles require reviewers to flip back and forth in your grant to see who you are citing.

How many references should I include in my grant? Like most scholarly endeavors, it depends on your field and funder, so look closely at your samples (chapter 6) and the application guidelines (chapter 7) to understand the expectations. If you're a guidelines person, the National Institute of Allergy and Infectious Diseases says to include fewer than a hundred citations.[87] As another data point, my most recent R03 grant to the National Institutes of Health had seventy-five references. When thinking about references, focus on the highest-impact ones. Think about which articles are foundational for your field, articles that have changed your field, articles that reviewers believe are high impact, and recent articles (within the last ten years).

Creating consistency is a lot of work. Will reviewers even notice?
Reviewers may not explicitly notice how consistent your grant is. Like observing master teachers, sometimes you don't know why an experience was lovely. You just know it was. You're trying to create a moving experience for reviewers. Every minute you put into creating a consistent grant enhances reviewers' experiences.

The Takeaway

Consistency makes it easy for reviewers to understand your work. At this point, you can draft all of your grant sections by using the inverted pyramid approach and applying consistency techniques across your grant. Note that this is just one way to approach writing your full draft. I chose this method because it's the simplest and fastest one to writing a compelling grant.

But please know you can and will veer from these strategies as you write more fundable grants. That's the beauty of grant writing. You learn what works best for you and the funders that love you.

Next, let's talk about a tool that makes it easy for reviewers to absorb information quickly: figures.

12

Go Figure

IMAGES THAT DELIVER VALUE

Use interesting visualization to help evaluation panels to understand and, most importantly, appreciate the uniqueness of your proposal.

—ROSDIADEE NORDIN[100]

WHEN I WAS LITTLE, flying from Texas to Taiwan was a thirty-hour trip. We had to go from Dallas to Los Angeles. Have an eight-hour layover. Fly to Tokyo. Have another eight-hour layover. Then we'd fly to Taipei. Nowadays, the trip can take as little as twenty hours. You can fly to Los Angeles, have a two-hour layover, and then fly to Taipei.

These two trips are an analogy for ways people approach understanding a topic.

Scholars generally prefer the first, longer trip. The first trip lets you meander as you learn. It's fun to explore a topic's tangents (an extra stop in Tokyo will be illuminating) and ponder the minutiae of a subject (layovers are fascinating). That curiosity is what drives many of us to earn terminal degrees. But remember, a grant isn't about you. Grants are written for reviewers.

Reviewers always prefer the second, shorter trip. The second trip is more enjoyable for people who are stressed and tired. It's easier and requires less energy. To stressed reviewers, unrelated tangents and unnecessary minutiae are burdens. Remember, reviewers want the simplest and most direct path to the information they need to evaluate your grant. Your job is to remove obstacles for reviewers in this journey.

Most people take this lesson to heart and streamline the writing in their grants. Apply this lesson to your figures as well. As George Savva writes, "I read a *lot* of grants, and I think in general the figures [people] use make them worse rather than better. Biggest problem is usually trying to put too much in (like 5 or 6 panels) with too little explanation. So make it easy to understand, and consider whether needed at all.[101]

Bad figures sink your grant faster than bad writing because reviewers like to spend time on figures. Figures are more fun to look at than writing. Even reviewers who aren't assigned to review your grant will be attracted to your figures when they skim your grant.

Bottom line, only use figures that add value. If the figure does not add value, the figure should be cut or revised. Otherwise, you're adding obstacles to reviewers' journeys and eating up precious space in your grant at the same time.

The **goal of this chapter** is to ensure that you use figures in your grant that deliver value. I focus on figures after your one pager, literature review, research plan, and creating consistency across your grant. I look at figures last in the drafting process because these other pieces will help you better understand where a figure could add value to your proposal.

Action Plan

- ☐ Understand ways to use figures
- ☐ Brainstorm how you want to use figures
- ☐ Create compelling figures

Understand Ways to Use Figures

Before you create your figures, decide why you want them. If you don't know what your purpose is, reviewers won't either.

Below I share several ways to use figures. This list isn't exhaustive. It's meant to help you brainstorm how you might want to use figures in your grant. Note that I'm using the term "figures" to encompass any image that appears in your grant. That could be pictures, maps, concept illustrations, tables, and more.

Potential Ways to Use Figures

A. **Organize information for reviewers**. Figures offer quick context for understanding your entire grant. They can show how you build from existing literature, illustrate mechanisms, or highlight deliverables.

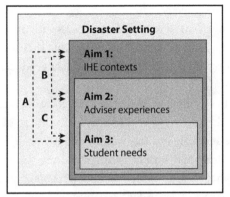

Notes: IHE = institutions of higher education; dashed lines
indicate assessment feedback loops.

FIGURE 11. Organize Information:
Disaster Student Recovery Theory

Conceptual models are often used for this purpose. As researcher
Aisha Dickerson notes, "I try to show a conceptual model early. That
way reviewers will understand the concepts even if they don't understand the rest of the proposal."

Example. Figure 11 is a sample conceptual model from a grant I wrote
   on IHEs (you saw the research plan and timeline for this grant in
   chapter 10, and a portion of this grant appears in chapter 11 to
   illustrate the inverted pyramid strategy). This figure's purpose was to
   organize information for reviewers so they could see how the study
   aims fit into a disaster student recovery theory. I also used the
   figure to highlight deliverables in the grant. The deliverables are the
   feedback loops labeled A, B, and C in the figure.

B. **Show something that's hard to explain in words**. Figures convey
   information quickly and more powerfully than words. You already
   know this. A common English proverb is "a picture is worth a thousand words." In Chinese, people say that "seeing it once is better than
   hearing a hundred times."[102]

Example 1. Researcher Susanne Brander cautions that you cannot
   assume "reviewers are directly in your field. Make your figures very
   clear even to someone who is skimming your grant." For example,
   Susanne was working on a National Oceanic and Atmospheric
   Administration grant that featured geoducks.[103] Susanne knew that

reviewers were likely to have questions about what geoducks look like. It's much easier to explain geoducks with a picture than words, so Susanne added a figure illustrating what they look like. (Fun side note, during this conversation I learned that geoducks is pronounced "gooey-ducks.")

Example 2. In our disaster work, the study location is critical to the research design. Maps of the study location can quickly explain the place and scale in a way words cannot.

Example 3. Measure descriptions are often long-winded and dense. A table of your measures can help reviewers quickly understand your independent and dependent variables, and how they are coded. Measure tables have the added benefit of saving room in your grant. Yet I don't always include measure tables in grants. I base this decision on whether a measures table will add value.

C. Showcase unique value added. Unique value could be access to special materials or something distinctive at your institution that positions you to do the work. Highlight what's special about your perspective.

Example 1. The Massachusetts Institute of Technology has an environmental chamber that measures gas-phase chemistry and secondary organic aerosol formation.[104] For some grants, this chamber would be a gateway to asking critical questions. In those cases, I would include a picture of the chamber and state why access to this chamber matters. I would only include a picture, however, if the chamber were directly related to questions posed in the grant.

Example 2. In our grant on schools and disasters (sample 2 in chapter 4), a critical contribution of the work was our ability to analyze diverse school types. We used a figure to highlight this unique value added (see figure 12). I included a benchmark so reviewers could understand how to interpret the values in the figure (i.e., the "State Average" column on the right).

D. Demonstrate you've put in the groundwork. Use figures to show your work is feasible, you know what the potential challenges may be, and you have a chance at success. Figures related to your pilot data are useful for this purpose.

Example. You may not think of literature reviews as pilot data, but you should. Figure 13 is an example of how Annette La Greca and I used

	Clear Creek ISD	Alvin ISD	Galena Park ISD	Pasadena ISD	North Forest ISD	State Average
Student population	37,142	16,591	21,409	51,923	7,662	7,630
% economically disadvantaged	23%	52%	77%	79%	99.9%	59%
% racial/ethnic minority	41%	63%	94%	89%	99%	67%
Total revenue	$362.2 M	$173.6 M	$216.3 M	$487.8 M	$71.9 M	$37.6 M

Note: ISD = independent school district; data from fiscal year 2010, http://ritter.tea.state.tx.us/perfreport/aeis/2010.

FIGURE 12. Unique Value Added: Demonstrating Diversity of Schools in Chosen Study Area

Study	Natural Disaster(s) Examined	Year(s)	Assessment Timing (Months Postdisaster)	% Sample in Trajectories			
				Chronic	Recovery	Resilience	Delayed
Fan et al. 2015[37]	Wenchuan Earthquake	2008	6, 12, 18, 24	11	20	65	4
Kronenberg et al. 2010[9]	Hurricane Katrina	2005	24, 36	23	27	45	5
La Greca et al. 2013[6]	Hurricane Andrew	1992	3, 7, 10	20	43	37	0
Liu et al. 2011[8]	Sichuan Earthquake	2008	6, 12	4	7	79	9
McDermott et al. 2013[38]	Cyclone Larry	2006	3, 18	8	72	16	3
Osofsky et al. 2015[39]	Hurricane Katrina; Hurricane Gustav	2005 2008	12, 24, 37, 49*	9	21	52	18
Self-Brown et al. 2013[7]	Hurricane Katrina	2005	3, 13, 19, 25	4	25	71	0

*Assessment timing given relation to Hurricane Gustav.

FIGURE 13. Groundwork: Summary of Person-Centered Child Disaster Research

a literature review as pilot data. For context, this chart is related to parts of a grant you've already read. You read this grant's one pager (sample 1 in chapter 4) and literature review outline (chapter 9). This table illustrates that we understood past findings on children's responses to disaster. We were underscoring variability in both the assessment timing and results across the literature.

E. Your timeline is feasible and you've got a plan. Reviewers love to look at timelines, often called Gantt charts. Timelines help reviewers understand how you are piecing together your work. Reviewers want to know if your work is feasible, as mentioned above. Showing your plan for the work helps them understand that you have a reasonable plan, approach, and a sense of how long the work will take.

Example. I showed you a Gantt chart for my IHEs grant in chapter 10 (figure 9). I organized the timeline around aims to give reviewers a clear structure to follow. I also used the timeline to highlight deliverables one more time. Reviewers need to speak to the outcomes of your work during review panels, so placing this evidence in multiple places ensures reviewers see it and view outcomes as integrated into your work. It makes their jobs easier. Discerning readers will notice this is the timeline that goes with figure 11's disaster student recovery theory. Notice that I matched the colors for the aims across both figures 9 and 11. Creating consistency like this is a subtle reminder to reviewers that you pay attention to details. It helps them feel confident in your ability to carry out a large-scale project.

Brainstorm How You Want to Use Figures

Look at the list of potential purposes above. Brainstorm one figure you could make for each purpose. Look at the sample grants you pulled in chapter 6 for extra inspiration. Then consider whether any of the figures you brainstormed add value to your grant. If so, create them. If not, don't.

If it helps to have a guide for the number of figures, many people I interviewed said they try to put one figure on each page. But keep in mind you want to think about value and quality before quantity. Remember to review the application guidelines on figures before you submit. You want to make sure your grant is compliant with the guidelines.

Create Compelling Figures

Now that you know how you want to use figures in your grant, it's time to think about what makes figures compelling. In short, the principles I covered about writing will make your figures compelling as well. You want figures to be clear and simple as well as consistent with your text and ideas.

But there are some extra considerations for figures:

1. **Figures should stand alone**. As researcher Christine Weirich notes, reviewers "should be able to understand the point of the figure *without reading your text.*"

   Do spend a lot of time tweaking a figure. Your title should be your takeaway message for the figure. As an example, look at figure 12. The title for that table is "Unique Value Added: Demonstrating Diversity of Schools in a Chosen Study Area." It is the takeaway message.

   Don't make reviewers read backward to understand your figure. For instance, don't say "aim 1" without giving extra context about what aim 1 is. Reviewers don't remember what aim 1 is. If you only say "aim 1" in a figure, reviewers have to go back to your one pager to remind themselves of what it is about. Do the hard work for them. That's why in figure 11, I say "Aim 1: IHE contexts." The extra words after aim 1 remind the reviewer that it is about IHE contexts. As another illustration of what not to do, the example I just gave forced you to flip backward in the book to look at figure 11. You don't want to force reviewers to go backward when reading. It slows down their momentum. (Unfortunately, in this section I will keep asking you to flip backward. In my defense, I had a figure limit for this book.)

2. **Design for accessibility**. Make sure all reviewers can view your figures. Otherwise, you've added an obstacle in their journey.

   Do make figures understandable in gray scale or black and white. You can use color, but if someone prints your grant with a black-and-white printer, the figures need to be readable.

   Don't use colors that are difficult for people with color blindness to understand (e.g., green/red, blue/gray, or green/brown). Don't make captions or notes too small. Generally, if your font is under eight points, no one can read it. Don't split a figure over two pages. For example, don't put the caption on one page and a drawing on another.

3. **Simplify**. Find ways to simplify figures so your core message comes across.

   Do consider how shapes and formatting influence your message. For example, when I was working on figure 11, I played around with using ovals to show that students are nested in adviser and institution contexts. I finally decided to use rectangles because simplifying to one shape type made the figure easier to read.

Don't repeat the same phrase multiple times. For instance, if you have a table that uses the same phrase multiple times, there's probably a repeat phrase you can delete and move to the column title.

4. **Have a consistent design**. This chunks information for reviewers, thus making it easier to read your grant. Be nitpicky. No detail is too small.

Do align shapes, stick to one size, and keep the formatting the same. To illustrate, look at figure 11. Notice that the letters A, B, and C all appear to the left of arrows and are centered in the arrows. The double arrows for B and C are the same size. Notice the alignment across the figure. Letters B and C are center aligned, and aims 1, 2, and 3 are left aligned down the figure. The explanations for the aims always appear in the second line. If you are using color, match colors across your figures.

Don't forget to think about spacing and sizes. If you look at the sample figures in this book, information that is conceptually grouped has the same width. For instance, in figure 13, the columns for percentages are all the same width. As another example, in the project timeline in figure 9, the columns for years are all the same width. The columns for quarter years are all the same width.

Tips and Frequently Asked Questions

Workshop your figures. Ask someone who isn't familiar with your grant for one minute of their time. If you show them your figure, what do they think is the point? Does this match what you think is the point? Do they have any feedback on how to improve the figure?

Can a figure ever really stand alone? Figures don't have much meaning without explanations in the text. It's true that figures are *best* understood by reading the full text. But let figures "stand alone" in the sense that they should have meaning without the full grant next to it. For example, look at the figures in this chapter. You can still get value from viewing them without reading a full grant.

Avoid including someone else's figures if that person isn't on your team. Researcher Youngjun Choe shares that he got this advice early in his career from a senior colleague. Youngjun notes, "This may not always be true. But using another scholar's figure shifts attention away from your work to someone else's work. Use figures to show your mindset."

Right before submitting, check the table and figure numbers as well as the formatting. When people draft grants, a lot of changes happen over time. Double check to make sure your final draft has sequentially numbered figures and tables. Misnumbered figures are a red flag for reviewers. It's a mistake that makes reviewers think you don't pay attention to details. You don't want that idea to enter reviewers' minds because you are trying to convince them that you can carry out a large-scale project successfully.

Do I need a figure at all? People are mixed on this. Personally, I like figures as they showcase how organized and sharp you are. Just make sure any figure you include has a purpose.

Where can I find more examples of figures? As I mentioned above, check out the sample grants you pulled in chapter 6. That will help you get a sense for figures typical for your funder and people who apply to your funder. For more examples, peruse grant samples online. I have a list of grant sample repositories at bettylai.com/samples. Beware of spending too much time viewing samples. The point isn't to wow reviewers with the flashiest figures humankind has ever seen. It is to quickly convey what you mean to do and why.

What software should I use? People use a range of software for figures such as PowerPoint, Adobe Illustrator, Excel, Google Drawings, and more. But thinking about software first can be limiting. Researcher Mason Garrison advises, "First draw/map out what you want a figure to look like. *Then* look for the software that will help you do it." Ask your networks for help. Technology changes quickly, and your networks are likely tapped into the newest tools.

The Takeaway

Make figures that deliver value. Design them with their purpose in mind and create compelling figures. If you're feeling overwhelmed, Alexa Riobueno-Naylor offers this encouragement: "Figures are a huge investment of your time. But figures pay off quickly. Figures help your grant. And figures can be used later in research papers, presentations, and abstracts."

At this point in the book, I've discussed everything you need to know to create a full draft of your grant. You know how to craft a one pager (chapter 4), literature review (chapter 9), and research plan (chapter 10). You have a way to flesh out your full grant and make your draft consistent (chapter 11). And you know when and how to add figures (this chapter). It's a lot of information. Remember that the framework in figure 1 organizes all the skills in this book for you.

In the next section of this book, "Task D," I'll teach you how to polish your rough draft so that reviewers say, "Wow. This was a well-written grant." First up, an important fact you need to understand about reviewers.

Polish Your Grant

13

Style Strategies

INCREASE READABILITY

Write and rewrite, and don't worry about terrible first drafts.

—SYLVIA PERRY

IT'S EASY to hate reviewers. So easy that "reviewer 2 strikes again" is shorthand on social media for everything people dislike about reviewers.

But hating reviewers isn't productive in grant writing. You'll write better grants when you empathize with them instead. And there's a lot to empathize with.

Here's what my life was like during my last review cycle. I had 430 pages of grants to review in less than two weeks. But I only had evenings to devote to review. That's because reviewing is service work. Reviewers evaluate grants on top of their regular jobs. I was reviewing grants while dealing with a global pandemic, spotty childcare, worrying about my tenure review, and juggling hybrid flex teaching.

These are the kinds of competing demands you're up against when you submit your grants for review.

As researcher Lauren Clay shares, "When you understand that reviewers are exhausted, you can see why it's hard for reviewers to see the science in your grant. Make it easy for them to understand your science."

Empathizing with reviewers means you make your work easy to read. You understand that reviewers are just scholars like you, committed to supporting quality scholarship. Reviewers care about the field, but they are tired.

The **goal of this chapter** is to fine-tune your grant writing so stressed reviewers breeze through the pages and your work steals the show.

Action Plan

☐ Understand what makes grants readable
☐ Practice style strategies

Understand What Makes Grants Readable

I ended the last chapter by summarizing all the pieces of your grant that you've learned how to draft.

But the good news is you've learned much more than just how to draft. You've also learned how to meet the needs of reviewers. You've been practicing empathy for reviewers this whole time.

Specifically, so far in this book you've:

- **Focused on what reviewers need** by understanding the evaluation criteria in chapter 8.
- **Mapped out the reviewer's journey** through the literature review in chapter 9.
- **Addressed reviewer questions about your work** through your research plan in chapter 10.
- **Structured your draft so reviewers know what to expect** through the inverted pyramid strategy and consistency techniques in chapter 11.
- **Focused on creating valuable and compelling figures for reviewers** in chapter 12.

These are "big picture" strategies for drafting your grant. Now I'm focusing on "small detail" strategies to polish your grant.

Style Strategies

A. Create white space. White space breaks up walls of text. White space matters because reviewers usually have hundreds of pages to read. You may be thinking, "But I have too much to pack into a tiny space." Packing in more doesn't mean your reviewers will read more. Reviewers read less when they're overwhelmed.

Example. I've created white space throughout this book to make it easier to read.

Action steps. At a minimum, each section should have one space above the header and titles. Put space around all of your figures so the text doesn't run into them, making it hard to read. Sarah Naumes offers this tip. You can write your grant in a fourteen-point font. After you finish drafting text, change to the correct font size for your agency. You now have extra room to create white space and add graphic elements.

B. Trim extra words. Any word that isn't needed should be cut. This helps reviewers focus on the words that matter. Famous writers have given different versions of this advice. Stephen King once said, "The road to hell is paved with adverbs."[105] Mark Twain observed, "When you catch an adjective, kill it."[106]

Example 1. My own previously published research clearly indicates that in almost all cases, A leads B, meaning that B is often preceded by factor A.

Revision 1. My research indicates A leads to B.

Example 2. Exposure to multiple stressors at the time of impact of disasters during the exposure period is associated with increased risk for mental health distress problems including posttraumatic stress, anxiety, depression, and suicidality.

Revision 2. Disaster exposure increases risk for mental health problems (e.g., posttraumatic stress and depression). [*Note*: I removed "anxiety" and "suicidality" to illustrate that you should only include terms directly relevant to the current project. Reviewers think any term you introduce has a purpose.]

Action steps. Delete adverbs, adjectives, clauses, or any word that is not needed to help a sentence make sense. Don't forget to look closely at your references as well. Are there references that aren't needed because they don't add to your point?

C. No jargon. Jargon creates a barrier between you and reviewers. Write so that your intelligent reviewers can read and understand your work without having to look up information.

Example 1. Utilizing serpentine, labyrinthine words sabotage your pithy precis.

Revision 1. Use simple words to make your point.

Example 2. The Patient Health Questionnaire Depression Scale 8 scores showed some promise of relationship to the Generalized Anxiety Disorder 7 screener scores.

Revision 2. Depression and anxiety scores were positively correlated. [Notice this revision prioritizes making the concepts easy to understand. If it's important for you to name measures for reviewers, you could say, "Depression scores (Patient Health Questionnaire Depression Scale 8)."]

D. **Short sentences only**. Bite-size ideas are easy to understand. If a reviewer has to read all the way to the end of a sentence to understand your meaning, you've lost them. Keep ideas together and avoid clauses. Look for any sentences that are more than two to three lines on the page. They may need to be cut. Antoine de Saint-Exupéry, the author of *The Little Prince*, once said, "Perfection is achieved, not when there is nothing more to add, but when there is nothing left to take away."[107]

Example 1. While important, many community and contextual factors influence mental health, and this information may inform the key stakeholders on strategies, if the stakeholders are interested in developing robust strategies for preparing schools to minimize the ultimate effects of a natural disaster on school recovery.

Revision 1. This information will inform strategies for preparing schools to recover from future disasters.

Example 2. We will evaluate risk and protective factors to see how these might influence outcomes for mental and physical health. We will conduct linear regression models and use two waves of data.

Revision 2. Linear regression models will evaluate risk and protective factors (wave 1) for mental and physical health outcomes (wave 2).

E. **Avoid acronyms**. It's hard to remember definitions for acronyms. Acronyms force reviewers to flip back and forth between pages in order to understand what you mean. What's more, some funders don't allow acronyms in review statements. In those cases, reviewers have to look up your acronym's exact definition each time it comes up in their review. That is one way to quickly annoy a reviewer. You've created a lot of extra work for them.

Example. We will use the YRBSS and BRFSS to understand DS and AS across development.

Revision. We will use the Youth Risk Behavior Surveillance Survey and Behavioral Risk Factor Surveillance System to understand depression and anxiety symptoms across development.

F. **Kill the ambiguous "this."** Any time you use the word "this," ask yourself if it is clear to the reviewer what "this" means.

Example. This largely ignores community-level factors that influence mental health.

Revision. Individual-level disaster theories of mental health fail to
include community-level factors.

G. Make a choice about voice. Should you write in an active or passive
voice? This is your choice to make. Choose based on conventions for
your field and the successful samples you pulled. What voice did they
choose? Lori Peek urges you to use a first-person active voice. "When
people write in passive voice ('the data will be analyzed,' 'children will
be interviewed'), it is not clear who is doing the analyzing or the
interviewing. That leaves your reviewers confused or second-guessing
who is doing what."

Example. Samples will be collected in year 1.

Revision. The graduate research assistant will collect samples in
year 1.

Practice Style Strategies

The biggest mistake scholars make is not being relentless enough in using style
strategies. Brutally edit your writing. Apply these strategies to every sentence
in your grant. You want reviewers to understand your work the first time they
read it.

Exercises

Read the sentences below and identify problems that interfere with readability.
Then revise each sentence. My answers are below.

1. One of the most challenging aspects of understanding infectious diseases
   is trying to understand the role of antimicrobial resistance in exacerbating
   and amplifying treatment effects and mechanisms.

2. When education is disrupted by a devastating disaster, children are at
   risk of failing to master important academic concepts and skills (e.g.,
   phonetic analysis, reading comprehension of math word problems, and
   making inferences), and this may ultimately contribute to a trajectory for
   a future of weak academic achievement across learning pathways and
   environments.

3. This has the potential to yield extraordinary results into how phenotypic
   diversity is generated through our use of ACMs that will hone in on
   PMs and MEs that influence the diversity of the HG.

Betty's Answers

1. *Problems.* It's hard to find the point of the sentence because it is not front-loaded. There are redundant words (e.g., exacerbating, amplifying, and understanding).

    Revision. Antimicrobial resistance is a serious threat to treating infectious diseases.

2. *Problems.* There are too many extra words and too much jargon. The sentence is too long and contains multiple ideas, and it includes an ambiguous use of "this."

    Revision. Disasters may interrupt children's learning of critical academic skills (e.g., phonetic analysis, reading comprehension of math word problems, and making inferences). Disrupted learning places children at risk for diminished achievement across their school years. [Note I kept in the reference to academic skills as it sometimes helps reviewers to have concrete examples. But only use examples that are relevant to your grant, as discussed earlier in this chapter.]

3. *Problems.* The acronyms are distracting and hard to understand. The overuse of adjectives makes the work sound padded. Notice that this sentence is so hard to read, you probably couldn't even rewrite it.

    Revision. Advanced computational models have the potential to yield insights into mutations and mechanisms that influence the diversity of the human genome.

Tips and Frequently Asked Questions

Read your grant out loud or have a program read your grant out loud. Sometimes it can help to use a different medium to test your grant's readability. Are the sentences short enough to be clear?

Read widely to understand what good writing looks like. Read work from professional writers and people you admire. Ask yourself what elements you like and what you might emulate. You may find it helpful to read general books on writing like William Strunk, Jr. and E. B. White's *The Elements of Style.*

What do I do if English is not my first language? Agencies acknowledge that reviewers may be biased against nonnative English speakers. Some funders take the important step of training reviewers to guard against this bias. Get feedback on your grant so that you can guard against this bias. For strategies on how to do this, see chapter 15.

Aren't some acronyms OK? I see them in other grants. Acronyms are always a burden to reviewers. Sometimes grant writers don't believe acronyms are a burden because an acronym is common for their field. Remember that not all reviewers (and program officers) are from your direct field and/or they may not use the acronym the way you do. Limit yourself to one to two acronyms at most. Consider the first one pager example in chapter 4 (sample 1). The main outcome was "posttraumatic stress symptoms." Because the term was used in almost every paragraph, I thought using one acronym, PTSS, would improve readability. Only use an acronym if it improves readability for *reviewers*. (Acronyms are often used because it makes writing easier for the *scholar*. Remember, grants are written for reviewers, not for you.)

Couldn't I take the shotgun approach and submit tons of imperfect grants to see what sticks? You get to decide what approach to grant writing works best for you. The shotgun approach works for some people. It may work for you, depending on your values and job expectations (chapters 2–3). Ask yourself, would you be OK if all the grants you submit happen to get funded? What level of quality do you feel comfortable being remembered for? As researcher Youngjun Choe shares, "You need to balance between the number of grants you submit and the quality of those grants. For a junior faculty member, it could make sense to submit a few proposals, learn from the feedback, and then perfect your grants after you've gone through the entire experience." Keep in mind that submitting sloppy grants has reputational risks. Reviewers and program officers will remember you for the wrong reasons.

Should I use left or full justification? Always go with the guidelines for your application. If you have a choice, choose the style you think is easiest for reviewers to read. I've written grants in both styles, and I don't think it matters. But some people are strongly team left justification or team full justification. Team left justification says that full justification is unreadable. Team full justification says that full justification creates cleaner grants (since the text lines up all the way down the page).

The Takeaway

Creating easy-to-read grants is the best way to empathize with your stressed reviewers. Implement these style strategies and keep practicing. You'll get better at these style strategies the more often you use them.

Next, let's talk about how to sell your expertise and team.

14

The Pick Me Factor

SELL YOUR EXPERTISE AND TEAM

The most difficult situations were when we had very junior investigators, and
it was very hard to determine who actually had the promise over someone else
at an early stage in their career.

—DIANA BIANCHI[108]

THE ODDS are not in your favor. In 2018, the National Institutes of Health
received 109,668 applications and awarded only 22,142.[109] In 2019, the Australian Research Council received 11,407 applications and funded only 2,303
projects.[110] In 2021, the American Council of Learned Societies received 1,300
applications for just 60 fellowships.[111]

I don't say this to discourage you. I know you can stand out in these large
pools. I've been able to do it. So have my friends and colleagues who've invested
in learning grant writing skills. You've already invested in learning these skills
by reading this far.

The point of mentioning the odds is this: you need to stand out. You can't
just sell your dazzling ideas and strong plan. You also need to sell why you and
your team are the perfect people to carry out the work.

You need reviewers to talk about you this way:

- "This principal investigator has so much promise."
- "I'm confident this team can deliver at a high level."
- "Look at their resources. They are set up for success."

Notice the level of excitement in these comments, which assume you are a rocket ship bound for success. Researcher Tom Cova shares this tongue-in-cheek saying about funders: "Funders want to add their sticker to rocket ships once the rocket is already at the launching pad, ready to take off." Communicate to reviewers you are at the launching pad.

If you don't, reviewers will say:

- "I'm not sure this principal investigator can produce repeatable experiments."
- "It's unclear whether this team can be successful."
- "It seems like this team is going to need _____, but it's not coming across in its description."

These negative comments open the door to doubts about your work and abilities. Instead of focusing on how to make your incredible ideas even better, reviewers look for the reasons why you and your team will fail.

The **goal of this chapter** is to up your pick me factor. In other words, I'm talking about how to sell your expertise and team.

Action Plan

- ☐ Understand how to excite reviewers
- ☐ Brainstorm what you bring to the table
- ☐ Build your dream team
- ☐ Reframe weaknesses
- ☐ Analyze a sample

Understand How to Excite Reviewers

You have what it takes to deliver on outstanding ideas. But it's not enough to tell reviewers you have outstanding ideas. They need reasons to believe in you as a scholar. Give reviewers evidence of your potential. Evidence excites reviewers and helps them advocate for you during reviews. As researcher Brittany Rudd explains, her mentor summed up this principle as, "Show me, don't tell me."

Here are three concrete strategies for showing reviewers evidence of your potential:

A. **Be precise**. Reviewers like numbers and data. Data is more convincing and memorable than vague statements. Vague statements can be said by any researcher or team. You want to stand out.

Vague example. This research project will *broaden the participation of* students from underrepresented and/or underserved communities.

Precise example. This research project will *broaden the participation of* students from underrepresented and/or underserved communities. The home institution of the principal investigators, Georgia State University, has an undergraduate student population with the following characteristics: 30 percent first-generation college students, 87 percent on financial aid, and 60 percent nonwhite (College Completion Plan 2012). The principal investigators are deeply committed to mentoring students from underrepresented groups; for example, two (50 percent) of four of Dr. Lai's current research assistants and two (66 percent) of three of Dr. Esnard's research assistants are from racially/ethnically minoritized groups.

B. **Showcase fit**. Reviewers need to understand why you, your team, and/or location are a combination that is absolutely perfect for the work. Convey that this perfect match between expertise, environment, and ideas did not happen by accident. This creates urgency for reviewers. Reviewers understand that if your grant is not funded, the opportunity for this level of fit may not happen again.

An example that sounds like an accident. Julie Schneider has unique expertise in environmental differences in language.

An example that showcases fit. Julie Schneider is uniquely positioned to answer questions about environmental differences in language due to her notable skill set (brain and environment interactions), location (e.g., the <u>Deep South</u>, an understudied but highly variable language site), and institution (e.g., which has <u>rural and urban</u> locations, necessary for understanding population influences).

C. **Tell the story**. Reviewers will have a CV or biosketch for you. Tell reviewers why information matters. You need to connect the dots for them. Explain the backstory: past collaborations, proximity, commitments, and so on. Reviewers will not search for this information. You may think the team members' roles are clear because you mentioned it on page 2. It's not. You may think it's clear that a collaborator is accessible to you because you're at neighboring institutions. It's not. Reviewers do not have time to hunt for clues.

Just the facts example. Lannister and Targaryen have the requisite expertise to carry out this project due to their backgrounds in digital literacies and folklore, respectively.

Story example that makes connections for reviewers. Principal investigator Lannister is an expert on digital literacies. Lannister completed
two scholar-in-residence trainings (Winterfell and the Wall). Lannister
developed five strategic plans cited by the *King's Landing Gazette* as
critical to the success of the Battle of Blackwater. Plans were publicly
deposited in DesignSafe. Coinvestigator Targaryen is an international
expert in dragon lore. Targaryen has successfully raised three dragons
to adulthood. Of note, Lannister and Targaryen are long-term
collaborators. They meet biweekly with their lab teams (ten students
total), and their offices are located within a hundred yards of each
other.

Brainstorm What You Bring to the Table

Now that you know how to excite reviewers, brainstorm what evidence you
want to show to them. Reviewers are looking for evidence that you have promise, you have a dream team, and your environment supports your work. They
don't have time to figure this information out on their own. Do the hard work
for them.

1. **You have promise**. We spend so long looking up to "experts" that it can
   feel cringeworthy to sell your expertise. Don't let this feeling stop you
   from finding success in grant writing. Clearly state what your strengths
   are (for tips on communicating clearly, see chapter 9). Becca Krukowski
   offers this reminder that your qualifications "are NOT just your
   publications and grades. If you have practical experience, that is also
   very relevant—make that clear!"[112]
   Researcher example. Katherine McNeill focuses on science education.
   In one of her recent grants to the National Science Foundation (now
   funded), Katherine made the case for her ability to bridge theory
   with practice. In the grant, she discussed her ability to build relationships with teachers and students. Katherine demonstrated this
   expertise by showing a figure of a tool that teachers could use in the
   classroom (to be concrete about how theory might translate into
   practice). She also gathered letters of support from schools and
   districts to show that there were people who wanted to work with
   her. And Katherine carefully thought about what information to
   present in her CV. Instead of presenting her theory-focused work,

she showcased her ability to bridge fields by including her professional development activities and practice-oriented articles.

Exercise. Identify any evidence that demonstrates you can do the work in your grant. Pull up your CV, and consider all of your training and collaborations to date. Concentrate on finding evidence that shows you can carry out your project.

Potential evidence. Publications. Committees. Awards. Presentations. Mentoring programs. Fellowships. Speaking engagements. Workshops. Courses. Undergraduate major.

2. **You have a dream team**. Make the case for why you have the perfect team. Reviewers tend to hyperfocus on these issues: whether you have the right expertise on your team, whether there's too much overlap in expertise, past evidence for collaboration, wanting to know who is in charge and how meetings will happen, and how and why time on the grant is allocated to collaborators and students.

Researcher example. Aisha Dickerson is an environmental neuroepidemiologist. She advises, "Create a dream team that's well rounded. Find people who will give input on the grant and be responsive. Sometimes people focus just on heavy hitters. But reviewers may see that your heavy hitters don't have time to work on the grant. You could get dinged for that."

Exercise. During the proposal development process, meet early on with collaborators and mentors. You need to discuss your plans for working together. Research development specialist Sarah Naumes asks her investigators to conduct a "kickoff" team meeting to explore issues like how to communicate, who's in charge, how the work will be divided, how to handle conflict, and how to ensure graduate students are able to let you know when there are problems. Your decisions from this meeting are evidence you can include in your grant. This exercise is especially important if you are working with a large or interdisciplinary team, where communication must happen across many people or fields.

Potential evidence. Areas of expertise for each team member. Key role of each person and how it contributes to the work. Ways you've collaborated in the past. Where and how you plan to meet. How you will mentor trainees. The plan for sharing information. Any unique aspects of your team that will impress reviewers (e.g., an all-female team, all members received Fulbrights, or junior/senior faculty diversity).

3. **Your environment is supportive**. Convince reviews you have what you need to launch the project. Weave this evidence into your full grant, not just into a facilities document or resources page.

Researcher example. Dana Rose Garfin has a K01 grant from the National Institutes of Health to develop a mindfulness intervention for trauma-exposed homeless women. Dana says that when she was writing her K01, she asked mentors at her institution for examples of how they wrote about facilities. She also carefully considered resources at her institution that were unique and stood out. For example, Dana wrote about its Center for Integrative Health, which was an especially relevant resource because of her grant's focus on mindfulness.

General example. Some research teams organize advisory boards for their grant. Advisory boards are groups of experts that convene to provide guidance on decisions, data to date, or future directions. Advisory boards have special advantages in that it's relatively easy to convince experts to serve because the workload is low. Plus advisory board members are clear stakeholders who will help disseminate your findings (i.e., more evidence that you've created a supportive environment for your work).

Exercise. Brainstorm any evidence that shows how your environment will help you carry out the work. The evidence could be formal or informal.

Potential evidence. Data on characteristics of your institution. Letters of support. Established partnerships or committees. Classes you teach. Information about your community. Pilot or even secondary data demonstrating that your work is feasible (e.g., preliminary data or published papers you've written). Instrumentation (e.g., a neutron microscope or large computer). Past numbers on recruitment. Attendance, engagement, retention, or acceptability in past work (including work that isn't your own but instead was carried out at sites that you or your collaborators will use). Alternative plans you've considered or attempted in the past, and how you've worked through problems. For training grants, why this grant sets you up for success. How you will help others when you succeed (e.g., depositing data in repositories). Situations where your institution will engage in **cost sharing** (i.e., where your institution will bear part of the cost of covering your grant work; check with your research administrators on issues related to cost sharing, as there are potential tax implications).

Build Your Dream Team

You just brainstormed evidence for why you and your team are phenomenal. But this process probably uncovered some of your weaknesses. Reasons why you might fail. Gaps in your expertise. A mismatch between your grant's goals and your team's experiences. That's OK. This is a normal part of the grant writing process.

Because the good news is, grants are about building the dream team. If you don't have the dream team yet, go out and create it.

Start with yourself. Bolster weak areas. Take courses, apply for fellowships and awards, publish, join other grants, secure seed funding, apply for mentoring programs, conduct a pilot project, act as a consultant, and so on. In short, seek out opportunities that are evidence you can oversee and complete a project. If you're applying for a training grant, you don't have to do all of these activities yet. Your grant can be about what the grant will allow you to do. But you need to identify opportunities that will launch you on a powerful career trajectory.

Build your dream collaborations too. Research dean Kirsten Davison shares that this is one of the most important skills in grant writing. "Consider whether you feel comfortable standing up and pitching yourself as the expert in a room. If you don't feel you can do that, find someone who is that expert." Fair warning, don't just add everyone who might have related expertise. Think carefully about who needs to be on the grant. Too much overlapping expertise makes reviewers question whether everyone has a real role.

If you're having trouble identifying a key expert in a new area, researcher Jessica Hamilton has helpful advice. Jessica recommends that you read deeply in that new area. See whose name keeps popping up. Start building a relationship with that expert by connecting via email. Your email could ask a question you had about the work, or you could note why their work was interesting to you. This relationship could eventually lead to a grant collaboration or that expert serving on a mentorship team for you.

Finally, create the dream environment. Figure out supports you need to carry out the grant work at a high level. Then get those supports. For example, say you are not at a Research I university but still want to make a case for having a supportive research environment. You could connect to a nearby Research I university by getting a secondary appointment, shadowing in a lab, or bringing on a coinvestigator. You may need to develop a track record of smaller grants to make the case for your environment. Or you could target opportunities geared toward institutions that are not Research I settings, such as an R15 grant at the National Institutes of Health.

Reframe Weaknesses

Sometimes, you can reframe weaknesses as strengths. Researcher Julie Schneider did this when she was in the state of Delaware. Julie knew that Delaware didn't receive as much funding as other states. This is a weakness that could have worked against her. She turned this into a strength. Julie argued in her postdoctoral grant application to the National Science Foundation that uneven funding across states is a critical social justice issue. She argued that therefore, her location in Delaware was a strength as this would play a role in redirecting funding to states that receive less funding.

Here's another example of reframing a weakness as a strength from researcher Andrés Castro Samayoa. Andrés was writing a grant to the W.K. Kellogg Foundation. On the surface, Andrés's work might seem like a bad fit for W.K. Kellogg. Andrés studies higher education, while W.K. Kellogg focuses on K–12 education. Yet Andrés and his mentor turned this potential mismatch into a key benefit of their work. They argued that minority-serving institutions in higher education offered a unique perspective and innovative approach to addressing inequalities in K–12 education.

Analyze a Sample

Here's a sample that uses this chapter's strategies. My notes on strategies are in brackets. This sample is based on a training grant I wrote. Notice that for training grants, you can focus on evidence of potential instead of your history of success. See if you can identify the weaknesses I was trying to anticipate. My answers are below.

Although I am not based in the Gulf region, I have actively sought out collaborations in the Gulf to address issues faced by youths in the region for the <u>last ten years</u>. [**Precision in terms of time.**] Notably, the team for this project builds on several key collaborations. [**Signal that I'm building a dream team.**] I will be working with Dr. Beth Auslander (school research expert) at the University of Texas Medical Branch. Dr. Auslander and I have already secured a commitment from the Galveston Independent School District, where we conducted our study of children's responses to Hurricane Ike in 2009. [**Precision. Tell the story of how we're connected.**

Reviewers have CVs, but they won't make this connection. Environment is supportive—in this case, the schools are willing for us to conduct the study.] In addition, Sam Brody (disaster expert) was a co–principal investigator of the National Science Foundation–funded Enabling the Next Generation of Hazards and Disasters Research Program, in which I was a fellow. [**Precision. Story of how we're connected.**] I am a former science teacher (Permanent New York State Science License), and I hold a master's degree in science education. [**Showcasing fit.**]

Answer: Weaknesses I was trying to anticipate.

- **Not being based in the Gulf region (since the funder focuses on the Gulf region).** I reframed this weakness by stating it up front and giving counter evidence that negates it.
- **Not enough experience in science education research.** I don't state this weakness explicitly. Instead, I built a dream team with expertise in schools, disaster research, and science inquiry.

Tips and Frequently Asked Questions

Won't I sound conceited? Researcher Mallika Nocco says, "People, especially women and those from underrepresented groups, are often hesitant to talk about the impact of their work. Grants are one place where you *need* to sell your impact. Adopt a 'swagger mindset.'" Mallika keeps a playlist of songs to build up her swagger mindset for grant writing.

How do I strike a balance between talking about my work and not going overboard? If you are asking this question, you are probably not the type of person who goes overboard. The short answer is, stick to concrete evidence. It's going overboard to say, "I'm the most amazing researcher of this century." But it's not going overboard to say, "I am an expert on _____. My expertise is demonstrated by ____ first authored paper on _____, my leadership on _____ monthly speaker series at _____ institution, and an honorable mention poster award for the quality and impact of my work from Division 12 of the American Psychological Association."

Does this concept of needing to sell your expertise differ by culture or funders? I can't speak for all cultures or funders, but I have not heard an exception to this principle. Interviewees for this book repeatedly mentioned the need for grant writers to demonstrate their expertise or trajectory for becoming an expert (e.g., for training grants). Reviewers and funders need to feel confident that you could carry out the work of the grant. They are investing in you as a scholar.

How much of a track record do I need? This is a tough question because like all questions related to research, it depends on your field, background, and so on. A quick way to gather data on this issue is to go back to look at the CVs you pulled in the usual suspects exercise in chapter 1. Do some cross-referencing. At the time the person of interest received a grant, how many publications did they have? But don't let fear of "not being ready" keep you from applying. Even without knowing your exact situation, I know you are ready to apply for funding. Don't wait. Apply. Keep building your CV. Gain new experiences. Get feedback. Keep searching for the right funders for your work.

What do I do if I don't fit into a neat problem space? I hear this question often from our wonderful interdisciplinary colleagues. Reframe what some consider a weakness as your advantage. Give evidence for how your unique expertise differs from common practice. Show why your perspective will help us address problems in our world. Look for funders that value or even require interdisciplinary collaborations. Calls for interdisciplinary work are becoming more frequent. Funders recognize how crucial interdisciplinary work is. More important, funders are *supporting* interdisciplinary work.

Is it OK that I didn't use up all the space in my grant? No. Use all the pages or words allowed. For instance, don't submit an eight-page research plan if the funder allows you to submit a ten-page one. When you write less, it looks like you ran out of steam or didn't have enough ideas or evidence to fill the space. Your grant is being compared to a pool of grants. You don't want your grant to stand out for having less material than the other ones. Using up space may seem contradictory to my earlier advice to use white space and short sentences (chapter 13). It's not. Make your grant easy to read. Streamline your grant. But also pack in compelling evidence about why your grant matters (one pager and literature review), why you have a strong approach (research plan), and why you, your team, and environment are ideal for the work.

The Takeaway

You're a scholar with enormous potential. But when you're starting out in grant writing, it's easy to get discouraged. You can feel like you're not good enough yet, no one will want to fund you, or it's a waste of time when the odds are this bad. You look at stars in your field, and their success is shocking and demoralizing.

These thoughts don't serve you. Focus on your goal of writing your next fundable grant. Practice the skills I've been discussing, and reviewers will understand why they need to pick you.

Next up, a secret that helps researchers at top universities get funded.

15

Critical Critiques

IDENTIFY WEAKNESSES

We all write through our own lens. It's hard to step back and see the larger picture. A pair of external eyes can help you to better shape your ideas and writing.

—ASHWINI TIWARI

RESEARCHER NANCY Kassam-Adams says there's a joke about the grant review system. "It's the worst system. Except for all the others." Most grant reviewers I spoke to felt this way. The grant review system is not perfect. But it's better than other systems we could use to evaluate grants.

Understanding the imperfections of the grant review system will help you get funded. Let me explain with data.

One major flaw of the review system is that reviewers don't agree. John Jerrim and Robert de Vries studied fifteen thousand peer reviews of four thousand grants to the Economic and Social Research Council.[113] They found that the correlation between reviewers' scores was only 0.2. This data shows that reviews are arbitrary.

The second flaw is that negative reviews have an outsize impact on your grant. Jerrim and de Vries found that a *single negative peer review* "reduced the chances of a proposal being funded from around 55% to around 25% (even when it has otherwise been rated highly)."[113]

This finding on the power of negative reviews is not a fluke. It's backed by experimental research. Elizabeth Pier and colleagues recruited forty-three seasoned grant writers to review National Institutes of Health grant applications.[114]

They found that grant ratings weren't associated with the number of strengths that reviewers identified. Instead, ratings were a reflection of an *absence of weaknesses*.

Taken together, these data tell us that weaknesses shape how your grant fares during review. To get funded, you need to remove weaknesses from your grant.

The **goal of this chapter** is to help you identify weaknesses in your grant. By the end of this chapter, you'll have a plan for weeding out your grant's weaknesses.

Action Plan

- ☐ Learn about red teams
- ☐ Form your red team
- ☐ Form a discussion circle
- ☐ Toss out weaknesses
- ☐ Pay attention to detail

Learn about Red Teams

I'm using the red team strategy to identify weaknesses in your grants. Red teams come from cybersecurity, an industry that depends on weeding out weaknesses. Red teams impersonate your nemesis. For instance, let's pretend I lead cyber-security for a bank. I'd hire a red team to impersonate robbers. The red team's job would be to break into the bank. The red team would try to steal money. Then the red team would report back on weaknesses in the bank's security system and return any money it took. (The red team is actually on your side, after all). Then I'd patch up and address the weaknesses the red team found.

Top universities use red teams for grant writing. Here's an example from Suhas Eswarappa Prameela. Suhas went through a training program that had a standing red team. His institution actually called it a red team. The red team was composed of senior investigators with a history of grant success and peer review experience. Team members impersonated reviewers. Suhas and his colleagues submitted grants to the red team, and the red team gave detailed feedback on weaknesses in the grants.

Stop and think about the power of this red team approach. Senior investigators identify weaknesses in your grant before those weaknesses count against you (i.e., before a real review cycle). This is a low-stakes review that saves you a whole grant review cycle.

This red team approach explains why researcher Ginny Vitiello made this discovery when she learned to write grants. Ginny notes that she was "surprised at how perfect a proposal has to be on the first try."

Here's the secret. The grants you're up against look perfect on the first try because it's *not* their first try. Those grants have been through rounds of red team polishing. As researchers Rebecca Brent and Richard Felder share, "NEVER let the funding agency or journal be the first to review your manuscript. Ask, beg, or bribe colleagues to read and severely critique manuscript drafts, and take their suggestions seriously."[115]

Let's make sure the grant you submit isn't your first try either.

Form Your Red Team

If your institution doesn't have a standing red team, it's time to get scrappy. Form your own red team. You are looking for people who are willing to read your grant and give you feedback. Ideally, find senior mentors who've received a grant from your funder and mechanism.

But most important, look for people who will be critical. Let me explain.

If someone tells you, "Your grant looks amazing. No changes. Wow!" They're being nice. They're trying to bolster your confidence. But those comments don't help you. They've wasted your time and their time.

Because your grant does have flaws. You need to know what those flaws are before reviewers find them. As Crystal Zheng shares, this means that "you need the right reader. Not someone who is supportive, but someone who can actually be critical."

Find readers who point out all the flaws in your grant. Researcher Matthew Fox says, "There's a joke in grant writing that you need feedback on your grant from the same people who will tell you your baby is ugly." In other words, you need readers who will tell you the truth instead of worrying about your feelings.

Ways to Find Critical Readers

1. **Tap your networks**. Who do you know in your institution or field that is committed to your success? Mentors, research deans, and faculty provosts are good first targets. If they can't help you, do they know someone who could? Think back to the meetings you set up in chapter 3. All of those people are potential red team members. You've already

established a relationship with them. When you reach out, make it clear you're wondering if they could provide critical feedback on your grant. Let them know when you will send a draft and how long of a turnaround time you'd need for feedback. This is why it's important to work far ahead on your grant. This strategy extends your grant writing timeline significantly—by a few weeks at least.

> *Example.* Researcher Melissa Osborne leveraged mentoring networks for her latest grant. As a new faculty member, Melissa discovered that it was easy to find readers for her grant. Her mentors were invested in her success as a new faculty member and did a full preview of her grant before she submitted it.

2. **Add a consultant or coinvestigator**. This idea comes from researcher Katie Edwards. As Katie notes, this strategy adds a leading expert to the team. And people in these roles are invested in giving you feedback on your ideas.

3. **Join a training or mentoring program**. This is a long-term strategy because you have to wait for a program cycle to open. But you are in this for the long haul. A program will help you build a network that will sustain you throughout your career. To find programs, ask mentors and peers, and study CVs. Keep a running list of programs and their due dates so you'll be ready to apply for the next cycle. Even if you aren't admitted during a cycle, you are getting your name on the radar. This benefits you beyond grant writing (for collaborations, symposia, papers, etc.). And it's compelling evidence when you apply the second time. Make sure to mention you are a second-time applicant. It shows persistence and organization.

> *Example.* I was privileged to join the Enabling Program, a hazards and disasters fellowship funded by the National Science Foundation. In the program, I was directly mentored by Ann-Margaret Esnard and Lori Peek. They read drafts of my work, met with me to discuss career development, and more. I continue to seek out Ann-Margaret and Lori's wisdom, as you may have noticed in this book. My program peers became my conference social hour buddies (important for an introvert like me), and we share new opportunities when we see them.

4. **Send a cold email to someone recently funded by your target funder**. You might not want to open with, Could you read my draft? But you could ask whether they'd be willing to meet with you for

twenty minutes to talk about their recent grant. You could ask questions about your grant idea at that time. If you feel comfortable as you develop a relationship with this person, you could eventually ask for feedback. Treat this as the start, though, to what will hopefully be a significant relationship. Remember that the worst response to a cold email is usually that someone says no or doesn't write you back. You're no worse off for having emailed.

5. **Hire a research development specialist**. Research development specialists are experts in proposal development and grant writing. If you have start-up funds or access to institutional funds, work with a research development specialist to get feedback on your grant. If you don't have these funds, ask mentors to advocate for your institution to create funds for research development specialists. Investing in your career is a win-win for you and your institution.

   Examples. In my first faculty position, my department paid for me to work with an external grants consultant, Janet Gross. Janet was instrumental in helping me refine my ideas and navigate the grants world. In the course of writing this book, I interviewed several research development specialists with keen insights into grant writing. Shout-outs to Alma Faust, Sarah Naumes, and Richelle Weihe.

6. **Network with peers**. Sometimes we focus too much on networking with senior colleagues. It's just as important in your career to network with peers. As research dean Kirsten Davison says, "Your fellow junior people become senior people." You are planting seeds for friendships and future collaborations.

Form a Discussion Circle

Red teams give high-level feedback on your grant on a onetime basis. (Sometimes more often if you are lucky). But you need to talk about ideas as you write your grant. Discussion helps you develop intuition around pitching and revising incredible ideas.

To generate these conversations, form a discussion circle, which are a group of peers working on grants. I had a small discussion circle with my colleague Matthew Magee. We'd meet for an hour every few weeks and rip apart drafts over coffee. I credit Matt with helping me launch my grant writing career.

To form your discussion circle, look for people who will offer and accept critical feedback. These people are hard to find. People have trouble hearing that their baby (their grant) isn't perfect. If your group isn't based on critical feedback, however, it's just a support circle that offers encouragement. That's not a bad thing. But it won't help you develop as a grant writer. You need to give and receive authentic feedback.

The essential task for a discussion circle is to identify weaknesses in the grant and how to improve it. If there is extra time, review application and evaluation criteria for the grants members are submitting. You don't need to be writing the exact same type of grant. Matt is an epidemiologist, and I'm a trauma psychologist. We were writing to different funders.

Here are the types of feedback you want:

A. **Do you buy the significance of this work? Do you care about it after reading this?** As we talked about in chapter 4, the pitch is the most important piece you need to get right for your grant. Keep working at it until your discussion circle has that "I'm in tears" reaction to your work.

   Prompts. Is it clear why this work matters? Does the impact seem big enough? Are the questions clear? Are the hypotheses specific enough to give new, incisive information? Where does your enthusiasm wane for the grant? What parts aren't convincing? Are there missed opportunities here to do more significant work?

B. **What are the red flags?** No problem is too small to identify now. Sometimes when you're writing, you say to yourself, "Oh, I hope reviewers don't think of this. Maybe if I don't mention it, reviewers won't notice it." Reviewers will notice the problems. They will write about these problems in their reviews. Get your readers to find and point the problems out to you now.

   Prompts. What are your concerns? Does the scope feel too big? Is there bias in the design? Are there problems you think I'll run into? Does the research plan match the questions? Are there issues with the plan and project timeline? What do you think about the generalizability of this work? Where do you think I could fail in this work? Do you understand what we plan to do to carry out the work?

   Sample ways red flags show up. This scope feels too big, given _____. Your project timeline doesn't match the aims. It's not clear why you chose this number of participants. You said you'd collect data over three years, but you're actually collecting two years of data. Your control group is contaminated because _____. The real weakness is _____. I'm concerned you're only doing _____. This is going to cause _____ problems. Not clear that you will be successful in _____. You overlooked _____ issue. Seems like there's insufficient planning for _____ terrible thing that could happen. How will you manage _____. Doesn't seem feasible to _____. Doesn't seem like you thought through _____. This equipment/method seems outdated. Your whole plan relies entirely on _____ or it will fail.

C. **What needs more justification?** Where do questions or glimmers of uncertainty show up? Remember, you are guiding reviewers on a journey (chapter 9). You want to know about places where reviewers might get distracted and move off the road map. For example, you say in the grant you're going to translate documents into Spanish, but you don't have anyone on your team who speaks Spanish or a plan for paying someone to translate. This starts reviewers down a detour of thinking, How will you get these translations? Why don't you have this expertise on the team? To keep reviewers on your road map, identify and wipe out these potential detours.

Prompts. Where did you have to make assumptions? What parts were you looking for that you didn't see? Are there things you think I should mention? Where are connections between concepts unclear? What parts feel vague, unconvincing, or confusing? Do you understand why I chose this design? Are you convinced we can do the work or get these outcomes?

Sample statements that indicate you need more justification. Not clear that you have access to _____ data needed for the work. You talked about _____, but your plan doesn't _____. The _____ are missing. Your benchmarks for success aren't clear. How are _____ and _____ connected? Feels like you are asking us to just trust you on _____ rather than justifying. It feels vague when _____. Why did you _____? Why didn't you talk about _____? Lack of detail on _____. I wasn't convinced that _____. You talked about focus groups, but that doesn't show up in your human subjects forms. How will you know when _____. You say you're collecting _____, but when and how?

D. **Story problems.** Story problems are related to justification, but this issue is about pacing. How could you tell the story better? Where does the urgency and argument feel sluggish?

Sample ways story problems show up. There seems to be a disconnect between these parts of the grant. Aim 1 is good, but not clear how aim 2 ties in. Was a lot of focus on _____, but you don't _____. You didn't address _____ part of the call. Why did you mention _____? Hard to understand why you didn't _____.

Toss out Weaknesses

I've talked about identifying weaknesses in your larger grant (red teaming) and individual sections as you are writing (discussion circles). Now it's time for *you* to actually get rid of weaknesses.

Tossing out weaknesses requires you to be vulnerable. To listen when people tell you there are weaknesses in your grant. That can be demoralizing. It's natural to want to defend yourself. To declare that readers missed the point or read too fast, and that comments are useless.

But being defensive doesn't serve you. Amy Summerville shares that a faculty member gave her this advice during graduate school: "You can't argue with the feedback, 'This was unclear.' Clarity is always in the eyes of the reader."[116] Take any feedback as information about how your grant reads to other people. As Vanessa Bohns writes, "Most of us have a tendency to treat our writing as too precious. I like to think of writing like you're putting together a jigsaw puzzle. If someone were to lean over your shoulder and say, "That piece goes over there," you wouldn't be offended and keep trying to jam it in over here."[117]

Address all feedback from red team and discussion circle readers. Don't feel discouraged if you received a lot of feedback. That is a gift. It means you've found critical readers who thought deeply about your work. They are pointing out how you can improve your skills.

Let's make this more concrete. Below I list the types of feedback from our section on discussion circles. Here's what each type often indicates, and how to troubleshoot those problems.

Decode Feedback and Troubleshoot

- **Significance problems**. Sometimes significance problems point to issues with your pitch. For pitch issues, go back to chapter 4 and look at "Evaluate a Structure for One Pagers." Are there aspects of this structure that you could refine to make a better case for your work? Are readers telling you that they don't feel invested in your ideas? If so, run through the "Build Your Pitch: Be a Prosecuting Attorney" skill from chapter 4. Can you think even more broadly about the significance of your work? Significance problems can also mean that you haven't built a strong enough case around the outcomes for your work. Look back at chapter 10's skill on "Offense: Build Your Case." Pay attention to the section on building good outcomes. What more could you add to your plan for good outcomes?

- **Red flags**. Red flags are usually specific, so address each one carefully. Consider whether your scope needs to shift, the design needs to be modified, or more. Grant writing is iterative. Shift and rework ideas to create the most polished grant possible.
- **Needs more justification**. Pay attention to where in your draft readers are bringing up issues. Issues in the one pager (chapter 4) and literature review (chapter 9) section often mean that your guidance statements need to be stronger, your evidence is too vague, or your evidence isn't aligned well enough with your guidance statement. Run through the "Become a Guide" skill in chapter 9 again. Are you making a strong enough argument about how we should move forward? Then test the strength of your evidence by going through the "Avoid Common Mistakes" skill in chapter 11. Remember, make evidence concrete and specific. If readers want more justification in your research plan, this usually means you need a stronger case for your research plan. Go back to chapter 10 and walk through the "Offense: Build Your Case" skill. Also look at chapter 14's skill "Brainstorm What You Bring to the Table" to amplify the evidence in your grant for why you have the right team and environment.
- **Story problems**. Story problems can indicate that you have either an inconsistent draft or structural issues. To ensure consistency, run through chapter 11's "Create Consistency across Your Full Grant" skills. To shore up the structure of your grant, reread chapters 11 and 13. And cut extra information relentlessly. Cutting builds momentum in your writing by removing dull text.

Pay Attention to Detail

You've worked too hard to let minor mistakes make a bad impression on reviewers. Before you submit, make sure you:

1. **Double check facts**. Reviewers are experts. They are miffed when they find "simple" errors.

    Examples of simple errors. Misnaming a measure. Missing the lower or upper end of your data range. Citing the wrong original publication. Referencing the wrong city because you modeled your plan on your previous work. These are details you do not want to get wrong.

2. **Check for consistency**. I spent a whole chapter talking about consistency (chapter 11). I bring it up again because inconsistency will sink your grant. Reviewers hate inconsistency. Work hard at creating a consistent grant. As researcher Nancy Kassam-Adams notes, "This is an iterative process. Sometimes two-thirds of the way through writing, you'll get a better idea and need to scrap earlier versions of your work. Make sure you go back and edit to create a compelling and consistent story."

    Example. In one part of the grant, you say you are recruiting people from minoritized groups. But your recruitment strategy only includes communities that are 90 percent white.

    Action steps. Make sure headings and aims are worded exactly the same way throughout the grant. Make sure the order of your information appears in the same order throughout the grant. Make sure the story you are telling matches across your grant. Go back to chapter 11 and run through all the consistency strategies before submission.

3. **Proofread heavily, especially at submission time**. Catch every typo and error. As Shannon Self-Brown notes, simple errors make reviewers "start to wonder if bigger problems exist. If you weren't careful here, where else could there be problems with the quality of this grant?"

    Actions steps. Plan extra time for proofreading and submission errors. Submission errors are hard to anticipate, but they are common. For example, sometimes labels you don't expect to appear will be visible to reviewers. That can be embarrassing (e.g., if you name a file "Last Ditch Attempt_Final_v10").

4. **Check the application guidelines one final time**. Your grant matters most for your career. Make sure your grant meets the application requirements. This is true even when you have research administrators and collaborators to help you. Scholars often run out of time or skip this step. I've heard many stories of grants being disqualified because the final edits accidentally made the grant go over the page limits, a

collaborator introduced an element that's not allowed, an important document was left out, and more. It's devastating when your grant is disqualified. Your grant isn't reviewed. You have to wait for another cycle, or if there are no more cycles, you missed your chance. Your hard work will go to waste for minor errors. Don't let this happen.

Tips and Frequently Asked Questions

What do I do if I hate my grant? It's a common journey in grant writing to get to a point where you don't like your grant. Negative feedback is demoralizing, and you spend a lot of time figuring out what's wrong with your grant idea. As researcher Beth Auslander shares, "You start out, and it's exciting. Then you reach a point when it becomes grueling. Get a partner to help unravel the knots and then get back on track so you're on your way." Take this roller coaster of feelings as a sign you're putting in the hard work of writing a captivating grant. And surround yourself with colleagues who can be critical and supportive.

What do I do if readers bring up conflicting issues? Similar to paper writing, address issues to the extent possible. Ask readers if they feel their concerns were addressed. Ultimately, this is your grant and you have final say. That's why you're writing the grant. (For reminders on why you want to do this work, see chapter 2.)

I'm having trouble finding weaknesses in my grant. I'm too close to it. In addition to red teaming and discussion circles, experiment to find strategies that give you a fresh look at your grant. Take time off to see if that helps. Try reading your grant out loud. Get a computer program to read your grant to you. Print key pages. Researcher Donald Moynihan offers two notable strategies: "Use conferences as a barometer. Call a family member. What are people excited about? What's compelling?"

I'm overwhelmed by all the potential problems that could come up when I carry out my grant. You cannot control everything that could come up in the future. Stay focused on the fact that your grant is your best guess in the present at understanding what might happen in the future.

Double and triple check any documents from collaborators and mentors. Yes, you can probably depend on collaborators or mentors to proofread their documents. But this is your grant too. Take the time to proof those documents.

The Takeaway

I've covered multiple strategies for polishing your grant: red teaming, discussion circles, tossing out weaknesses, and paying attention to detail. When you weed out weaknesses in your grant, you ensure reviewers will read your grant and say, "Amazing. This is so perfect on the first try." You'll know the secret. Your grant is absolutely not your first try. But reviewers don't need to know this. They can just enjoy your amazing ideas.

Conclusion

The role models I look up to the most aren't those who always succeed, but
rather those who confront failure and adversity and work to make things
better for the people who follow them.

—JEN HEEMSTRA[118]

MY FAMILY is not athletic. Growing up, we'd max out our library card's
twenty-book limit every weekend instead of going outdoors. My little
sister took *xin suan* (mental math abacus classes) in her free time. I never
willingly watched a professional sports game until I met my husband (go
Patriots!).

So imagine my surprise when my older sister called me during graduate
school to say she signed up for the Chicago half-marathon. I was floored. A
person in my family running 13.1 miles. She asked if I wanted to join her. On
a whim, I said yes. Despite the fact that I wasn't able to run even a mile at the
time.

It took all of my psychology training to pursue this big goal. I broke 13.1
miles down into smaller goals. I made mindset shifts. I found a buddy (my
friend Lisa). And I made myself accountable by paying the $125 registration
fee and training in the Miami heat for three months.

The day of the Chicago half-marathon, it poured. It rained so hard we made
ponchos out of trash bags. We couldn't see the mile markers. But we did it. We
made it across the finish line.

You signed up for your own Chicago half-marathon when you decided to
write a grant. In this book, I walked through everything you need to reach this
big goal:

- **Your smaller goals** (find available grants, determine your values and external values, the one pager, writing timeline, evaluation criteria, the literature review, the research plan, figures, and your pick me factor).
- **Mindset shifts** (be a guide, not a peer; focus on clarity, consistency, and readability).
- **Finding your buddies** (aspirational peers, mentors, program officers, research administrators, red teams, and discussion circles).

Now it's time to make yourself accountable and train in the heat.

Be Accountable

Apply the strategies in this book, get feedback, reread chapters, and keep polishing your work.

Most important, submit. You may want to push off deadlines and wait for the next deadline. That's fine. Just don't delay too long. Submitting is how you get the top people in your field to engage with your ideas and give you feedback.

Then celebrate when you submit. This is a momentous achievement that took a lot of hard work.

Train in the Heat

Your grant probably won't be funded the first time you submit. At the National Science Foundation, only about 36 percent of new investigators receive their first award on their first attempt.[119]

These statistics may make you think the deck is stacked against you. That's true if you only play once. You have to play again. (I know, I'm mixing metaphors.)

The point is, grant writing really is a marathon. Don't give up. Keep revising and submitting. If we go back to National Science Foundation statistics, principal investigators submit about 2.3 proposals for every award they receive.[119] Every grant you write gets you one of those 2.3 submissions under your belt. Keep going.

You are building skills that will sustain your career over your lifetime. The short term is not what matters. Stay the course. Here are some success stories for inspiration:

> Ya-Hui Yu submitted three fellowship applications before receiving her first one. "Even if you think you're not ready, just give it a try. Having a first draft gives you a start. It's easier to revise a draft when it exists."

Kelly Shaffer submitted her first grant in graduate school. Her grant, an F31 to the National Institutes of Health, was not discussed on the first round. When she resubmitted, her grant scored in the third percentile and was funded. Kelly says, "Keep the faith. Even if your grant is not discussed, it doesn't mean there isn't merit to it. Persistence matters."

Jessica Schleider was developing a line of research in a new area: single-session interventions. When she started, many people didn't think single-session interventions could work. But Jessica believed in the power of this work. So she applied to "any funders that might listen." And Jessica notes that "resistance to single-session interventions declined exponentially once I got my foot in the door with my first grant." She knew this because the "hit rate" on her grants went up after she received her first major grant. That first grant made it "safer" for other funders to invest in this new area.

All of that being said, rejection is hard. Give yourself time to grieve and process the disappointment. Then pick yourself up and run again. Here's how:

A. **Remember it's not personal**. If your grant isn't funded, it's not that you don't have an important idea or you're not good enough. Many smart people were rejected right alongside you. There's a video where Diana Bianchi shares a grant rejection letter she received early in her career from Eunice Kennedy Shriver. This letter is hilarious because Diana now *directs* the Eunice Kennedy Shriver National Institute on Child Health and Human Development. Diana says, "The moral of the story is don't let your self-worth or career choices be influenced by failure to get funding. . . . Believe in yourself."[108]

B. **Get as much feedback as you can**. Make an appointment with your program officer to learn from the reviews. Research administrator Rosemary Panza says, "Summary statements don't always say enough. Making the call may uncover information for you." And talking to your program officer helps you build your relationship with a program officer and the program. Some agencies and foundations don't provide feedback. You can still reach out and ask. Researcher Ryan Landoll says he's had success with this strategy about 50 percent of the time. If you're able to obtain a meeting, treat it like a red team discussion. It's a chance to listen and learn. It's not a chance to argue for your work.

C. **Revise and resubmit**. Read reviews carefully. Talk to your collaborators. Similar to paper writing, figure out how you can use the feedback to make your work stronger. Resubmit to the same funder or submit to a new funder if you think there may be a better fit for your work (see chapter 5).

D. Nothing is lost work. Experts thought deeply about ideas you created. And researcher Dennis Kao shares, "Submitting any grant proposal shows you are sharpening your grant writing skills. You have promise and are working toward your research agenda. This is true even if your grant is rejected." And rejected grant applications can be listed in your annual reviews. They can also be repurposed for new grants, concept papers, smaller pilot projects, your promotion packet, and more.

Last Thoughts

I opened this book by thinking about social justice issues in grant funding. Our funding systems are biased. We need systemic solutions to our structural problems. I'm heartened to see many funders taking action to create more just systems of funding.

I wrote this book to uncover one barrier to equity and access: the hidden curriculum of grant writing. Scholarship should not be built around "insiders" and "outsiders." Scores of experts agreed and shared their best advice. I hope we've given you the power to create the career and life you choose.

You have a role to play here too. Submit. Join the conversation. Let us hear your voice. This matters for you and all the people looking up to you. Because grant writing can change your life and theirs. Two of my colleagues describe grant writing this way:

Matthew Magee: "Grant writing is the opportunity to grow your skills and intellectual capacities. It's my favorite part of my work because it's the chance to dream."

Claire Spears: "Grant writing sounds daunting, but it can be a fun and creative process. And it's what keeps you on top of emerging research."

You've read this far. I know you have what it takes to write a fundable grant. You've got big dreams and the guts to turn those dreams into reality. Go out. Write more fundable grants. And most important, make our world a better place.

Task A: Develop an Idea

Chapter 1. The Landscape: Find Available Grants

- Am I too early in my career to begin applying for grants?
- What do I do if I have trouble finding CVs?
- The usual suspects exercise lets us track the careers of a few people. How else do people hear about grants?
- I work in an area that isn't a high priority for funding. How do I find people who might support my work?
- What are the success rates of grants?
- How long does it take to write a grant?
- What are the differences between funders?
- Are there other ways besides grants for researchers to support their work?

Chapter 2. Your Values: Generate Ideas

- Find your North Star.
- Is it a problem if my ideas don't cover every pillar?
- Avoid proposing ideas that are too big to be feasible.
- At the same time, avoid proposing ideas that are too small.
- Which comes first, the idea or the funding target?
- Should I start with "safe" or "risky" ideas?
- Is it harder to get funded for more controversial topics?

Chapter 3. External Values: Further Your Career Goals

- Won't people steal my idea?
- How do I get past feelings of intimidation in order to email experts?

- Should I start with small or big grants?
- How many grants should I be writing at one time?
- Should I focus on leading my own grant or being a collaborator?
- How do I find collaborators?
- How do I choose collaborators?
- Are there other ways to build out my network?
- What advice do you have for people who've had success with small grants but haven't landed that big grant yet?
- What advice do you have for people who are not citizens in the country where the funder is based?
- Are there other benefits to grant writing?

Chapter 4. The One Pager: Create Phenomenal Pitches

- How many aims do I need?
- How big should the scope of my aims be?
- Do I always need aims or hypotheses?
- What should I do if I'm overwhelmed and not sure where to start?
- What should I do if my work differs from common practice or conventional wisdom?
- Does the guidance here differ if I'm a bench scientist versus a clinical scientist versus a humanities scholar?

Task B: Target a Funder

Chapter 5. Talk to a Program Officer: Fit with a Funder

- Should I feel bad when my work doesn't align with a funder's mission or priorities?
- How closely do ideas need to be aligned with the program or funder? Does it need to be an exact match?
- Is it OK to speak to more than one program officer?
- Are there other times I can speak with the program officer?
- What do program officers say is a common mistake from new grant writers?
- Will every program officer give feedback?
- What if no one gets back to me?
- Are there other strategies for finding fit with a funder?

Chapter 6. Get Samples: Signal That You Belong

- Is an unfunded sample still helpful?
- What if I can't find a sample of a grant that was funded by my program?
- Does my sample need to be from someone in my field?
- I'm intimidated by my samples. How am I supposed to live up to them?
- Are there other ways to get access to samples?
- Can program officers provide samples?

Chapter 7. A Grant's Anatomy: Outline and Timeline

- What's the best place to begin in terms of writing?
- Figure out what time of day is most productive for writing; guard that time.
- More on budgets, because they are tricky.
- What are fringe rates?
- Divide and conquer.
- Define roles early.
- Don't reinvent the wheel.
- What is a letter of intent?
- Read all instructions carefully.

Chapter 8. Evaluation Criteria and the Mission: Make It Easy to Advocate for You

- Is it a problem if my work doesn't address all aspects of the funder's mission?
- Make sure you also directly address the solicitation or request for applications (discussed in chapter 2).
- Who are my reviewers?
- How do funders make sure reviewers don't have conflicts of interest?

Task C: Draft Your Grant

Chapter 9. The Literature Review: Clear and Simple Communication

- Evaluate the literature reviews in your samples.
- How long should a literature review be?
- Make sure you include foundational works from your field in your grant.

- No sentence in your literature review should span more than three lines.
- I'm feeling stuck. How can I get started?
- When can I begin to get feedback?
- How would you modify this advice for people working on training grants?

Chapter 10. Your Research Plan: Living up to the Hype

- Why do you recommend drafting the one pager and literature review before the research plan?
- How long should my research plan be?
- Does my final research plan need to cover every single question from the activity about brainstorming your research plan?
- How do I know if I've chosen the best methods?
- What do I do if my methods go against conventional wisdom?
- What can I do if I don't have much pilot data?
- If I introduce ways my plan can fail, won't reviewers hyperfocus on problems with my work?
- What if there isn't enough money in the budget to do the work I want to do?
- Wouldn't the optimal strategy be to add tons of experts to my grant?
- Don't hoard your data.
- Are research plans set in stone? Meaning, could a research plan be flexible if I run into problems later?

Chapter 11. Structure Your Draft: Consistency Is Comforting

- Where should I invest the greatest amount of time: the one pager, literature review, or research plan?
- How do I come up with a good title for my grant?
- How do I handle the different writing styles of my collaborators?
- What reference style should my references be in?
- How many references should I include in my grant?
- Creating consistency is a lot of work. Will reviewers even notice?

Chapter 12. Go Figure: Images That Deliver Value

- Workshop your figures.
- Can a figure ever really stand alone? Figures don't have much meaning without explanations in the text.

- Avoid including someone else's figures if that person isn't on your team.
- Right before submitting, check the table and figure numbers as well as the formatting.
- Do I need a figure at all?
- Where can I find more examples of figures?
- What software should I use?

Task D: Polish Your Grant

Chapter 13. Style Strategies: Increase Readability

- Read your grant out loud or have a program read your grant out loud.
- Read widely to understand what good writing looks like.
- What do I do if English is not my first language?
- Aren't some acronyms OK? I see them in other grants.
- Couldn't I take the shotgun approach and submit tons of imperfect grants to see what sticks?
- Should I use left or full justification?

Chapter 14. The Pick Me Factor: Sell Your Expertise and Team

- Won't I sound conceited?
- How do I strike a balance between talking about my work and not going overboard?
- Does this concept of needing to sell your expertise differ by culture or funders?
- How much of a track record do I need?
- What do I do if I don't fit into a neat problem space?
- Is it OK that I didn't use up all the space in my grant?

Chapter 15. Critical Critiques: Identify Weaknesses

- What do I do if I hate my grant?
- What do I do if readers bring up conflicting issues?
- I'm having trouble finding weaknesses in my grant. I'm too close to it.
- I'm overwhelmed by all the potential problems that could come up when I carry out my grant.
- Double and triple check any documents from collaborators and mentors.

SUBMISSION CHECKLIST

Here's a checklist of items to evaluate before you submit. The items are structured to match the order of book chapters.

- ☐ **Application instructions.** Have you met all required proposal elements?
- ☐ **Evaluation criteria.** Have you included good headings and emphasis words throughout your proposal (i.e., sound bites)?
- ☐ **Funder's mission.** Have you indicated at least one statement in your grant about how you address the mission of the funder?
- ☐ **Funder's strategic plan.** Have you thought through and stated how your work addresses the funder's strategic plan?
- ☐ **Request for proposals.** Have you stated in your grant how your work directly addresses the request for proposals?
- ☐ **Guidance versus statements.** Does your proposal make arguments for how the work moves the field forward (i.e., guidance) rather than focusing on descriptive statements? Are there places where you make tepid statements? Could those be strengthened?
- ☐ **Build your case.** Does your research plan explain why you have a solid plan, chose the right methods, you'll be able to do the work, and why the funder can expect good outcomes?
- ☐ **Anticipate reviewer questions.** Have you thought about the questions reviewers will have about your research plan? Did you address those questions?
- ☐ **Inverted pyramid.** Does every paragraph have a clear guiding statement? Within each paragraph, does the evidence fit the guidance at the start of the paragraph? Have you identified conflicting evidence? Have you removed "filler" material, focusing instead on concrete numbers, data, studies, and so on?
- ☐ **Signposts.** Do you have signposts throughout your grant?

- ☐ **Mirroring**. Have you mirrored the structure of every section in your grant?
- ☐ **Repetition**. Have you used the same terms throughout the grant?
- ☐ **Emphasis techniques**. Are your emphasis techniques consistent? Is it clear why you are using an emphasis technique? Are there any places where emphasis techniques are not needed and could be removed?
- ☐ **Front-load your point**. In every sentence and paragraph, is the point front-loaded? (As a refresher example, this checklist is front-loaded. The main points appear at the beginning of each bullet and are bolded.)
- ☐ **Figures**. Does every figure have a purpose? Can you understand the figures without having to read the text? Are the figures accessible? Is the font large enough to read? Are the figures as simplified as they can be? Are the figures consistent with regard to alignment, colors, size, and formatting?
- ☐ **White space**. Have you created white space on every page?
- ☐ **Trim extra words**. Have you gone through the entire grant and trimmed every word that could be cut?
- ☐ **No jargon**. Do a last check of your grant to remove any jargon that may be removed.
- ☐ **Short sentences only**. Are all of your sentences under three lines of text? Could any sentences be shortened further? Do you have any compound sentences that could be simplified or split?
- ☐ **Avoid acronyms**. Have you removed acronyms wherever possible?
- ☐ **Kill the ambiguous "this."** When you search for the word "this" in your grant, is it always clear what "this" means?
- ☐ **Voice**. Did you write in an active voice? Or if you wrote in a passive voice, is it clear who is in charge?
- ☐ **Be precise**. Have you made your case with numbers and data instead of general statements?
- ☐ **Showcase fit**. Have you explicitly stated why you and your work are unique?
- ☐ **Tell the story**. Have you made connections for reviewers to help them understand how the people and work are related?
- ☐ **Build your dream team and reframe weaknesses**. Have you considered the weaknesses reviewers will identify in you, your team, or environment? Have you bolstered those weaknesses or reframed them as strengths?

☐ **Critical critiques.** Have you addressed all the weaknesses readers raised?

☐ **Final fact-checking.** Are all of your facts accurate? Did you check that all of your measure names are correct? Do you have the right data ranges? Have you cited the correct articles?

☐ **Final consistency check.** Are the headings and aims worded consistently? Is the information presented in the same order every time? Did you use the same terms with the same spelling throughout?

☐ **Final proofing.** Have you checked for all spelling and grammar errors? Referencing errors? Did you recheck the figure numbers one last time, including any places where the figures are referenced in the text?

☐ **Final check of application requirements.** Have you ensured that all of your final documents meet the application requirements?

GLOSSARY

Grant terms are defined below with a note for the chapter where the term is discussed. Grant terms are bolded the first time they appear in a chapter.

Authorized organization representative (sometimes called the AOR) (chapter 7). This person is authorized to sign and submit your grant on behalf of your institution. Remember that grants are usually awarded to your institution, not directly to you. This is why you are not typically the person who signs and submits your grant.

Buy out (chapter 2). This is how people often refer to covering a person's time on a grant. For example, you can buy out of a course. That means the grant is paying for the time you would normally spend teaching one course.

Coinvestigator (chapter 3). Sometimes referred to as "co-i's," coinvestigators are collaborators on the grant, but they do not lead the grant. The principal investigator (also known as a PI) leads the grant and is responsible for the project. For promotion, some institutions require or encourage you to secure grants as a principal investigator. Other institutions will be happy to see you secure grants as a coinvestigator. Use your meetings from chapter 3 to divine this information. Note that funders often have many labels for the team on the grant. You may also see coprincipal investigator, multiple principal investigator, project leader, or other significant contributors.

Conflicts of interest (chapter 8). These are situations where it will be difficult for a person to be objective. Funders pay special attention to reviewers' conflicts of interest and try to eliminate them so that grants receive unbiased reviews. For example, funders usually do not allow reviewers to review grants written by a mentor, mentee, or someone at their current institution. Most funders ask reviewers to explicitly identify situations that present potential conflicts of interest.

Cost sharing (chapter 14). This means that part of the expenses for the grant are not covered by the funder. Instead, your institution or someone other than the funder is willing to bear those costs. Sometimes funders require cost sharing. Sometimes people donate their time in "in-kind" support to make a case for their commitment to a grant. In past grants, I've used cost-sharing examples as evidence that I am in a supportive environment. For instance, I have noted cases where my institution is committed to funding student stipends for students who will contribute their time to work on the grant. That is cost sharing because the costs for the student stipends does not come from the funder.

Curiosity gaps (chapter 4). Curiosity gaps are spaces between what we know and what we need to know.[48] Curiosity gaps motivate people to keep reading because people want to discover what you will reveal. For example, in *Game of Thrones*, we know Ned Stark claims to be Jon Snow's father. We don't know who Jon Snow's mother is, but it's clear that this information is important to the story. That gap piques our curiosity. In grant writing, you create a space between what is known in your field and what needs to be known to move your field forward.

Direct costs (chapter 3). These are the costs that you budget for your work. This includes items like salaries, participants, equipment, and travel.

Federal grants (chapter 1). Federal grants refer to government-funded grants in the United States. This would include grants from the National Science Foundation and National Institutes of Health, for example.

Foundation grants (chapter 1). These are nonfederal grants. Foundations may be public or private. Examples include the Spencer Foundation, Jacobs Foundation, or William T. Grant Foundation.

Fringe rates (chapter 7). These are the costs for health insurance, retirement plans, tuition reimbursement, social security, or unemployment/worker's compensation. Fringe rates vary by institution and personnel on the grant. At Boston College, fringe rates for 2020–21 were 30.7, 48.3, and 7.65 percent for professional, nonprofessional, and part-time staff, respectively.[67] This means that if a professional staff person is paid $10,000 in salary on the grant, I also have to budget 30.7 percent on top of that salary to cover the benefits (i.e., $10,000 plus $3,070 for fringe). Because the rules are complex, check with your research administrator about fringe rates.

Gantt charts (chapter 10). These are charts that illustrate your project timeline. Use Gantt charts to show that your project is feasible and cohesive, and that you have a clear plan for carrying out your aims. For a Gantt chart example, see figure 9.

Hard money position (chapter 3). These are positions funded by an institution. People in hard money positions are not required to bring in grants or contracts. In contrast, soft money positions require individuals to bring in a portion of their salary through grants or contracts. Hard money positions usually rely on teaching or other activities (e.g., clinical work) outside of grants and contracts to cover salary. For example, I am in a hard money position where I teach four courses per year.

Ikigai (chapter 2). Ikigai is a Japanese concept that translates to your "reason for being." In this book, I focus on an interpretation of Ikigai to help you generate grant ideas: What does the world need? What do you love? What are you good at? What could you be paid for?

Indirect costs (also known as indirects or IDCs, overhead, or facilities and administration or F&A) (chapter 3). These are the costs of the grant that go toward overhead (e.g., keeping the lights running and paying administrators). Indirect costs get charged to federal agencies at a set negotiated rate by each institution. Some foundations also allow institutions to charge indirect costs. Indirect costs are based on a set percentage of a grants' direct costs. At Boston College, for example, our current indirect cost rate for on-campus research is 56.5 percent.[120]

Internal grants (chapter 1). These are grants from your institution. They are usually listed on your institution's website or in email newsletters.

Letter of intent (chapter 7). Sometimes abbreviated as LOI, letters of intent are usually short, one- to two-page documents indicating that you plan to apply for a grant. Funders often have specific rules about letters of intent. Read the application guidelines carefully. For example, sometimes you are only allowed to apply if you submit a letter of intent. Funders request letters of intent for various reasons, including to identify applications that will align best to a call for grants, gauge interest, or provide feedback.

Letter of support (chapter 7). These are letters that you include with your grant to show that you have support from collaborators, mentors, consultants, your institution, organizations, or people with materials you might need. People typically use letters of support as evidence to demonstrate they will be able to carry out the work in the grant and make an impact. Not all funders allow letters of support, and some have strict rules for letters. Make sure you read the application guidelines carefully.

Mechanisms (chapter 1). These are grants for specific purposes, activities, or audiences. People sometimes use the term to refer broadly to different types of awards (e.g., grants, contracts, or cooperative agreements). But more often people use "mechanism" to refer to specific types of grants. Examples of mechanisms include R21s, R01s, CAREER grants, Spencer postdoctoral fellowships, and so on.

Office of Sponsored Programs (sometimes referred to as the Grants Administration Office or University Research Services and Administration [URSA]) (chapter 7). This is the central office at your institution that manages funding. This is typically where you send your grant for final approval, sign off, and submission. People in this office are a trusted and valuable resource to you during your grant writing journey. Sometimes institutions have a separate office that handles foundation funding. Check with your colleagues to understand these nuances.

One pager (also referred to as specific aims) (chapter 4). The one pager introduces your grant idea. It is the document that pitches why your work matters and how you will carry it out. This is the most widely read section of your grant. When program officers are advocating for your grant, they often circulate your one pager. A one pager is frequently one page long, but it could be as long as two or three pages. For two funded examples of one pagers, see chapter 4.

Postaward (chapter 7). Postaward means people who work with you after your grant is awarded. Postaward work involves tasks like helping you spend the grant, review budgets, or complete annual or final reports to the funder.

Preaward (chapter 7). Preaward refers to people who work with you before you submit your grant. Preaward administrators usually help you put together your budgets and materials for submission, complete internal paperwork, and route your submission to your authorized organization representative.

Principal investigator (also known as a PI) (chapter 3). This is the person who leads the grant. Institutions vary with regard to how much they value principal investigator status versus coinvestigator status (i.e., the person who collaborates on and supports the grant work). Use your external values meetings in chapter 3 to understand how your institution and field values these roles.

Program (chapter 1). Programs are designated areas of focus for a funder. For example, my program at the National Science Foundation is Humans, Disasters, and the Built Environment. This program focuses on (as you probably guessed) humans, disasters, and the built environment. Find programs that are searching for scholars like you by using the usual suspects exercise in chapter 1.

Program officer (also known as a PO, program director [PD], or program official) (chapters 1 and 5). Program officers are employees of the funder. A program officer's job is to build and oversee a portfolio of grants for a program. Program officers are often scholars themselves. They identify research opportunities, set priorities, convene reviewers, and speak with interested scholars about the program.

Protected time (chapter 2). Protected time refers to the idea that when a grant is covering portions of your time, that time cannot be used for nongrant-related activities (e.g., extra courses, clinic days, or other projects). It "protects" your time by earmarking how that time may be used.

Requests for applications (sometimes referred to as RFAs, requests for proposals or RFPs, or funding opportunity announcements or FOAs, also pronounced as "foh-ahs") **(chapter 2).** These are announcements from your funder about the types of grants they are seeking to fund. Pay special attention to these requests for applications. They are meant to guide you in terms of how to create a great match between your idea and what the funder is seeking.

Research administrator (chapter 7). Research administrators are employees of your institution. They are experts who understand the rules of different funding agencies. They help you and your institution comply with those rules.

Research plan (chapter 10). A description of how you will carry out the work of the grant. Research plans go by different names, depending on the funder. Some common names for research plans include: research strategy, project description, project plan, methods section, research narrative, or the research design.

Review panel (chapter 1). When reviewers meet to discuss the grants they reviewed, this is called a review panel. Not all funders convene review panels. Speak to your mentors and program officers to understand how the review process works at your funder. And try to serve on a review panel (for ideas on how to do this, see chapter 6).

Social proof (chapter 1). Social proof refers to the idea that people feel more comfortable when they see others engage in a behavior. In our case, funders are more likely to want to fund you when they see the social proof that others have funded your work.

Soft money position (chapter 3). These are positions that require a portion of the salary to be covered by grants or contracts. They are usually compared to hard money positions, which do not have these requirements.

Specific aims (chapter 4). This is how the National Institutes of Health refers to one pagers.

Subcontracts (also referred to as subs and subawards) (chapter 7). Subcontracts are official contracts between institutions. If you lead a grant but have a collaborator at another institution, your institution "contracts out" part of the grant work to your collaborator's institution. This allows the other institution to pay your collaborator. Subcontracts require many forms and signatures (i.e., they take a lot of time).

Summer salary (chapter 3). For those in nine- or ten-month positions, summer salary refers to the salary paid for your summer months. If you are in a nine-month position, for example, you have three months that are not covered by your contract. Grants could cover those three months. This translates to 33 percent of your yearly salary paid "on top" of your regular salary. Funders and institutions have different rules for whether summer salary is allowed.

Triage (chapter 8). Triaging means that the lowest-scoring grants don't get discussed during the review panel because they are unlikely to be funded.

ACKNOWLEDGMENTS

THIS BOOK would not have been possible without the following people.

Princeton University Press. I am grateful to my editor, Peter J. Dougherty, for believing in and championing this work. Peter was always available for a call or check-in, guiding me to resources and experts at every step of this process. Thank you to press director Christie Henry for your leadership, vision, and support. Thanks go to editor Alena Chekanov for your wizardry and guidance. To editor Matt Rohal, thank you for your encouragement and support in this process. Lisa Black's expertise on permissions was invaluable; Lisa fielded many questions, big and small. I'm grateful to Lauren Lepow for her editorial feedback on this manuscript. Lauren saved me from making many copyediting and manuscript preparation mistakes. Copy editor Cindy Milstein gave this manuscript a professional polish. Cindy offered much appreciated insight and encouragement in the final mile. I also want to thank production editor Karen Carter, cover designer Matt Avery, production specialist Lauren Reese, and publicists Alyssa Sanford and Kathryn Stevens.

Inspiration. I attended a training by the OpEd Project in 2020 to learn how to write opinion pieces. But I left with much more. The workshop facilitators, Katie Orenstein, Anya Tudisco, and Chelsea Carmona, spoke about why we need to hear from missing voices in the op-ed world. I am thankful to all at the OpEd Project for ensuring that diverse voices are heard. The OpEd Project's call to action compelled me to write this book. We need to hear from our missing voices in the grant writing world. I hope you read this book and know how much your voice matters.

Publishing expertise. Laura Portwood-Stacer explained the entire academic publishing system, making it accessible. Laura helped me believe this book could become a reality. I highly recommend her book proposal workshop and her *The Book Proposal Book* as the ultimate guides to crafting a scholarly book proposal. I owe Laura a debt of gratitude as well for introducing me to my editor, Peter. I am also thankful to the following scholars who shared their experiences with publishing: David Blustein, Belle Liang, Gabrielle Oliveira, Scott Seider, Dennis Shirley, and Usha Tummala-Narra. It is a joy to have colleagues who make academia a kind and generous space.

Readers. The following scholars provided expertise and comments on drafts of this book: Samantha Aubé, Kathryn Becker-Blease, Clare Conry-Murray, Joanna DeMeyer, Kate Guastaferro, Barbora Hoskova, Ngoc Phan, Alexa Riobueno-Naylor, Hoa Lam Schneider, and Clara Shim. I am humbled that they lent their time and insights to make this work better (in the middle of a pandemic, no less). I am also grateful to the three reviewers commissioned by Princeton University Press. Lori Peek, Don Waters, and Reader C were the ultimate red team. Their wisdom and sharp insights made this book stronger.

Grant expertise. Incredible people shared their experiences for this project. They cared about helping others find success in this mysterious world of grant writing. I am ever grateful to these people: Eva Alisic, Ananda Amstadter, Michael Armey, Beth Auslander, Angela Boatman, Susanne Brander, Sam Brody, Andrés Castro Samayoa, Donald Chi, Youngjun Choe, Lauren Clay, Rebekah Levine Coley, Dan Cooper, Tom Cova, Carolyn Anh Dang, BreAnne Danzi, Kirsten Davison, Michelle Desir, Aisha Dickerson, Shanta Dube, Katie Edwards, Nicole Errett, Ann-Margaret Esnard, Suhas Eswarappa Prameela, Joe Evans, Alma Faust, Erika Felix, Stephanie Fitzpatrick, Kristin Flower, Matthew Fox, Dana Garfin, Mason Garrison, Emily Gates, Michelle Gittens, Mary Beth Grimley, Janet Gross, Kate Guastaferro, Cal Halvorsen, Jessica Hamilton, Summer Hawkins, Jen Heemstra, Daphne Henry, Kathleen Holland, Lisa Ibañez, Dennis Kao, Nancy Kassam-Adams, Nathan Kearns, Mathew Kiang, Annette La Greca, Ryan Landoll, Emily Lattie, Sarah Lowe, Becca Lowenhaupt, Natalie Lundsteen, Shannon Mace, Matthew Magee, Valerie Maholmes, Natasha Malmin, Meghan Marsac, Katherine McNeill, Donald Moynihan, Raquel Muñiz, Sarah Naumes, Mallika Nocco, Nicole Nugent, Gabrielle Oliveira, Ponmile Olonilua, Kimie Ono, Melissa Osborne, Caille Ostrolencki, Rosemary Panza, Maggi Price, Ido Rosenzweig, Donna Roybal, Brittany Rudd, Andrew Rumbach, Jessica Schleider, Hoa Lam Schneider, Julie Schneider, Scott Seider, Shannon Self-Brown, Kelly Shaffer, James Shulman, Erin Sibley, Jim Slotta, Brian Smith, Billy Soo, Claire Spears, Deb Thomas,

Ashwini Tiwari, Ginny Vitiello, Jon Wargo, Don Waters, Richelle Weihe, Christine Weirich, Sam Westcott, Dan Whitaker, Haorui Wu, Ya-Hui Yu, and Crystal Zheng.

Family. This book exists because of my husband. He moved mountains (and homes) to support my career. He fills our house with joy, lighting up all the bath toys because it makes the kids laugh. He also brought Jeanne and Lee into my life, the best in-laws ever. I am grateful to Jeanne and Lee for their emergency childcare, Thanksgiving stuffing, and the huge loving family they raised. Finally, thank you to my parents for putting education first. They opened every door they could for us. They wanted us to dream big and see results from hard work. I hope to pay some of this gift forward with this book.

Stay in touch! Sign up for my newsletter at bettylai.com/newsletter.

REFERENCES

1. "Workshops," OpEd Project, 2020, accessed December 3, 2020, https://www.theopedproject .org/seminars#about-our-programs.

2. "Impact of NIH Research," National Institutes of Health, May 1, 2018, accessed January 6, 2022, https://www.nih.gov/about-nih/what-we-do/impact-nih-research/our-society#:~:text =With%20a%202018%20budget%20of,a%20share%20of%20this%20investment.&text =In%20FY%202017%2C%20NIH%20extramural,billion%20in%20economic%20output%20 nationwide.

3. Diego F. M. Oliveira, Yifang Ma, Teresa K. Woodruff, and Brian Uzzi, "Comparison of National Institutes of Health Grant Amounts to First-Time Male and Female Principal Investigators." *JAMA* 321, no. 9 (2019): 898–900, doi:10.1001/jama.2018.21944.

4. Donna K. Ginther, Walter T. Schaffer, Joshua Schnell, Beth Masimore, Faye Liu, Laurel L. Haak, and Raynard Kington, "Race, Ethnicity, and NIH Research Awards," *Science* 333, no. 6045 (2011): 1015–1019, doi:10.1126/science.1196783.

5. "Average Age and Degree of NIH R01-Equivalent First-time Investigators," National Institutes of Health, 2016, accessed March 31, 2022, https://grants.nih.gov/grants/new_investigators /Age_Degree-First-Time-117-16_RFM_lls_25march2016_DR-Approved.xlsx.

6. Holly O. Witteman, Michael Hendricks, Sharon Straus, and CaraTannenbaum, "Are Gender Gaps Due to Evaluations of the Applicant or the Science? A Natural Experiment at a National Funding Agency," *Lancet* 393, no. 10171 (2019): 531–540, doi:10.1016/S0140–6736(18)32611–4.

7. Sindy N. Escobar Alvarez, Reshma Jagsi, Stephanie B. Abbuhl, Carole J. Lee, and Elizabeth R. Myers, "Promoting Gender Equity in Grant Making: What Can a Funder Do?," *Lancet* 393, no. 10171 (2019): e9–e11, doi:https://doi.org/10.1016/S0140-6736(19)30211-9.

8. Anna Severin, Joao Martins, Rachel Heyard, François Delavy, Anne Jorstad, and Matthias Egger, "Gender and Other Potential Biases in Peer Review: Cross-sectional Analysis of 38 250 External Peer Review Reports," *BMJ Open* 10, no. 8 (2020): e035058, doi:10.1136/bmjopen-2019 –035058.

9. "Budget," National Institutes of Health, October 31, 2014, accessed November 30, 2020, https://www.nih.gov/about-nih/what-we-do/budget.

10. "FY 2020 Budget Request to Congress," 2019, accessed November 12, 2020, https://www .nsf.gov/pubs/2019/nsf19005/nsf19005.pdf.

11. "EPA's Budget and Spending," United States Environmental Protection Agency, February 8, 2013, accessed November 30, 2020, https://www.epa.gov/planandbudget/budget.

12. "UK Research and Innovation," GOV.UK, accessed April 23, 2021, https://www.gov.uk /government/organisations/uk-research-and-innovation.

13. Donna K. Ginther, Shulamit Kahn, and Walter T. Schaffer, "Gender, Race/Ethnicity, and National Institutes of Health R01 Research Awards: Is There Evidence of a Double Bind for Women of Color?," *Academic Medicine* 91, no. 8 (2016): 1098–1107, doi:10.1097/ACM.0000000000001278.

14. Travis A. Hoppe, Aviva Litovitz, Kristine A. Willis, Rebecca A. Meseroll, Matthew J. Perkins, B. Ian Hutchins, Alison F. Davis, et al., "Topic Choice Contributes to the Lower Rate of NIH Awards to African-American/Black Scientists," *Science Advances* 5, no. 10 (2019): eaaw7238, doi:10.1126/sciadv.aaw7238.

15. Jennifer Reineke Pohlhaus, Hong Jiang, Robin M. Wagner, Walter T. Schaffer, and Vivian W. Pinn, "Sex Differences in Application, Success, and Funding Rates for NIH Extramural Programs," *Academic Medicine* 86, no. 6 (2011): 759–767, doi:10.1097/ACM.0b013e31821836ff.

16. National Science Foundation and National Science Board, *Merit Review Process: Fiscal Year 2019 Digest*, accessed January 6, 2022, https://www.nsf.gov/nsb/publications/2020/merit_review/FY-2019/nsb202038.pdf.

17. Robert Rohm, "Tip: You Miss 100% of the Shots You Don't Take!," April 28, 2017, accessed November 30, 2020, https://www.personality-insights.com/tip-you-miss-100-of-the-shots-you-dont-take/.

18. Michael S. Lauer and Deepshikha Roychowdhury, "Inequalities in the Distribution of National Institutes of Health Research Project Grant Funding," *eLife* 10 (2021): e71712, doi:10.7554/eLife.71712.

19. Matthew Hayes and James Hardcastle, *Grant Review in Focus: Global State of Peer Review Series*, Publons, 2019, 4, 16, 37, https://publons.com/community/gspr/grant-review.

20. Danielle B. Rice, Hana Raffoul, John P. A. Ioannidis, David Moher, "Academic Criteria for Promotion and Tenure in Biomedical Sciences Faculties: Cross Sectional Analysis of International Sample of Universities," *BMJ* 369 (2020): m2081, doi:10.1136/bmj.m2081.

21. Lindsay R. Pool, Robin M. Wagner, Lindsey L. Scott, Deepshikha Roychowdhury, Reddit Berhane, Charles Wu, et al., "Size and Characteristics of the Biomedical Research Workforce Associated with U.S. National Institutes of Health Extramural Grants," *FASEB Journal* 30, no. 3 (2016): 1023–1036, doi:https://doi.org/10.1096/fj.14-264358.

22. "Fact Sheet: National Science Foundation," National Science Foundation, February 19, 2019, accessed November 30, 2020, https://www.nsf.gov/news/news_summ.jsp?cntn_id=100595.

23. "NSF's Merit Review Process Determines Which Research Has the Greatest Potential," National Science Foundation, YouTube, June 21, 2014, accessed April 9, 2021, https://www.youtube.com/watch?v=WMoGdIFgy5o.

24. Michael Levitt and Jonathan M. Levitt, "Future of Fundamental Discovery in US Biomedical Research," *PNAS* 114, no. 25 (2017): 6498–6503, doi:10.1073/pnas.1609996114.

25. "Where Can I Find Statistics on Foundation and Corporate Giving?," Candid Learning, accessed June 17, 2021, https://learning.candid.org/resources/knowledge-base/giving-statistics.

26. "Pivot-RP: Accelerate Your Research Funding," Ex Libris, accessed November 25, 2020, https://exlibrisgroup.com/products/pivot-funding-opportunities-and-profiles/.

27. "Funding Mechanisms," National Cancer Institute, StatFund, accessed April 16, 2021, https://statfund.cancer.gov/funding/mechanisms.html.

28. "About Grants.gov," Grants.gov, accessed November 24, 2020, https://www.grants.gov/support/about-grants-gov.html.

29. "Grant Fraud Responsibilities," Grants.gov, accessed June 17, 2021, https://www.grants.gov
/learn-grants/grant-fraud/grant-fraud-responsibilities.html.
30. "Get the Information You Need to Do Good," Candid, accessed November 25, 2020,
https://candid.org/.
31. "Daniella Zalcman," Writers' Co-op, accessed February 15, 2021, https://www.thewritersco
oppod.com/episodes/daniella-zalcman.
32. Adrienne R. Carter-Sowell, Danielle Dickens, and Katie Edwards, "Where to Begin with
Grants: Good Ideas Can Become Fundable Projects" (Webinar for Division 35 of the
American Psychological Association, February 26, 2021), https://bit.ly/398XQJq.
33. OECD Directorate for Science, Technology, and Innovation, *Effective Operation of Competitive Research Funding Systems*, 2018, 57:7, doi:10.1787/2ae8codc-en.
34. Kyle Hart, @KyleHartPhD, accessed November 25, 2020, https://twitter.com/KyleHartPhD
/status/1331230297640329217.
35. "Functional Neuroanatomy of Social and Perceived Internal Threat in Anxious Youth at
High-Risk for Bipolar Disorder," NIH RePORTER, accessed April 27, 2021, https://reporter
.nih.gov/search/FQSaR1leuUmg5rFOq5VWtQ/project-details/9927709#details.
36. "006: Rock Star Neuroscientist, Ken Mogi's 5 Pillars of Ikigai," Ikigai Tribe, January 19, 2020,
accessed February 12, 2021, https://ikigaitribe.com/ikigai/the-5-pillars-of-ikigai/.
37. Carlos, @cabr92, accessed November 25, 2020, https://twitter.com/cabr92/status
/1282220389117067264.
38. "Ikigai," Wikipedia, February 13, 2021, accessed February 14, 2021, https://en.wikipedia.org
/w/index.php?title=Ikigai&oldid=1006572995
39. Chris Myers, "How to Find Your Ikigai and Transform Your Outlook on Life and Business,"
Forbes, February 23, 2018, accessed February 12, 2021, https://www.forbes.com/sites
/chrismyers/2018/02/23/how-to-find-your-ikigai-and-transform-your-outlook-on-life
-and-business/.
40. Jessica Wei, "Our Greatest Fear Should Not Be of Failure: Francis Chan," *Due*, January 12,
2016, accessed February 15, 2021, https://due.com/blog/our-greatest-fear-should-not-be
-of-failure-francis-chan/.
41. Paula S. Strickland, "Grant Writing for Success: Preparing a NIH Grant Application," You-
Tube, October 13, 2017, accessed February 14, 2021, https://www.youtube.com/watch?v
=EX4gO69AGo0.
42. "Indirect Costs," Harvard University, accessed November 25, 2020, https://research.fas
.harvard.edu/indirect-costs-0.
43. "With Federal Funds, Harvard Helps Drive Local Economy," *Harvard Gazette*, March 1,
2020, accessed November 25, 2020, https://news.harvard.edu/gazette/story/2020/03
/harvard-attracts-federal-funding-supports-economy/.44. Michelle Pebole, @MPebole,
April 13, 2021, accessed April 13, 2021, https://twitter.com/MPebole/status/138206508543
9442944.
45. Valerie Grant, "Insider's Guide to NIH Peer Review for Applicants," National Institutes of
Health Center for Scientific Review, YouTube, February 25, 2016, accessed February 22,
2021, https://www.youtube.com/watch?v=DuNYjugBMXM&feature=emb_title.
46. David Kosub, "All about Grants Podcast: Considerations for a Research Plan," accessed
March 16, 2021, https://grants.nih.gov/podcasts/All_About_Grants/episodes/Research
-Plan.htm.

47. Vernita Gordon, "Assessing the Roles of Biofilm Structure and Mechanics in Pathogenic, Persistent Infections." National Institute of Allergy and Infectious Diseases, 86, accessed August 2, 2021, https://www.niaid.nih.gov/sites/default/files/1-R01-AI121500-01A1 _Gordon_Application.pdf.

48. Joanna Wiebe, "Should You Use a Curiosity Gap to Persuade Your Visitors to Click?," *Copyhackers*, April 15, 2014, accessed April 22, 2021, https://copyhackers.com/2014/04/curiosity -gap/.

49. Eugene Wesley Ely, @WesElyMD, February 21, 2021, accessed June 21, 2021, https://twitter .com/WesElyMD/status/1363503685725270021.

50. Mathew Kiang, "Things to Consider Before Applying for a K99/R00," *MathewKiang(.com)*, June 12, 2020, accessed April 2, 2021, https://mathewkiang.com/2020/06/12/applying-for -a-k99/.

51. Caroline Ashley, @cashley122, February 28, 2021, accessed August 2, 2021, https://twitter .com/cashley122/status/1366021418731925506.

52. Mary Hertz, @MaryBSweets, October 26, 2020, March 2, 2021, https://twitter.com /MaryBSweets/status/1320762486057029637.

53. Joan Didion, "Quotes," Goodreads, accessed June 21, 2021, https://www.goodreads.com /quotes/264509-i-don-t-know-what-i-think-until-i-write-it.

54. Parag Mahanti, @ParagMahanti, February 21, 2021, accessed February 23, 2021, https:// twitter.com/ParagMahanti/status/1363537314832596993.

55. Samantha (Sam) J. Westcott, @sjwestcott, February 10, 2021, accessed February 23, 2021, https://twitter.com/sjwestcott/status/1359626800951828483.

56. Kayden Stockwell, @KaydenStockwell, December 2, 2020, accessed February 23, 2021, https://twitter.com/KaydenStockwell/status/1334256589360926721.

57. National Institute of Mental Health: Job Vacancy Announcement. Health Scientist Administrator (Program Officer)—Research Training and Career Development. Accessed February 25, 2021. https://www.nimh.nih.gov/about/careers/job-vacancy -announcement-health-scientist-administrator-program-officer-research-training-and -career-development.shtml.

58. "Clinician-Scientist Investigators Curriculum: NIH Overview by Dr. Diana W. Bianchi (Full Lecture)," Eunice Kennedy Shriver National Institute of Child Health and Human Development, YouTube, September 24, 2020, accessed April 6, 2022, https://www.youtube .com/watch?v=mBqMIEdsGIk.

59. Artstor, accessed April 8, 2021, https://www.artstor.org/.

60. NIH staff, "Program Officials Are Here to Help," Extramural Nexus, October 5, 2020, accessed February 23, 2021, https://nexus.od.nih.gov/all/2020/10/05/program-officials-are -here-to-help/.

61. Australian Research Council, *Annual Report 2014–15*, accessed April 6, 2022, https://www .arc.gov.au/sites/default/files/minisite/static/396/2014-15/preliminaries/australian -research-council.html.

62. Ale Babino, reply to Vanessa Bohns, "What's your favorite piece of writing advice?," @AleBabino, accessed March 2, 2021, https://twitter.com/AleBabino/status/136600461203 4084869.

63. "Peer Reviewers," U.S. Department of Justice, Office of Justice Programs, accessed August 2, 2021, https://www.ojp.gov/funding/peer-reviewers.

64. "The NSF Reviewing Process," Oregon State, accessed August 2, 2021, https://web.engr .oregonstate.edu/~grimmc/NSF/TheNSFReviewingProcess.html.

65. Terrinieka W. Powell, @DrTerriPowell, accessed October 14, 2021, https://twitter.com /DrTerriPowell/status/1366202781544173569.

66. Amanda Aykanian, @aykanian, accessed October 13, 2021, https://twitter.com/aykanian /status/1366056546552193026.

67. "Sponsored Programs," Boston College, accessed July 21, 2021, https://www.bc.edu/bc-web /research/sites/vice-provost-for-research/sponsored-programs.html.

68. National Science Foundation Board, *National Science Foundation's Merit Review Criteria: Review and Revisions*, accessed March 10, 2021, https://www.nsf.gov/nsb/publications /2011/meritreviewcriteria.pdf.

69. Duncan MacGregor, @blueapex, March 4, 2021, accessed June 15, 2021, https://twitter.com /blueapex/status/1367518209130307588.

70. "Racial Equity Research Grants," Spencer Foundation, accessed August 2, 2021, https:// www.spencer.org/grant_types/racial-equity-special-research-grants.

71. "Jacobs Foundation Research Fellowship Program," Jacobs Foundation, accessed March 11, 2021, https://jacobsfoundation.org/en/activity/jacobs-foundation-research-fellowship -program/.

72. "The Art and Science of Reviewing Proposals," accessed April 9, 2021, https://blog.valdosta .edu/research/2018/09/25/nsf-releases-video-with-tips-for-peer-review/.

73. Russell Brunson, *Dotcom Secrets: The Underground Playbook for Growing Your Company Online with Sales Funnels* (Carlsbad, CA: Hay House Business, 2020).

74. Ernest Hemingway, "Quotes," Goodreads, accessed July 16, 2021, https://www.goodreads .com/quotes/1192680-easy-reading-is-hard-writing.

75. "CSR Insider's Guide to Peer Review for Applicants," NIH Center for Scientific Review, accessed December 7, 2020, https://public.csr.nih.gov/ForApplicants/InitialReview ResultsAndAppeals/InsidersGuide.

76. Yingru Liu, "Experimental Gonococcal Vaccine," National Institute of Allergy and Infectious Diseases, 79, accessed April 8, 2022, https://www.niaid.nih.gov/sites/default/files//R44 -Liu-Application.pdf.

77. Patricia Garrett, "Rapid Test for Recent HIV Infection," National Institute of Allergy and Infectious Diseases, 116, accessed August 2, 2021, https://www.niaid.nih.gov/sites/default /files//2r44ai098567-03_garrett.pdf.

78. Toma Susi, "Heteroatom Quantum Corrals and Nanoplasmonics in Graphene (HeQuCoG)," *Research Ideas and Outcomes* 1 (December 17, 2015): e7479, accessed August 2, 2021, https:// riojournal.com/article/7479/.

79. Monica Gandhi, "Hair Extensions: Using Hair Levels to Interpret Adherence, Effectiveness and Pharmacokinetics with Real-world Oral PrEP, the Vaginal Ring, and Injectables," National Institute of Allergy and Infectious Diseases, 135, accessed August 2, 2021, https:// www.niaid.nih.gov/sites/default/files/2-R01-AI098472-06_Gandhi_Application.pdf.

80. Rosie Redfield, "Regulation of CRP-S Promoters in *H. influenzae* and *E. coli*," University of British Columbia, Department of Zoology, 12a, accessed August 2, 2021, https://www .zoology.ubc.ca/~redfield/proposals/Sxy%20proposal.pdf.

81. Jessica Burnett, "Using Integrated Population Modelling in Decision-Support Tools to Connect Science and Decision Makers," Figshare, 1, accessed August 2, 2021,

https://figshare.com/articles/online_resource/burnett_jessica_2019_mendenhall_usgs
/13120247.

82. Arun Durvasula, "Research Proposal to the National Science Foundation," Github, 1, accessed August 2, 2021, https://github.com/ybrandvain/GRFP/blob/master/Arun
_Durvasula_Research_Proposal_2018.pdf.

83. Chengwen Li, "Enhance AAV Liver Transduction with Caspid Immune Evasion," National
Institute of Allergy and Infectious Diseases, 34, accessed April 8, 2022, https://www.niaid
.nih.gov/sites/default/files/R01_Li_Sample_Application.pdf.

84. Truman Capote, AZ Quotes, accessed April 8, 2022, https://www.azquotes.com/quote
/599388.

85. Seth Fried, "Murder Your Darlings," Tin House, April 15, 2013, accessed April 2, 2021,
https://tinhouse.com/murder-your-darlings/.

86. Olga Onuch, @OOnuch, accessed August 2, 2021, https://mobile.twitter.com/oonuch
/status/1366169639814893570.

87. "Write Your Research Plan," National Institute of Allergy and Infectious Diseases, accessed
January 10, 2022, https://www.niaid.nih.gov/grants-contracts/write-research-plan.

88. Raul Pacheco-Vega, @raulpacheco, accessed October 14, 2021, https://twitter.com
/raulpacheco/status/1323578948425601024.

89. Daniel Gould, @DJGould94, accessed October 14, 2021, https://twitter.com/DJGould94
/status/1366092815554416640.

90. Samuel Perry, @socofthesacred, accessed October 14, 2021, https://twitter.com
/socofthesacred/status/1366003013597487107.

91. Stanley Schmidt, AZ Quotes, accessed January 12, 2022, https://www.azquotes.com/quote
/538833.

92. Lawrence A. Palinkas, Sarah M. Horwitz, Carla A. Green, Jennifer P. Wisdom, Naihua Duan,
and Kimberly Hoagwood, "Purposeful Sampling for Qualitative Data Collection and Analysis
in Mixed Method Implementation Research," Administration and Policy in Mental Health and
Mental Health Services Research 42, no. 5 (2015): 533–544, doi:10.1007/s10488-013-0528-y.

93. NVivo, QSR International, accessed April 8, 2022, https://www.qsrinternational.com/.

94. Matthew B. Miles and A. Michael Huberman, Qualitative Data Analysis: An Expanded
Sourcebook, 2nd ed. (Thousand Oaks, CA: SAGE Publishing, 1994).

95. Betty S. Lai, Annette M. La Greca, Beth A. Auslander, and Mary B. Short, "Children's
Symptoms of Posttraumatic Stress and Depression after a Natural Disaster: Comorbidity
and Risk Factors," Journal of Affective Disorders 146, no. 1 (2013): 71–78, doi:10.1016/j
.jad.2012.08.041.

96. Laurence E. Lynn, Teaching and Learning with Cases: A Guidebook (London: Chatham
House Publishers, 1999), 2.

97. Delphine Grynszpan, Virginia Murray, and Silvia Llosa, "Value of Case Studies in Disaster
Assessment?," Prehospital Disaster Medicine 26, no. 3 (2011): 203, doi:10.1017/S1049023
X11006406.

98. Shannon Hale, @HaleShannon, accessed January 11, 2022, https://twitter.com
/haleshannon/status/636907891379736576?lang=en.

99. Alma Faust, @AZFaust, accessed March 31, 2021, https://twitter.com/azfaust/status
/1276231182959738883.

100. Rosdiadee Nordin, @rosdiadeem, March 4, 2021, accessed June 22, 2021, https://twitter .com/rosdiadee/status/1367487350150860800.

101. George Savva, @georgemsavva, April 7, 2021, accessed August 2, 2021, https://twitter.com /georgemsavva/status/1379917805382946817.

102. "Talk: A Picture Is Worth a Thousand Words," Wikipedia, September 2, 2020, accessed May 25, 2021, https://en.wikipedia.org/w/index.php?title=Talk:A_picture_is_worth_a _thousand_words&oldid=976317499.

103. Susanne Brander, @smbrander, March 10, 2021, accessed October 14, 2021, https://twitter .com/smbrander/status/1369526028062789633.

104. "Laboratory Facilities," MIT Atmospheric Chemistry, accessed August 3, 2021, http:// atmoschem.mit.edu/resources/laboratory/.

105. Maria Popova, "Stephen King on Writing, Fear, and the Atrocity of Adverbs," *Marginalian*, March 13, 2013, accessed April 2, 2021, https://www.brainpickings.org/2013/03/13 /stephen-king-on-adverbs/.

106. Mark Twain, "Quotes," Goodreads, accessed April 2, 2021, https://www.goodreads.com /quotes/495945-when-you-catch-an-adjective-kill-it-no-i-don-t.

107. Antoine de Saint-Exupéry, "Quotes," Goodreads, accessed July 12, 2021, https://www .goodreads.com/quotes/19905-perfection-is-achieved-not-when-there-is-nothing -more-to.

108. "Clinician-Scientist Investigators Curriculum: NIH Overview by Dr. Diana W. Bianchi (Full Lecture)," NICHDVideos, YouTube. September 24, 2020, accessed November 25, 2020, https://www.youtube.com/watch?v=mBqMIEdsGIk&feature=youtu.be.

109. "Success Rates," NIH RePORT: Research Portfolio Online Reporting Tools, accessed June 3, 2021, https://report.nih.gov/success_rates/Success_ByIC.cfm.

110. "NCGP Trends: Success Rates," Australian Research Council, September 18, 2020, accessed April 12, 2021, https://www.arc.gov.au/grants-and-funding/apply-funding/grants-dataset /trend-visualisation/ncgp-trends-success-rates.

111. "American Council of Learned Societies Names 60 New ACLS Fellows," American Council of Learned Societies, accessed April 11, 2022, https://www.prweb.com/releases/american _council_of_learned_societies_names_60_new_acls_fellows/prweb17860914.htm.

112. Becca Krukowski, @DrBeccaK, accessed October 14, 2021, https://twitter.com/DrBeccaK /status/1286728713711882240.

113. John Jerrim and Robert de Vries, "Are Peer-Reviews of Grant Proposals Reliable? An Analysis of Economic and Social Research Council (ESRC) Funding Applications," *Social Science Journal* (2020): 1–19, doi:https://doi.org/10.1080/03623319.2020.1728506.

114. Elizabeth L. Pier, Markus Brauer, Amarette Filut, Anna Kaatz, Joshua Raclaw, Mitchell J. Nathan, Cecilia E. Ford, and Molly Carnes, "Low Agreement among Reviewers Evaluating the Same NIH Grant Applications," *PNAS* 115, no. 12 (2018): 2952–57, doi:https://doi.org /10.1073/pnas.1714379115.

115. Rebecca Brent and Richard M. Felder, "New Faculty Members May Not Know How to Teach, but at Least They Know How to Do Research . . . Right?," *Chemical Engineering Education* 504, no. 4 (2016): 252.

116. Amy Summerville, @RegretLab, accessed October 14, 2021, https://twitter.com/RegretLab /status/1366056225184440324.

117. Vanessa Bohns, @profbohns, February 28, 2021, accessed July 13, 2021, https://twitter.com/profbohns/status/1366001709294747648.

118. Jen Heemstra, @jenheemstra, March 20, 2021, accessed August 2, 2021, https://twitter.com/jenheemstra/status/1373321228782567427.

119. "Merit Review Facts," National Science Foundation, accessed August 2, 2021, https://www.nsf.gov/bfa/dias/policy/merit_review/facts.jsp#2.

120. "Institutional Profile," Vice Provost for Research, Boston College, accessed July 21, 2021, https://www.bc.edu/bc-web/research/sites/vice-provost-for-research/sponsored-programs/institutional-profile.html.

INDEX

abstracts, 17
accountability, 194
acronyms, 166, 169
administrators, research, 83–86
advice beacon approach, 24–25
advisory boards, 175
aims, 51–52, 55–56, 147
ambiguous terms, 116
American Council of Learned Societies, 170
American Medical Association, 149
American Psychological Association, 149
Amstadter, Amanda, 38, 88
application, guidelines/instructions within, 80–83, 190–91
approach to content, as sample signal, 75
arguments, bolstering, 53–54
Artstor, 62
Ashley, Caroline, 56
aspirational peers, 16, 34–35, 72
Auslander, Beth, 23–24, 191
Australian Research Council, 60, 170
authorized organization representative, 86
Aykanian, Amanda, 87

Babino, Ale, 74
benefits, guidance regarding, 112, 113–14
Berry, Mary, 91
Bianchi, Diana, 170, 195
bias, within funding, 1, 196
Bohns, Vanessa, 188
Boston College, 88, 208
brainstorming, 107–9, 125–28, 156, 173–75
Brander, Susanne, 40

Bremer, Andrew, 61
Brent, Rebecca, 183
broader impacts, as evaluation criteria, 94–96
Brody, Sam, 29
budgets, 88, 137
building a case, 128–32
Burnett, Jessica, 111
"buy out," for collaborations, 21
buzzwords, 74–75

Capote, Truman, 114
CAREER grant, 21, 29, 75
Chan, Francis, 25
Chi, Donald, 24, 40, 87
Choe, Youngjun, 88–89, 158–59, 169
clarity: feedback regarding, 188; within figures, 153–54; within research plans, 124, 129–30; within terminology, 116; within writing, 104, 114–15
Clay, Lauren, 75, 163
coinvestigator, 36, 184
Coley, Rebekah Levine, 39, 60, 74
collaborations: benefits of, 40; building, 176–77; expense of, 21; expertise within, 174; finding, 40; kickoff meeting for, 174; proofreading from, 191; with research administrators, 83–86; writing styles within, 149; for writing timelines, 86–87
collaborators approach you approach, 26
communication, 63–64, 84
community partners, 87
conflicting issues, 191

conflicts of interest, 100
confusion, myths regarding, 104–6
connections, making, 115
consistency: checking for, 190; creation of, 146–48; example of, 140; within figures, 158; of master teachers, 139; purpose of, 139–40; for reviewers, 150; through emphasis techniques, 147–48; through front-loading, 148; through mirroring, 146–47; through repetition, 147; through signposts, 146
consultant, as red team member, 184
content, approach to, as sample signal, 75
Cooper, Dan, 44
cost sharing, 175
Cova, Tom, 55, 75, 79, 171
COVID-19 vaccine, 43
critical readers, 183–85
curriculum vitaes (CVs), 16–17, 18, 173–74, 179

Danzi, BreAnne, 92
Davison, Kirsten, 36, 176
deadlines, 86
debriefing, following program officer meeting, 66
Delaware, 177
Desir, Michelle, 61–62, 75
detail, attention to, 189–91
Dickerson, Aisha, 30, 153, 174
direct costs, 32
discussion circle, 185–88
discussion fuel approach, 24
disqualification, of grant applications, 81, 82
Durrant, Valerie, 43, 103
Durvasula, Arun, 111

easy peasy approach, 24
Edwards, Katie, 18, 30, 72, 82, 184
Einstein, Albert, 59
The Elements of Style (Strunk and White), 168
Ely, Eugene Wesley, 54
emailing, 63–64, 73, 84, 184–85
emphasis techniques, 147–48

emphasis words, 94–96, 97
Enabling Program, 184
environment, support within, 175
Environmental Protection Agency, 1–2, 13
Errett, Nicole, 40, 89
Esnard, Ann-Margaret, 38, 49–51, 184
Eswarappa Prameela, Suhas, 182
Eunice Kennedy Shriver National Institute of Child Health and Human Development, 27, 195
evaluation criteria, 93–94, 99–100, 199
Evans, Joe, 25, 74
evidence, 141, 144, 145, 175
existing data approach, 26
expertise, 174, 178–79, 201
explanatory example, within research plan, 130
external values: aspirational peer meeting regarding, 34–35; importance of, 31; indirect costs and, 33; mentor meeting regarding, 35–36; overview of, 32–33; senior administrator meeting regarding, 37; uncovering, 34
extra words, trimming of, 165

facts, double checking, 190
faculty provosts, as red team members, 183–84
Faust, Alma, 55, 107, 139
feasibility, within research plan, 130–31
federal grants, 13, 17, 32
feedback, 117, 186–89, 195
Felder, Richard, 183
fellowships, funding opportunities through, 18
figures: accessibility through, 157; attraction to, 152; brainstorming for, 156; clarity within, 153–54; consistency within, 158; creation of, 156–58; examples of, 153, 155, 159; explanations for, 158; feasibility explanation through, 154–55; frequently asked questions regarding, 158–59, 200–201; as information organization, 152–53; mistakes within,

159; simplification of, 157–58; software for, 159; as stand-alone, 157; timelines through, 156; tips regarding, 158–59, 200–201; unique value showcasing through, 154, 155; usage ways for, 152–56; value within, 152

filler statements, 145–46

final draft, 79

Fitzpatrick, Stephanie, 40

follow the energy approach, 24

foundational works, inclusion of, 117

foundation grants, 13, 17, 33

Fox, Matthew, 89, 183

Freedom of Information Act, 72

fringe rates, 84–85, 88

front-loading, 148

full justification, 169

funders: bias of, 1, 196; differences between, 19; frequently asked questions regarding, 67–68, 198; identification of, 28–29; interests of, 59; key words regarding, 68; mission of, 99–100; policies of, 138; role of, 92; studying program and operation of, 64–65; tips regarding, 67–68, 198. *See also specific funders*

Game of Thrones, 207–8

Gandhi, Monica, 111

Gantt chart, 128, 129

Garfin, Dana Rose, 98, 175

Garrett, Patricia, 110

Garrison, Mason, 69, 79–80, 159

Gates, Emily, 75–76, 91, 92

general samples, 70–71

Georgia State University, 14–15

Gittens, Michelle, 83

Gould, Daniel, 117

grant mechanisms approach, 25

grants: career impact of, 4; consistency within, 146–48; feasibility issue regarding, 55; finding, 18; frequently asked questions regarding, 17–19, 29–30, 38–42, 87–89, 168–69; hating, 191; idea selection for, 38; limiting beliefs regarding, 3–5;

mindset shifts regarding, 194; readability of, 164–67; road map of, 14; roles within process for, 14–15; small goals within, 194; small *versus* large, 39, 41; statistics regarding, 1, 11; success rates of, 18; time process regarding, 18, 79–80; tips regarding, 17–19, 29–30, 38–42, 87–89, 168–69. *See also specific types*

Grants Administration, 83

Great British Baking Show, 91

Grimley Prieur, Mary Beth, 11

Gross, Janet, 52, 81, 89, 185

groundwork, through figures, 154–55

Guastaferro, Kate, 11

guidance, within inverted pyramid approach, 141, 142–43, 144

guide, peer *versus*, 106–9

Hale, Shannon, 135

Hamilton, Jessica, 39, 176

hard money position, 39

Hart, Kyle, 20

Harvard University, 32–33

headings, 94–96, 97

Heemstra, Jen, 75, 76, 94, 193

Hemingway, Ernest, 104

Hertz, Mary, 56

Hewlett Foundation, 62

hidden curriculum, 2–3, 65, 196

Hollywood, Paul, 91

Humans, Disasters, and the Built Environment (National Science Foundation), 15

Hunger Games, 106–7

ideas, 26–28, 38, 197

Ikigai, 22–26

imposter syndrome, 17, 73

incentives, for participants, 20–21

indirect costs (IDCs), 32–33

institution, grant process role of, 14–15

instructions, 80–83, 89

intellectual merit, as evaluation criteria, 94–96

intellectual wandering, 24

internal grants, 13, 17
inverted pyramid approach, 140–46

Jacobs Foundation, 13, 98–99
jargon, 165–66
Jerrim, John, 181
jumping off point approach, 23
justification, 169, 187, 189

K99/R00 mechanism, 61–62, 140
Kao, Dennis, 196
Kassam-Adams, Nancy, 27, 140, 181, 190
K award, 21, 33
Kearns, Nathan, 73
key words, for funder strategies, 68
Kiang, Mathew, 45, 54, 82, 140
King, Stephen, 165
Krukowski, Becca, 173

La Greca, Annette, 26, 47–49
Landoll, Ryan, 59, 195
Lattie, Emily, 53, 80
leaders, 16, 72
left justification, 169
letter of intent, 89
letter of support, 87
Li, Chengwen, 112
limitations approach, 23
limiting beliefs, confronting, 3–5
literature review, 109–17, 144, 199–200
Liu, Yingru, 110
logic, importance of, 115
Lowenhaupt, Becca, 21, 24

mad libs, 75–76, 108–9
Magee, Matthew, 185–86, 196
Maholmes, Valerie, 55–56, 61–62
Mandalorian (film), 74
marathon, 193, 194
marketing, general rule within, 104
master teachers, consistency of, 139
Matchmaker portal (National Institutes of
     Health), 13
McNeill, Katherine, 21, 173–74

"me" grantee, 55
Mellon Foundation, 88
men, funding statistics for, 1
mentoring programs, 184
mentors/mentoring, 35–36, 89, 183–84,
     191
mentor texts, samples as, 74
methods section. See research plan
Military Operational Medicine Research
     Program, 59
mirroring, 146–47
mission, 64, 98–100
moving away approach, 24
Moynihan, Donald, 105, 191
Muñiz, Raquel, 20, 22

names, clarity regarding, 116
National Institutes of Health: abstracts of,
     17; applications for, 81; as federal grant,
     13; funding from, 3; investment within, 1;
     K award from, 21; Matchmaker portal
     within, 13; negative reviews from, 181–82;
     Posttraumatic Stress grant one pager for,
     47–49; program officer role within, 60;
     statistics regarding, 4, 170
National Science Foundation: abstracts of,
     17; evaluation criteria from, 93–96; as
     federal grant, 13; Humans, Disasters, and
     the Built Environment, 15; investment
     within, 1; School Recovery grant one
     pager for, 49–52; statistics regarding,
     4, 194
Naumes, Sarah, 174, 185
negative reviews, 181
networking: finding critical readers through,
     183–84; with peers, 185; process of, 41,
     83; with program officers, 67; specific
     samples from, 71
next steps approach, 22
Nocco, Mallika, 53, 99, 178
Nordin, Rosdiadee, 151
North Star, finding, 29
Nugent, Nicole, 23, 75, 98, 115
numbered styles, for references, 149

Office of Sponsored Programs, 83

one pager: aims within, 51–52; argument bolstering on, 53–54; common mistakes within, 54–55; construction of, 54; frequently asked questions regarding, 55–56, 198; inverted pyramid approach for, 143–44; overview of, 44–45, 143–44; pitch building for, 52–54; purpose of, 119; significance within, 53–54; simplification within, 55; structure of, 45–52, 143–44; timeline for, 148; tips regarding, 55–56, 198

Onuch, Olga, 115

operation, 63–66

Osborne, Melissa, 30, 87, 184

Ostrolencki, Caille Taylor, 31

other fields approach, 23–24

outcomes, within research plan, 132

Pacheco-Vega, Raul, 117

pain point, 111, 113

Panza, Rosemary, 62, 195

papers, grant writing *versus*, 107

paragraphs, 115, 140–43

participants, paying, 20–21

partnership, 83–86, 87

past research, building from, 111–12, 113

payoff argument, within inverted pyramid approach, 141, 142–43

Pebole, Michelle, 39

Peek, Lori, 39, 40–41, 117, 127, 184

peers, networking with, 185

Perry, Samuel, 117

Perry, Sylvia, 163

persistence, 60, 87

perspective approach, 23

pick me factor, 171–75, 176–79

Pier, Elizabeth, 181

pilot data, 136

pitch, 44, 52–54, 188–89

Pizzie, Rachel, 18–19

postaward functions, 83

Posttraumatic Stress grant one pager, 47–49

Powell, Terrinieka W., 79

pragmatic purpose, program officer role regarding, 62–63

preaward functions, 83

precision, use of, 171–72

principal investigator, 36, 71, 83

problem approach, 23

program, 15, 64–65

program officers: debrief following meeting with, 66; frequently asked questions regarding, 67–68, 198; grant process role of, 15; influence of, 65; learning from, 61–63; meeting with, 65–66; operational purpose of, 63; pragmatic purpose of, 62–63; reaching out to, 63–64; review panels and, 76; roles of, 60–61; scientific purpose of, 61–62; tips regarding, 67–68, 198

project description. *See* research plan

project plan. *See* research plan

proofreading, 190

proposal elements, 81–82

protected time, 21

Quiller-Couch, Arthur, 115

R01 grant, 23, 36, 87, 111, 112

R03 grants, 11, 26

R44 grant, 110

Racial Equality Research Grants program (Spencer Foundation), 96–98

readability, 164–67, 168–69, 201

Redfield, Rosie, 111

red flags, 186–87, 189

red teams, 182–85

references, 149–50

rejection, 195, 196

repetition, consistency through, 147

requests for application, 25

research administrators, 83–86, 183–84

research development specialist, 185

research plan: anticipating reviewer questions within, 132–34; brainstorming for, 125–28; budgets and, 137; building your case within, 128–32; clarity within, research plan (*continued*)

124; data sharing within, 137–38; defensive strategy within, 132–34; defined, 120; development of, 125; drafting, 134–35; feasibility within, 130–31; flexibility within, 138; frequently asked questions regarding, 135–38, 200; guidelines for, 121; instilling confidence through, 136–37; inverted pyramid approach for, 144; length of, 135; offensive strategy within, 128–32; outcomes within, 132; overview of, 120–25; pilot data within, 136; project timeline for, 128; research questions within, 125, 126–27; reviewer exercises for, 133–34; sample, 121–24; tips regarding, 135–38, 200; troubleshooting for, 130

research questions, 125, 126–27

resubmission, 195–96

reviewers: clarity for, 151; conflict of interest of, 100; consistency for, 150; criticism of, 163; empathy for, 163; within evaluation process, 93; excitement generation for, 171–73; grant process role of, 15; inverted pyramid approach and, 141; red teams approach and, 182–83; research plans and, 133–34, 136; reviewing process of, 103–4; role of, 43–44, 76–77, 92; types of, 100

review panel, 15, 76–77

review system, flaws within, 181

revision, process of, 145, 195–96

Riobueno-Naylor, Alexa, 159

Rosenzweig, Ido, 84

Rudd, Brittany, 171

Rumbach, Andrew, 132

Russell Sage Foundation, 60

SafeCare, 27

Saint-Exupéry, Antoine de, 166

Samayoa, Andrés Castro, 63, 92, 177

samples: analyzing, 177–78; emailing requests for, 73; frequently asked questions regarding, 77–78, 199; general, 70–71; of inverted pyramid approach, 142–43; literature review, 109–14; as mentor texts,

74; overview of, 70; research plan, 121–24; review panel and, 76–77; signals within, 74–76; specific, 70, 71–72; tips regarding, 77–78, 199

Savva, George, 152

Schleider, Jessica, 109, 195

Schmidt, Stanley, 119

Schneider, Julie, 11, 177

School Recovery grant one pager, 49–52

science, 61–62, 65

Seider, Scott, 75

Self-Brown, Shannon, 27, 87, 115, 190

senior administrator, 37

Shaffer, Kelly, 195

short sentences, 166

shotgun approach, 169

Shulman, James, 43, 62

signals, within samples, 74–76

significance problems, 188–89

significant area, 110, 113

signposts, 146

simplicity, within writing, 103–4

Singleton, Daniel, 44–45, 55

sloppiness, 80, 169

Slotta, Jim, 41

Smith, Brian, 61, 82–83

social proof principle, 12

soft money position, 40

solid plan, 129–30

solution, example of, 111, 113

sound bites, 94–98

Spears, Claire, 23, 196

specific aims page, 44. *See also* one pager

specific samples, 70, 71–72

Spencer Foundation, 13, 36, 92, 96–98

Star Wars (film), 74

story problems, feedback regarding, 187–88, 189

storytelling, within grants, 172–73

Strickland, Paula, 26

structure: acronym avoidance within, 166, 169; checklist for, 203–5; common mistakes regarding, 144–46; extra word trimming within, 165; frequently asked questions regarding, 148–50, 199, 200; of full proposal, 143–44; inverted pyramid approach for, 140–43; jargon elimination within, 165–66; of literature review, 110–16, 144; of one pager, 45–52, 143–44; of paragraphs, 140–43; precision within, 171–72; readability within, 164–67; of research plan, 128–35; revision and, 145; as sample signal, 75; short sentences within, 166; showcasing fit within, 172; storytelling within, 172–73; style strategies within, 167–68; tips regarding, 148–50, 199, 200; using all space within, 179; voice choice within, 167; white space within, 164–65

Strunk, William, Jr., 168
style strategies, 167–68
subcontracts, 87
submission, 190, 195–96, 203–5
summer salary, 37, 41–42
Summerville, Amy, 188
Susi, Toma, 111, 112
swagger mindset, 178

takeaway message, 112, 114
team, 174, 176–77, 182–83
technicals, 91
terminology, choosing, 116
thank you notes, 66, 84
theories approach, 23
"this," avoidance of, 166–67
Thomas, Deb, 88
tiger time, 87–88
timelines, 128, 156, 199
titles, 148–49
Tiwari, Ashwini, 149, 181
track record, 179
training grants, 21, 117, 177
training programs, 184
triaging, 93
troubleshooting, 130, 145, 146, 188–89
trust, regarding specific samples, 71
Twain, Mark, 165

UK Research and Innovation, 2
unique position approach, 25
unique value, 154
University Research Services and Administration, 83
usual suspects, identification of, 16–17

vagueness, 129–30, 171–72
values, 22–26, 197–98
Vitiello, Ginny, 23, 183
voice, choosing, 167
Vries, Robert de, 181

Wargo, Jon, 36, 144
Waters, Don, 55, 88
weakness, 177, 178, 179, 188, 191, 201
web-based assessment, 27
"we" grantee, 55
Weihe, Richelle, 185
Weirich, Christine, 117, 157
Westcott, Sam, 83
where is it approach, 23
Whitaker, Dan, 27
White, E. B., 168
white space, 164–65
William T. Grant Foundation, 13
W.K. Kellogg Foundation, 177
women, funding statistics for, 1
worldview, painting, 110–11, 113
writing: clarity within, 104, 114–15, 116; dividing and conquering within, 88–89; frequently asked questions regarding, 87–89; planning timeline for, 86–87; process of, 87; roles within, 89; simplicity within, 103–4; tiger time for, 87–88; tips regarding, 87–89
writing styles, 149
Wu Roybal, Donna, 21, 33

Yu, Ya-Hui, 18, 194

Zalcman, Daniella, 16
Zheng, Crystal, 18, 183

CPSIA information can be obtained
at www.ICGtesting.com
Printed in the USA
JSHW081153140223
37601JS00004B/4

A practical guide to effective grant writing for researchers at all stages of their academic careers

Grant funding can be a major determinant of promotion and tenure at colleges and universities, yet many scholars receive no training in the crucial skill of grant writing. *The Grant Writing Guide* is an essential handbook for writing research grants, providing actionable strategies for professionals in every phase of their careers, from PhD students to seasoned researchers.

This easy-to-use guide features writing samples, examples of how researchers use skills, helpful tips, and exercises. Drawing on interviews with scores of grant writers, program officers, researchers, administrators, and writers, it lays out best practices, common questions, and pitfalls to avoid. Betty Lai focuses on skills that are universal to all grant writers, not just specific skills for one type of grant or funder. She explains how to craft phenomenal pitches and align them with your values, structure timelines and drafts, communicate clearly in prose and images, solicit feedback to strengthen your proposals, and much more.

Ideal for course use, *The Grant Writing Guide* is an indispensable road map to writing fundable grants. This incisive book walks you through every step along the way, from generating ideas to finding the right funder, determining which grants help you create the career you want, and writing in a way that excites reviewers and funders.

Betty S. Lai is an associate professor in the Lynch School of Education and Human Development at Boston College. Her research has been funded by the National Science Foundation, the National Institute of Mental Health, and the Gulf Research Program of the National Academies of Sciences, Engineering, and Medicine, among others. Her work has been recognized with awards from the American Psychological Association and the American Psychological Foundation. Twitter @BettySLai

"Betty Lai shepherds readers through every logistical—and emotional—step of securing a major grant. This will undoubtedly become the go-to grant writing guidebook for scholars of every stage, from graduate student to full professor. It's the book I wish I had twenty years ago when I started my career as an academic!"
—Anthony Christian Ocampo, author of *Brown and Gay in LA*

"If you've ever wondered about how to develop a winning grant, this book is for you. From concept to submission, this highly engaging work offers useful advice informed by Lai's own distinguished research career and numerous interviews with other successful grant writers. It's a must-read for scholars at every career stage."
—Lori Peek, University of Colorado Boulder

"Betty Lai's *The Grant Writing Guide: A Road Map for Scholars* translates the unspoken insider language that keeps access to resources in the hands of those who already have resources. Her book deftly supports an equity-driven narrative vision with an engineer's analytic specificity."
—James L. Shulman, American Council of Learned Societies

"*The Grant Writing Guide* recognizes that fundraising is not a solitary process. It shows researchers how to build networks of administrators, mentors, and peers who are supportive yet critical in helping to generate persuasive grant proposals. This book's detailed and elegantly presented advice is much needed and long overdue."
—Donald J. Waters, former senior program officer, Andrew W. Mellon Foundation

Skills for Scholars

PRINCETON
press.princeton.edu

EDUCATION | REFERENCE
ISBN 978-0-691-23188-4

90000

9 780691 231884

Cover design: Monograph / Matt Avery